Federal Aid to the Disadvantaged, What Future for Chapter 1?

Education Policy Perspectives

General Editor: **Professor Ivor Goodson**, Faculty of Education, University of Western Ontario, London, Canada N6G 1G7

Education policy analysis has long been a neglected area in the United Kingdom and, to an extent, in the USA and Australia. The result has been a profound gap between the study of education and the formulation of education policy. For practitioners such a lack of analysis of the new policy initiatives has worrying implications particularly at such a time of policy flux and change. Education policy has, in recent years, been a matter for intense political debate — the political and public interest in the working of the system has come at the same time as the consensus on education policy has been broken by the advent of the 'New Right'. As never before the political parties and pressure groups differ in their articulated policies and prescriptions for the education sector. Critical thinking about these developments is clearly necessary.

All those working within the system also need information on policy-making, policy implementation and effective day-to-day operation. Pressure on schools from government, education authorities and parents has generated an enormous need for knowledge amongst those on the receiving end of educational policies.

This series aims to fill the academic gap, to reflect the politicalization of education, and to provide the practitioners with the analysis for informed implementation of policies that they will need. It will offer studies in broad areas of policy studies. Beside the general section it will offer a particular focus in the following areas: School organization and improvement (David Reynolds, University College, Cardiff, UK); Social analysis (Professor Philip Wexler, University of Rochester, USA); Policy studies and evaluation (Professor Ernest House, University of Colorado-Boulder, USA); and Education and training (Dr Peter Cuttance, University of Edinburgh, UK).

Education Policy Perspectives

Federal Aid to the Disadvantaged: What Future for Chapter 1?

Edited by

Denis P. Doyle and Bruce S. Cooper

Foreword by

Sally B. Kilgore

The Falmer Press
(A member of the Taylor & Francis Group)
London • New York • Philadelphia

USA   The Falmer Press, Taylor & Francis Inc., 242 Cherry Street, Philadelphia, PA 19106-1906

UK   The Falmer Press, Falmer House, Barcombe, Lewes, East Sussex, BN8 5DL

First published 1988

Library of Congress Cataloging in Publication Data is available on request

ISBN 1 85000 368 8
ISBN 1 85000 369 6 (pbk.)

Jacket design by Caroline Archer

Typeset in 11/13 Bembo by
Mathematical Composition Setters Ltd, Salisbury, UK

Printed in Great Britain by Taylor & Francis (Printers) Ltd, Basingstoke

Contents

Contents

List of Tables and Figures

Foreword

Improving the educational performance of disadvantaged children and young people is central to our nation's efforts to achieve economic competitiveness. While we, as a nation, have made some measurable advances in the education of such young people, our standards of equity and excellence suggest that we have, yet, some miles to cover. Central to our democratic structure is the commitment to literacy for all; central to our tradition of ingenuity is the belief that we can do it better.

It is within this larger context that the Special Studies Division of the Office of Research in the US Department of Education convened policy analysts from all over the country to consider strategies for improving compensatory education. Combining the wisdom of hindsight with the challenge of the future, the authors provide an historical context of the Federal and state roles in providing compensatory programs, challenge old assumptions, and propose alternative standards and policies. Such evaluation and reconsiderations are healthy and part of the responsibility of the Office of Research as we seek to invigorate the marketplace of ideas about the education of our young. As with a good democracy, the authors are not necessarily of one voice. While many facts are agreed upon, the implications of those facts, or the relative viability of certain solutions, vary by author. That is as it should be. Nothing herein should be taken as the official position of the US Department of Education.

I encourage all of you who enter the pages of this book to ponder the implications, to imagine the possibilities, and to reflect upon your practice. Once done, I hope that policymakers, researchers, and practitioners will discover new insights worthy of further exploration in research or practice.

While acknowledgements are seldom adequate or exhaustive, some individuals, in particular, deserve whatever recognition such statements can provide. The efforts of Ron Anson, Project Officer for this conference, and Denis Doyle, chair for the conference, provided the conceptual framework and required tenacity to transform a bright idea into reality. Beatrice Birman, Director of the Special Studies Division, provided guidance and wisdom to the endeavor. Barbara I Williams, with Research and Evaluation Associates, provided the logistical support — a challenge never to be underestimated. The outcome testifies to the dedication of each of them.

Sally B. Kilgore
Director, Office of Research
US Department of Education

1
Introduction: Title I in Retrospect, Chapter 1 in Prospect

Denis P. Doyle and Bruce S. Cooper

This timely book is a product of the United States Department of Education's Congressionally mandated study of ECIA *Chapter 1*. Many of us, of course, still say *Title I*, a throwback to the program's original designation in the Elementary and Secondary Education Act of 1965. Difficulty in adjusting to the new name is, of course, a commentary on the power of habit. But it is more than that. It reminds us of just how naive and ambitious we were two decades ago. *Title I* was a product of President Johnson's 'War on Poverty', a full fledged assault that would bring opportunity and success to all. It was part of a grand plan to lift the nation out of poverty. Education — particularly of the very young — would be the first step. Poverty would gradually disappear. Or so we hoped.

Title I sought to help the nation's poorest, lowest achieving children to 'compensate' for their academic and social disadvantages. Thus was born the major federal initiative in 'lower' education, a 'crusade' to help the poor which remains with us to this day.

It was a grand dream and a noble ambition, no less so because it is still unrealized. But unrealized it is, and it is clear as we look to the future that we must think about ways to improve *Chapter 1*. The issue is specially important as reauthorization approaches, for if the mood of the mid-60s was unbridled optimism and confidence about our ability to improve the lives of all our citizens, the mood of the present is one of resignation, even cynicism, about our ability to do much of consequence on the domestic front.

Two decades ago, three events had made it possible to think

seriously about solving the problems of poverty: the social sciences matured after the Second World War; the high speed computer became accessible to scholars and analysts, making it possible to manage and manipulate huge data sets; and Lyndon Baines Johnson became President. He was nothing if not an optimist, and was convinced that government — big government — could be a force for lasting social change. As Franklin Roosevelt had rescued the nation from the Great Depression — and forever shaped Lyndon Johnson's thinking about the role of government — Johnson thought the federal government could solve the problems of poverty. Above all else, he had an abiding faith in the power of education.

Johnson's enthusiasm was matched by the confidence — perhaps *hubris* is the better word — of social scientists, who thought that lasting social change was simply a matter of designing the 'right programs'. As Senator — then Professor — Daniel Patrick Moynihan observed, social science promised to finally solve the problem of poverty.

In retrospect, such confidence and enthusiasm seem almost quaint. How worldly and jaded we seem today. Will any social programs work? Can we ameliorate — not solve — the problems of the poor? Can we increase the power and scope of *Chapter 1*? The issue is a real one because of the inability of *Chapter 1* to measure up to the educational and social promise held out by the program's original architects. Politically, the program more than measures up — its popularity is real and, in terms of the program's reach at least, is justified.

The difficulty in finding 'sustaining effects' in *Chapter 1* programs, however, is now well known. The most extensive study is Herbert Walberg's; more recently Terry Hartle, then of the American Enterprise Institute, now of Senator Kennedy's staff, combed the literature. To their surprise, if not consternation, they find little measurable impact over time. Does this mean that *Chapter 1* doesn't 'work'? It appears to mean that *Chapter 1* doesn't produce the unambiguous, long–term academic results its architects had hoped it would, but there are two responses to this point. First, there is more to such a program than test scores. It is clear, as this volume reveals, that *Chapter 1* provides the services it is meant to, relatively smoothly, over time, in thousands of different sites across the nation.

It is also clear that *Title I* enjoys substantial goodwill, even from hard-headed analysts who might otherwise be more finicky about what the data shows. This generosity is revealed in the opening remarks of

Paul Peterson:

> There are lots of other forces that were at work at the same time, but I thought that it was another bit of evidence that somehow this program had had or had contributed to or had been part of an effort, a broader effort in our society to do something about our needy populations that on the margins had a beneficial effect.

It reaches all of the nation's Congressional districts, the administrative machinery at the Federal and state level appears to be well-oiled, and the various parties to program administration work well together. From this perspective the program is a success.

But it is also the case that *Chapter 1* shows stronger results in some configurations than others. As Mary Kennedy's work reveals, concentration appears to work. Paul Peterson and Mike Smith also argue that concentration appears to work. Bob Koff thinks that inadequate funding masks program effects, and that full funding would reveal more robust results. Other strategies are also important, and provide reason for cautious optimism or at least careful inquiry. As Nathan Glazer notes, such things as after school or summer programs — rather than same day 'pull out' programs — look promising. But both greater concentration and after school or summer school supplemental programs fall outside the mainstream of *Title I* and require a more flexible reauthorization permitting administrative flexibility both in Washington and among the states.

From a political and budgetary standpoint, however, the most important implication of greater concentration is not increasing efficacy but its zero sum dimension. By increasing the resources in one site, resources in another are decreased. The tried and true political remedy for such a problem is to increase the size of the pie rather than cutting pieces of different size. But the reality of the deficit makes even the most optimistic skeptical about big increase in *Chapter 1* or any other domestic programs.

For our purposes, however, the most important aspect of *Chapter 1* is that it is a mature program, a fertile field for study and analysis, and one about which we know a good deal. Indeed this is the second major study of *Chapter 1* mandated by the Congress. In addition to what we know about *Chapter 1*, we also know much more about education in general, and how it works or doesn't work, than we did two decades

3

ago. There is now a fairly substantial research base and convincing evidence about the education process. While much remains to be learned, we stand on a firmer foundation of knowledge and practice than we did when *Title I* was originally enacted. There is every reason to believe that we have learned enough over the past twenty years to actually improve the program's educational outcomes, if there is the will.

As it happened, the question as to whether or not policy could or would be actually shaped by 'knowledge' became a central point of discussion in the conference. As the reader will see this came up most forcefully in the first session, but was a theme woven through the conference as a whole. This is hardly surprising given the nature of the participants, many of whom have held positions of public trust and all of whom regularly advise policymakers. If they did not worry about the quality *and* utility of their advice it would be most unusual.

Beneath *Chapter 1's* placid political exterior, then, the problem of 'sustaining effects' is a nagging one, more perhaps for intellectual than political reasons. It is a problem to analysts even if it is not a problem to policymakers because education programs are supposed to have educational outcomes. It is a special problem if policy research means to be genuinely useful, as those of us in the field think it should be. If policymakers were to use research findings to make policy decisions then a program that does not produce the results it is ostensibly designed to produce would find itself in trouble. Thank God for small blessings, the program recipient might say. But put most starkly — at least in policy analytic terms — if it will not solve the problems of poverty is it worth continuing support? There is, it would seem, no immediate risk. But a program that does not do what it asserts it will may be a program at long term risk. Although as we noted earlier, *Chapter 1* is a 'popular' program, that will only protect it for a while. It will not guarantee its continuance indefinitely. Success will.

Doubters need only remember 1981, and the rapidity and severity of education budget cuts then. Two major programs were wiped out altogether, both of which had been enormously popular. Until 1981 social security benefits for orphans, half-orphans and dependent children of disabled workers continued until age 22 *if the beneficiary was a full-time student*. It was the biggest single 'education' program in the federal budget; it was enormously popular with beneficiaries; the public at large — insofar as it knew about the program at all — thought it was fair and sensible. Only budget cutters cared enough to try to kill it. They succeeded.

The Middle Income Student Assistance Act (MISSA) died the same way. Enacted under the Carter Administration, it provided subsidized loans to middle income college students. It was enormously popular (though badly misguided) and fell to the budget axe without much dissent.

One lesson in these two stories may be that programs for orphans and college students are easier to cut than programs with powerful constituencies. If that is true, what chance does *Chapter 1* have over the long haul? If it is to remain a major federal program — and it has not kept pace with inflation; in real dollars it is smaller today than it was a decade ago — it could be more confident of long-term survival if it did a better job, educationally. Education pork barrel is not enough. The reauthorization challenge before the Congress is precisely to fashion a more effective *Chapter 1* program.

It is well known, of course, that a political strategy to protect a program can take one of several forms; change the program, change its name or change its purpose. Occasionally, all three expedients are tried. In the case of *Title I* one has already been tried, though desultorily. The name change was as much omission as commission. While it has sown some confusion and not a little irritability, it seems to be a change of little consequence and little impact.

What about program change or changes in program purpose? The commissioned articles that make up this book (and the conference at which they were presented) examined the other two alternatives. As the reader will see, this they do admirably. The authors and the commentators at the conference at which the articles were presented in November 1986, are a 'who's who' of American education policy analysts. Most of them have had both academic and government experience, and all are thoughtful and seasoned observers of the education scene. The articles and reaction to them are briefly described in this introductory chapter.

As the reader will note, this introductory narrative moves in parallel with the table of contents. It does two things the individual chapters do not that commend it to the reader. First, in this chapter we briefly discuss the exchanges that took place in the conference, weaving in some of its give and take. It was lively, spirited and productive, punctuated by wit and insight in equal measure; we have tried to capture some of that. Second, we attempt to weave together the intellectual strands of the conference and draw some preliminary conclusions.

The reader should also know that the articles were not 'read' at the conference; for the most part, they were available well in advance for review and comment. At the conference, the briefest of summaries was presented and animated discussion ensued. There was, then, a continuing colloquy among authors and reactors. Finally, authors had the opportunity to revise their articles after receiving the good counsel of their fellow authors and reactors. A verbatim transcript of record was maintained, permitting direct and accurate quotation.

While it is correct to observe that the conferees were uniformly civil, even courtly, there were no holds barred. It was a serious conference about a serious subject. And although there were strong differences among the participants, we all shared a commitment to a revitalized *Chapter 1* program. We care about the effective education of low income children.

Before turning to the theme of this book, it is important to offer a brief comment on the role of the Department of Education and the program officers who worked with us as we commissioned the articles, planned the conference, and then conducted it, Beatrice Birman, Ron Anson, Richard Jung, Martin Orland and Gilbert Garcia. They were unfailingly cooperative and responsive, encouraging us — and the conferees — to call the shots as we saw them. They insisted we set our sights high, and pushed and prodded us intellectually, but in the final analysis left us to our own devices. As a consequence we owe them a debt of gratitude, but must assume all responsibility for any errors of fact or opinion that may have crept into the text. We alone are responsible.

Equally important was the unflagging support we received from the staff of Research and Evaluation Associates, particularly Barbara Williams, Peggy Richmond and Joan Michie. Their patience and unfailing good humor was a continuing source of reassurance. Without their calm professionalism and steady hand at the helm, this effort could not have gone forward successfully.

It hardly needs stating, but the authors of the articles are solely responsible for their content. They have been copy-edited but substantively are the exclusive province of the author.

The book, as was the conference, is divided into three broad categories of description and analysis. First is *The Federal Role*, second is *Selected Issues of Access and Accountability* and third is *Lessons for Implementation*. Our objective was to provide historical and intellectual continuity, and to provide enough structure to encourage an active interchange between authors and reactors. It worked.

Section I: The Federal Role

The lead session on the federal role was organized around four articles and two invited reactors, Nathan Glazer of Harvard and Robert Koff, Dean, School of Education, SUNY-Albany who provided spirited commentary on these and other chapters. Glazer, a prolific author and noted analyst, has written widely on the questions of education and poverty. Koff is a past member of the National Advisory Council on the Education of Disadvantaged Children.

The opening chapter of this section (the second chapter in this book) 'The Evolution of the Compensatory Education Program' by Paul Peterson, Barry G Rabe and Kenneth K Wong of The Brookings Institution provides a brief political history of the federal role in *Title I-Chapter 1*, stressing its purposes and effects. The article is best characterized as 'cautiously optimistic'. As Peterson noted in his opening remarks, 'things are good, but they could be better, and I want to explain why we thought things were much better than we had anticipated'.

Peterson then goes on to examine what the federal interest has been to date, and identifies three stages of development. The authors see an organic evolution over time, because 'intergovernmental programs ... (are) ... a solution to a collective action problem'. The issue, according to Peterson, is that states and localities won't act on their own, because 'if one does ... and nobody else does ... the one that does try to meet the needs of that population is going to get swamped'.

The argument emerges from political economy, attributing political behavior to economic motives. The federal government 'takes upon itself the responsibility because everybody thinks other communities get a free ride'. The first phase of the program, then, was characterized by 'very vague guidelines written in the heyday of great expectations that Lyndon Johnson's rhetoric provided'. Because of misappropriation and under-utilization, the Federal government entered phase two: 'detailed regulations on how the money was to be spent making sure that it was supplement not supplant' and that maintenance of effort occurred.

Phase two, then, was a period of 'over-regulation', seriously complicating the life of 'locals'. The most serious effect of over-regulation, Peterson argues, was the creation of the 'pull out problem'. The simplest way to demonstrate compliance with federal rules and regulations was to 'pull out' *Title I* students. Good accounting makes for bad pedagogy.

The third phase emerged in the late seventies, and it was 'the phase of accommodation where the feds began to relax a bit on their regulations'. This was reasonable because by then the locals 'had a commitment to the program that went well beyond stereotypical following of rituals'. They had begun to identify with program goals. Not surprisingly, the program ran more smoothly as the period of accommodation entered full flower. Indeed, even 'though there was a great deal of deregulation ..., there was very little change in practice at the state and local level'.

In light of the moderate administrative successes they see, Peterson and his co-authors believe that 'the main way the program can be improved is by targeting schools, not students'. The penchant of Congress and of school districts is a little something for everyone, a 'thinning' effect, in which the virtues of concentration are lost. Peterson observed that

> Mary Kennedy and the other members of the *Chapter 1* study team's interim report shows that living in a poor neighborhood is just about as bad as being poor yourself. When you put the two together you have a very severe learning problem, and that is where the monies need to be concentrated.

He concludes by saying, 'if you want to reduce it to a slogan, I would say "Target schools, not students"'. Peterson believes that it 'is going to be very difficult to do politically'.

In the final analysis, Peterson believes that 'more of the same' is probable, but that it is also reasonable to think that today 'knowledge' makes a difference; policymakers may not be consumed with a passion for 'pork barrel' politics and it is worth trying to shape policies on the basis of what we have learned from research. It is an exciting vision; would that it works.

Chapter 3, 'Program Strategy and Design: Options for Federal Action in Education' was written by Paul Hill of The Rand Corporation. In addition to Hill's expertise as a policy analyst, he was the Director of the first major study of *Title I*, conducted in the 70s at the direction of Congress by the National Institute of Education *for* the Congress. It was a study of unusual size and scope, and was conducted with the utmost skill by Hill and a small senior staff.

In this article, Hill develops a taxonomy of different service delivery strategies and options, relying on existing models that are either in place or that have been tried. Hill develops three dimensions: 'who pays, who delivers services, and who chooses what services are delivered'. Hill then creates a large table and assigns 'existing programs to try to understand, from looking at the patterns of empty and full cells — are there some kinds of program designs that are intrinsically more likely to be workable than others'.

Hill's effort produces a 36 cell paper,

> each a possible program design. There are three clusters that look interesting . subsidy programs, in which the Federal Government pays for services which are delivered and chosen by the state and local education agency.

The second kind of 'cluster' was one in which 'the Federal Government pays for services which are chosen and delivered by independent organizations like contracts by the school'.

The third is one in which the Government 'pays for services delivered by private organizations, but chosen by parents and students'. He then assessed these three broad categories on four dimensions: goals, funding, political constraints and organizational capacities.

In contradistinction to Peterson, Hill argues that change in federal programs, particularly large, popular ones, is incremental and slow, and that research findings will have only limited impact on program design. He believes that experimentation or 'demonstration projects' are potentially fruitful and could be sold to the Congress.

Hill raises the all-important tactical and political question concerning state and local support for federal innovations such as *Title I*. He argues, persuasively, that 'subsidy' programs such as this one have a 'much broader basis of current and political support than a contract based program', since they 'work through the existing educational bureaucracies, and the parent-teacher organization, and therefore have stable support'. He prefers, then, federal reform through the system, rather than working around it. In summary, Hill concludes that

> it is very hard to see, to imagine, a nationwide, high volume federally funded program that is not basically a subsidy program, though we wonder how services will be distributed equally to all children — even those in religiously affiliated schools — if federal programs are viewed as mainly a subsidy to the existing public school system.

Chapter 4, 'Increased State Capacity and Aid to the Disadvantaged', is by Susan Fuhrman of the Center for Policy Research and Education at the Eagleton Institute for Politics, Rutgers University. Fuhrman is one of the nation's leading authorities on state and local government, and she argues that a revolution of competence has occurred in the states, particularly over the last decade. No longer the province of political hacks and hangers on, the states are sophisticated and capable. As Fuhrman noted in her opening remarks, 'you have come a long way baby'. But the question remains. Do the states care about disadvantaged youngsters and will they deliver for them? Fuhrman says the jury is still out.

She notes that 'States have come a long way in regard to education in general and perhaps in regard to low achieving students, but that it remains an open question.'

The Fuhrman chapter develops the theme of continued state growth in providing education resources, though 'compensatory education' is often the first to be cut and often the last to be funded. 'Historically, or at least up to the early eighties, there was never a very strong state commitment for the disadvantaged or low achieving students'. In competition with 'general' programs, state governments find it easier to reduce resources for special children, rather than to reduce the funds to school districts for general equalization. It does seem quite clear, however, that since the early days of *Title I*, when the states were new to the 'war on poverty', the state education apparatus has greatly improved its abilities to serve the local communities: they have, in Fuhrman's words, 'modernized and matured'. In part, she explains, the states have increased their fiscal capacities and their imagination in helping the children in both public and private schools. State legislatures, the last vestiges of 19th century government, have improved in representation, appointment, and effectiveness. She lists the major state reforms, many of which are responses to the funding of schools by the federal government: improved teacher training and certification; better teacher compensation; revisions in school governance and finance; strengthened school curriculum, attendance, and programs; higher graduation standards; and better testing and preparation.

Over time, however, Fuhrman found that commitment to compensatory education has seriously eroded, as budgets were tightened. She found that 'weak political support accounts for the rather discouraging state commitment to the disadvantaged'. Politicians, it seems, win and lose elections not on how they support compensatory programs but how well they maintain the general aid to schools across the states. Often, in fact, special needs programs are 'folded into' the general program, giving local boards more discretion and weakening the ability of compensatory programs to succeed as separate, definable programs.

A new generation of reform in the states is under way. It shows, Fuhrman argues, new support for 'at risk' children that extends beyond the work of the federal government. These programs are often coupled with general improvement schemes. For as states raise their graduation and promotion requirements, the needs of low-achieving students are increased, as is the demand for compensatory services. The impact of these new-wave reforms on programs such as *Chapter 1* in the states is not yet known.

As Fuhrman observed at the conference, the '$64,000 question is what about all those new, recent state reforms and disadvantaged or low achieving children?'

Chapter 5, 'The Federal Role and Chapter 1: Rethinking Some Basic Assumptions', was written by Michael W Kirst of Stanford University. The former Chairman of the California State Board of Education and one of the first employees of the original *Title I* office in 1964, Kirst brings a wealth of knowledge and policy analytic skill to this chapter. (Kirst was the first program person hired by the original *Title I* office in 1965.) He argues that it is now time to move beyond 'process' and begin to think about a federal role with a substantive component. Historically, Washington has done no more than pass out money (with fairly rigorous accounting requirements) and has left pedagogy and content to the states and localities. There is now enough of a knowledge base to do more.

What does Kirst advocate in this chapter? The government should move from funding to 'technical assistance', the use of the bully pulpit, and teacher training — rather than acting as an auditing and regulatory agency. Kirst argues that the role of government is more than a money dispenser; that it should become vitally concerned about education quality.

In his opening comments at the conference, Kirst remarked that:

> I think that a new focus of the Federal Government ought to be on the curricular content that these pupils are exposed to and what knowledge and content they need to understand and on instructional strategies for teaching ... this ought to be a key part along with fund concentration that Paul Peterson spoke about ...

Kirst found that the federal government has six alternative roles to play in education: to give general aid to schools, stimulate change through differential funding, to regulate, disseminate new knowledge and ideas, and provide technical assistance, and finally, to exert moral suasion, the bully pulpit. In carrying out these roles, the government has undergone some major changes, from minimal to increased support of private education; from a large to a 'mitigated federal role; from mistrust to a strong reliance on state and local agencies to improve schools; and from categorical to more unrestricted financial aid to schools'.

Kirst makes a key point of the conference: that as the government in Washington, D.C., and the state capitols became basically program managers (under *Chapter 1*), or as Kirst calls them, 'policy administrative generalists', they lost their ability to give leadership in curriculum and instructional areas. This shift — from educators to administrators — meant that less attention was paid to the quality of education — and more on how to dispense funds. Curriculum became 'slowed down' for these kids and 'we have made it over simplified and boring. Therefore, they get farther and farther behind'. Ironically, *Chapter 1* managers worried more about fiscal 'supplanting' and less about *educational* supplanting. Kirst goes on to note that 'We have frustrated attempts to integrate *Title I* more closely with the core curriculum in the regular classroom.'

Kirst argues for greater attention to curriculum, program, and teaching, supported, perhaps, by a national network of educators, curriculum experts, and government people at all levels. This shift from attention to administrative detail to the core of the educational process is long overdue. Government can play a vital role, Kirst believes, in this process: 'it will not be easy to blend a core curriculum approach, teacher training, and school improvement with financial accountability and targeting the neediest pupils'. But until we do, the essence of programs like *Chapter 1* will be lost and its impact blunted. Kirst concluded his conference presentation by noting that

> The states' focus is increasingly on curricular leadership, on instructional strategies. They have moved away from the administrative fiscal strategy as their sole repertoire of leadership and it is about time the Federal Government followed the lead.

The first respondent at the conference was Nathan Glazer, and he observed that the most powerful idea to emerge in the first four papers was the concept of targeting. He went on to note that it was an old idea in government programs, and that whatever intellectual interest it presented, it also presented serious political problems. By way of illustration, he described the targeting discussions that were a part of the model cities planning process. Once the intellectual decision was made to 'target', to reach a 'critical mass', targeting decisions were proposed. Within minutes the list of cities to be targeted had climbed to 150. Glazer's point, and a powerful one, is that however attractive 'targeting' might be intellectually and programmatically, it is very difficult to pull off politically.

With an elegant play on words, Glazer moved from fund concentration to 'concentrating' on study. On what should *Chapter 1* students concentrate? Is it possible to give real curricular leadership from the federal level? What kinds of concrete suggestions might be made? Is there more to the study of mathematics than 'drill and practice', for example? Calculators? Glazer, as were the other participants, was fascinated by the prospect of significantly increased flexibility in the use of *Chapter 1* resources, particularly for such things as after school rather than pull out programs. Citing the experience in Miami schools with this alternative, Glazer suggested that this kind of novel and practical experimentation be encouraged and expanded.

He concluded by noting that there were really three approaches presented in the opening papers: concentrate, focus on curriculum, or give the funds to the parents and let them decide what to do. The

13

unifying thread among these otherwise disparate ideas is that each goes against the grain of current practice.

Bob Koff, Dean of the School of Education at SUNY-Albany was the second respondent and he was concerned by the treatment two questions received — or failed to receive. He was concerned that a preoccupation with a narrow federal program mandate distracted us from the more important question of 'academic failure' among children generally. He observed that:

> We are so preoccupied with complying with various mandates and regulations that we have forgotten that *Chapter 1* was designed, at least initially, to focus on the whole child.

Koff stressed the issue of funding levels for *Chapter 1*, both at present and over time. He believes that inadequate funding partially explains the difficulty of finding sustaining effects, and that it creates serious questions of horizontal or cross district equity. More precisely, he believes that the political decision to fund every district means that serious inequities occur, exacerbated by inadequate funding. Koff uses the hypothetical of one eighth grader getting help if he reads at a seventh grade level in one district, and an eighth grader in another district not getting help if he reads at a fifth grade level.

Of all the articles and various presenters, Koff marshalled the most impressive commentary on the lack of congruence between the core curriculum of the school and the curriculum of the 'pull out' programs. He cited research findings indicating almost no fit at all; classroom teachers who had no idea what was being taught in the pull out program and pull out teachers having no idea as to the school or classroom curriculum. Koff took the argument to its logical conclusion: the existing system segregates children, and *weakens* the incentives in the school to redesign their curriculum to take into account the needs of the disadvantaged. Thus, supplement not supplant had worked too well; it had produced the paradoxical outcome that *Chapter 1* students were less rather than more integrated into the school.

Recognizing the academic importance of targeting, Koff nevertheless is convinced that targeting — at least at present levels of funding — raises very thorny political questions. Citing New York State's 'Comprehensive Assessment Plan' which collects data on each school and every school district, 'you end up with the bottom 10 per cent of which 400 (or there about) are located in New York City'. Koff asked, rather plaintively, 'now that you have identified all the schools with very serious problems, and they are all located in places that you know ... what do you do about it?' Koff goes on to propose that each school in the state develop a plan and that a central state source allocate funds, including such funds as PL 94–142 (which Koff argues are in important respects 'compensatory' education funds).

Section II: Selected Issues of Access and Accountability

The second session on access and accountability was organized around four papers with three reactors, Constance Clayton, Superintendent of Schools, Philadelphia; Charles Glenn, Director of Desegregation, Massachusetts Department of Education; and David Kirp, School of Public Policy, University of California at Berkeley.

Chapter 6, 'Selecting Students and Services for Chapter 1', was written by Marshall Smith, Dean, Graduate School of Education, Stanford University. Smith advances a carefully reasoned and worked argument on the desirability of increasing the concentration of resources on schools rather than individuals. He proposes that fewer schools get more money, that 'pull out' programs be largely abandoned and that existing financial accounting requirement be left in place. It is essentially a strategy of doing more for fewer children, one which may be pedagogically sound but politically difficult to pull off.

Smith's argument is based on his prevailing belief that *Chapter 1* is basically sound and working. Where weaknesses occur, he says, some 'technical assistance' may be useful. In particular, Smith advises that *Chapter 1* be targeted to students in the greatest need and in the deepest poverty. He strongly emphasizes in this chapter that 'We must expand the level of allocation to schools with the highest concentrations of poverty students'. To accomplish this in a time of constrained resources, funds must go to fewer schools. This theme of greater funding, concentrated on fewer students, for greater effect, was common throughout the conference. But politically, to cut out school districts with few poor, low achieving pupils may be difficult, though Peterson, Kirst and Smith all agree that some effort must be made to see that only schools and children with severe poverty and disadvantage receive the bulk of federal funds. In sum, Smith makes a strong case for greater 'efficiency' in targeting schools, in seeing that the best use of money be determined at the 'schoolhouse door', and that good outcome, or output measure be used to strengthen the incentives for *Chapter 1* programs to improve. Improve whole schools, for everyone, and be concerned less for fine-tuning the allocation system to each child — this is the major message of this chapter.

Chapter 7, 'Funding the Individual? An Essay on Chapter 1', was written by Denis P. Doyle of The Hudson Institute, and Bruce Cooper of Fordham University. The United States Supreme Court, in *Aguilar v Felton* has ruled against *Chapter 1* programs in religiously affiliated schools, undoing two decades of successful collaboration. The decision is notable for a number of reasons, not least that it undermines a fragile coalition of support for disadvantaged youngsters that bridges traditional public-private school differences. The authors conclude, perhaps pessimistically, that aid to poor students in private schools is probably doomed.

The authors suggest that unless some device can be found to fund *Chapter 1* families — rather than public school systems — the chance of providing equitable services to students in parochial schools is unlikely. A number of models are possible: vouchers for *Chapter 1* students are probably most efficient — certainly more efficient than the elaborate and expensive 'off-site' means now being used since the Court outlawed 'on-site' methods.

The authors also consider other means of funding the individual: the simplest and most direct would be for the Secretary to declare that parents are 'bypass agents', using the same logic used to 'bypass' SEAs in Virginia, Wisconsin and Missouri where state constitutions prohibit provision of services to religiously-affiliated schools.

The authors argue that unless the government moves quickly to restore *Chapter 1* to private school students, they will be eliminated from the program simply because they 'exercised' their religious rights and selected a parochial school. Further, they argue that the loss of private school leaders from the political coalition that has supported *Chapter 1* since its inception in 1965 may put the program as a whole at risk. They conclude by noting that it is disingenuous of the public sector — which secured passage of the original law only with private school support — to sit idly by while the private schools are removed from the program.

Chapter 8, 'The Problem of Quality in Chapter 1' by Richard F. Elmore of Michigan State University, raises the issue of quality in the opening sentence of his article 'How can federal policy enhance the quality of local programs in *Chapter 1?*'. The issue is hardly an idle one, particularly in light of the discussion the idea raised in the conference, well before time for Elmore's presentation occurred. As he notes, however, 'relatively little attention has been focused explicitly on the issue of quality in *Title I/Chapter 1*, and there is relatively little systematic understanding or analysis of the issue in the evaluation literature growing out of the program'. The silence on the issue is the more peculiar because, as Elmore notes, everyone — 'members of Congress, federal, state and local administrators, teachers, parents, evaluators and analysts' — is concerned about quality. Elmore observes that most of us, the public as well as specialists, think that *Chapter 1* is designed to bring about changes in educational performance that will make a difference, 'that this money is assumed to provide the difference needed to pull a significant proportion of the educationally disadvantaged into the educational mainstream'.

He goes on to note that the single most important aspect of *Chapter 1* is that it is a 'marginal' program. By this he does not mean that it is unimportant — to the contrary, it can be very important if it is well used — but that it exists by 'augmenting' existing programs. Insofar as they are good, *Chapter 1* may be good; insofar as they are weak so too is *Chapter 1* likely to be weak. The 'quality' of services, then, 'is heavily dependent on the setting in which services are delivered'. To better understand how 'quality' might be used to better shape federal policy, Elmore develops three working definitions:

> the resources applied to a local program (inputs), the operating characteristics of local programs (process), and the consequences of local programs for students (outputs), and I will speculate about the strengths and limitations of using each of these approaches as a basis for policy.

Input standards raise the classic set of problems associated with input measures in education generally. They are not sensitive to regional or even building variations in the mix of students to be served, they do not establish the kinds of incentives for local behavior that would be desirable, and they 'focus attention on the allocation of resources to schools and classrooms, rather than the characteristics of the student population served'. This is a particularly severe shortcoming, Elmore argues, in light of the strong findings that student performance is 'strongly related to the race, family income and family resources of students', and that 'the higher the concentration of minority, low income students, the lower the achievement level of the school'.

'Process' standards offer little more about which to be optimistic. They permit the purchase of 'certain packages of instruction', but they too are not sensitive to differences among communities and schools. Process standards, Elmore observes, 'focus local administrators' and teachers' attention on educational practice, rather than on the allocation of dollars'.

While this is an improvement over input standards, 'process standards have their own set of problems'. They lack the kind of flexibility necessary to effective program management; indeed, the very idea would strip local teachers and administrators of much authority and judgment about how best to design and implement a program best suited to their community and school.

By way of contrast, 'output standards' relate to what it is a student learns, not how much in the way of resources are put behind him or what kind of 'instructional package' is made up to serve him. As Elmore notes, output measures are a vote of confidence in the wit and wisdom of the local staff, at least implicitly asserting that they know best how to proceed. Output standards say, in effect, 'do whatever is necessary to produce these effects with this amount of money'. They present a serious technical problem, however, for it is difficult to measure them. First it is difficult to know what standard to apply and second, it is difficult to know how that standard might be measured. There is no education 'bottom line', at best none that is widely accepted. Elmore includes a lively and interesting discussion of some of the other 'technical' and methodological problems, as well as some of the political pitfalls associated with tests and measures. Should standards be set too high, failure appears to be endemic still. Set too low, the standards appear to be a farce. Any standard, of course, produces incentives and disincentives, not least on the part of the participating school, which, after all, depends on meeting the standard to assure its income.

Having sketched in the limits and opportunities of these three different approaches to the question of quality, Elmore notes that there is little likelihood of the federal government imposing quality standards on states and localities. Even if they know what to do, the political realities make it impossible. In light of the limited capacity to use known quality mechanisms effectively, and the impossibility of 'regulating' quality, is the federal government a helpless giant? Elmore thinks not. He believes that a federal concern for quality can be 'manifested in ways that are consistent with a limited federal role and with the serious practical and conceptual issues that underlie alternate definitions of quality'.

In this connection, then, Elmore sketches in three alternative federal strategies, *jawboning, piggybacking, and bootstrapping*. In addition to being colorful, these approaches 'do not require extensive departures from existing practice'. By jawboning Elmore means the 'systematic use of information to draw attention to either good or bad behavior'. If jawboning sounds like the 'bully pulpit' that is because that is exactly what it is. But it is more as well, for it includes within itself 'invidious' comparisons, including reports of bad as well as good performance. It is a flat repudiation of the notion that seems to have gripped some educators, that ignorance is bliss. Jawboning is based on the notion that it will actually change behavior.

Piggybacking is the 'use of discretionary funding to reward and claim credit for local successes'. It too involves the identification of exemplary schools or behavior, but goes jawboning one better — it puts its money where its mouth is. As Elmore notes, 'publicizing their efforts lends authority to a view of *Chapter 1* as aggressively searching out and rewarding creativity'.

The final strategy is bootstrapping, the 'use of discretionary funding to underwrite program development in the most difficult circumstances, with the least likelihood of success, and to claim credit for success against the odds'. Elmore concludes that these strategies are not likely to be popular among the traditional friends of *Chapter 1*; indeed, for them, ignorance is bliss. But these are approaches that over the long haul could make a significant difference both to the program and the students in it.

Chapter 9, 'How Fiscal Accountability and Program Integrity Can Be Insured For Chapter 1', is the work of Allan Odden of University of Southern California. One of the nation's leading authorities on school finance, Odden argues that fiscal accountability is effective and adequate, and that the means for implementation are now fully developed. He also argues that program quality is a function of district quality, which is beyond direct federal government influence. He concludes with a five-part program of recommendations to strengthen program quality on the basis of what we now know about *Chapter 1*.

Odden reinforces ideas developed in the Kirst chapter — that until we recognize that *Chapter 1* is only part of a total school program, that until federal efforts are harnessed to local efforts to improve schools, until schools themselves have a strong and effective program, then *Chapter 1* cannot be successful. Odden argues, rightly, that first all schools with *Chapter 1* programs must have school-wide education improvement plans integrated with *Chapter 1*; second, *Chapter 1* services should be 'aligned' with the regular school program; and third, *Chapter 1* funds should be conditional on the school's using effective schools and teaching strategies; and fourthly creating new *Chapter 1* programs as model or demonstration projects to foster new curricula and approaches for low-income students.

Odden concludes by noting that his chapter has two basic points — the first is that the 'current structure of *Chapter 1* — the law and accompanying rules and regulations — is adequate for assuring fiscal accountability'. He believes that the means for implementing this structure at the state and local level are firmly developed and 'function relatively well'. His second point is that the effectiveness of the program depends on the quality of the local schools — its curriculum and teaching — two 'arenas essentially beyond direct influence by the federal government'. He is, nevertheless, confident that four broad strategies are available to the federal government to increase quality.

Odden would require all *Chapter 1* sites to have a 'school wide education improvement program'. He would also require that *Chapter 1* service be 'aligned' with the regular program. He would condition receipt of *Chapter 1* funds on schools implementing 'research-based effective teaching and school strategies'. And finally, he would provide funds to develop 'model curriculum guides', improved testing, and supplemental instructional strategies and materials. The Odden paper, perhaps because of Odden's unavoidable absence, was the subject of animated and good natured discussion. Kirst, in the context of discussing other papers, ably summarized the paper and Glazer, in an enthusiastic mood, observed that the ideas developed were not likely to work in the real world. Requiring schools to develop plans which would incorporate the best research findings about effective schools or effective *Chapter 1* programs was an invitation to dissimulation at best, and outright chicanery at worst. Schools, eager to receive their allocation would 'promise anything, so long as it was *Chapter 1* compliance'. The issue, at a serious level, would be compounded by compliance problems; to attempt to monitor school compliance with promised adherence to school effectiveness research is a daunting problem.

Odden's absence was a great disappointment, because he is an articulate and sophisticated analyst and would have rejoined skillfully and effectively. The point remains, however, and Odden is on target in his insistence that 'alignment' is essential. A cosmetic, add-on program, that has little direct relationship to the day to day life of the school is one that is guaranteed not to work. In addressing both Odden's and Smith's paper Kirst noted that the ideas developed by Elmore mirrored the other two. In particular, Elmore's notion of jawboning, piggyback-ing, and bootstrapping were reminiscent of Smith's view that radical experimentation and demonstrations should be tried. In the context of the Odden paper, it became clear that the authors and conferees were concerned about the 'nitty gritty' aspects of the program — what works and why?

Dr Constance Clayton approached her reading of the papers from the perspective of a big city superintendent. She too was concerned about the 'nitty gritty'; as she told the conferees, '*Chapter 1* is an essential component of the school district education program ... it is from that perspective that I read the papers ... and from which I express both concurrence and reservation'. Dr Clayton concurred actively and enthusiastically with the idea that it was impossible to build effective *Chapter 1* programs without effective school programs. She found both Elmore's and Odden's characterizations on target, Elmore's notion of 'marginality', *Chapter 1* as an add-on, and Odden's notion of 'align-ment'. She also agreed that fiscal accountability does not assure program quality. But she did not agree that fiscal accountability was effective or acceptable:

> If we were to calculate both the transaction costs and the opportunity costs of the prevailing regulatory structures, we might find that it was possible to develop alternative mechan-isms capable of insuring more certainty, less anxiety and more effective utilization of the opportunities to reach the targeted populations.

More important than the limitations of fiscal accountability, according to Dr Clayton, is the 'reality that the prevailing regulatory environment is not neutral on issues of educational quality. Rather, the regulatory environment, in many instances ... tends to deter, impede and undermine educational improvement and reform'. Dr Clayton was not sanguine about jawboning either. She asserted that 'rhetoric, no matter what the source, or the volume, or the flourish, will not in and of itself solve real problems'. She went on to observe that concrete, programmatic interventions are required.

She was more enthusiastic about piggybacking, but noted that the development of exemplary programs takes time. She was most enthusiastic about bootstrapping, Elmore's third proposal. But most important was Dr Clayton's reading of a recent study on the fit between Philadelphia students and their schools. In summary form, the poorest and the most disadvantaged are today's clientele — the better off, black, white and Hispanic — have gone. And the public school is the only institution left for these communities. Most important, they cannot go it alone. They need the help of other institutions.

Superintendent Clayton closed with a recommendation notable for its novelty and interest, 'education enterprise zones', areas in which schools could escape the reach of federal rule and regulation and state imposed program specific guidelines.

Charles Glenn, Director of Desegregation in Massachusetts, observed that in his experience 'top down' reform strategies simply did not work, communities and schools had to have some feeling of ownership and participation. One of the strengths of an effective desegregation strategy, for example, is that it releases new energies in a school. Bad programs turn people off, they lose interest and energy, become passive.

Glenn found the articles persuasive in one particular that would have immediate utility to him in dealing with the Board of Education, and that was the target of reform should be the school building not the school system. Not only does identifying the school get out from under problems with school districts, it permits the program to be school wide and not stigmatize students.

David Kirp, alert to the perversity everywhere apparent in public policy, described an amusing but potent anecdote about California's incentive program. A group of high school juniors in Chico approached their principal and told him they would do poorly on the statewide incentive examination — a high score on which would have entitled the school to a state bonus — unless he restored certain privileges. Upon his refusal they scored low, and the school's opportunity costs turned out to be high.

Kirp's more general cautionary note was well placed also. A skeptic by temperament, training and experience, Kirp cautioned the conferees against the dangers of being overly narrow, of focusing on the schools most in need of help, but by so doing, hoping to find a panacea, a cure.

Section III: Lessons for Implementation

The first session of lessons for implementation was organized around three articles with three reactors, David Savage, formerly the chief education writer for *The Los Angeles Times* (now covering the Supreme Court); Joan Davis Rattaray, Head of the Institute for Independent Education; and Milbrey McLaughlin, Professor at the Graduate School of Education, Stanford University.

Chapter 10, 'Effective Public Schools; Choice and Diversity', is by Charles Glenn, Director, Desegregation Programs, State of Massachusetts. Glenn, drawing on more than a decade of experience as the Director of desegregation programs for the State of Massachusetts, argues that magnet schools and other means of parental and family choice among public schools permits them to enjoy some of the flexibility and responsiveness usually associated with the private sector. The chapter sums up Glenn's experience, and provides a rich array of empirical evidence.

Glenn highlights the human side of *Chapter 1*, its impact on the life and times of children in schools: he remarks on the role of integration, for example, in producing solid 'respect and friendship across racial difference', involved and constructive parents and teachers, and schools where great improvement has occurred in his State of Massachusetts. He concentrates on the old concerns of racial integration, wherein the state targets schools with high percentages of minority students. Where integration is not possible, extra effort is expended to upgrade the program through assessment programs, technical assistance, and new materials and leadership.

His chapter details the desegregation process in his state, and its impact on children and their community. He found that 'schools do make a difference, that other children in the schools matter (isolation of poor, underachieving children is unacceptable), that programs for these children can have a positive effect'. He argues that 'pull-out' programs, while sometimes necessary, should be rethought and redesigned, as too disruptive and destabilizing for students. He ends his valuable chapter with some practical advice for school administrators, teachers, and policymakers, including the need for good coordination to locate students with special needs, for a 'cohesive sense of mission', for a unified faculty, for new programs, including the extended day and year, and the continued need for desegregation and improvement. The value of this chapter is its state-level perspective and its strong, practical slant on the improvement of compensatory education for those who need the assistance.

Chapter 11, 'The Way that Schools Are: Lessons for Reformers', was written by Larry Cuban, the new Assistant Dean of Education at Stanford. Cuban, a former school Superintendent, speaks to the issue of reform at the schoolhouse level. He is pessimistic about the ability of higher levels of government to make a lasting difference, and only somewhat less pessimistic about the willingness of local schools district to actually make a difference. Nevertheless, he is convinced that reform, if it occurs at all, will be initiated locally.

Cuban argues in his chapter that federal/state level reform is a 'blunt tool', since only those on the premises can truly be responsive to the needs of children. We should, we must, he says, learn from history, from the development of reform over the last 100 years. From his grand historic view, Cuban carefully culls some sage advice which is particularly pertinent to the future of *Chapter 1* and compensatory education.

First, he explains, prescription is useless, since schools and classrooms vary widely. Second, the corollary of one, improvement must be tied to each school site. Third, without greater independence for teachers and administrators, he continues, these educators cannot hope to respond to the critical needs of the students. Reform by 'remote control' is neither wise nor effective. Fourth, effective change in schools, Cuban explains, relates closely to what on-site implementers think and need — and the support they receive from parents, central office and unions. Fifth, start in the elementary schools, since their size, simplicity, and scheduling make improvement possible.

Cuban argues forcefully for continued state and federal involvement in education, though unless these agencies realize the importance of the school level, the role of teachers and administrators, and the centrality of local commitment, these national efforts will fail. He writes of the 'need for strategies of school improvement that focus less on control through regulation and more on vesting individual schools and educators with the independence to reach explicit goals and standards — within flexible and fair ways of holding educators responsible'.

Chapter 12, 'Effective Schools and the Problems of the Poor', is by John Chubb of The Brookings Institution. Certainly the most provocative chapter in the book, it is a fitting way to conclude the discussion of *Chapter 1*. Chubb argues that organizational climate makes the difference between 'good' and 'bad' schools, that school effects of the kind observed by Rutter and his colleagues in the UK or Coleman and his colleagues in the US, appear most fully developed in the private sector. He also argues that these effects can by their nature not appear in as robust a form in the public sector as the private, and concludes with support for education vouchers. He does not believe that *Chapter 1* by itself can be the agent of reform; it is too little too late.

The Chubb chapter calls attention to school organization as a critical variable in school reform and improvement. What goes on inside the school, and how that school is structured, are probably central in explaining school outcomes. He maintains that structure is more than how teachers teach and administrators lead; effectiveness is also related to such other qualities as discipline and homework, the common beliefs in the school and so on, qualities that seem more evident in private than in public schools. Using data from the *High School and Beyond* survey, Chubb was involved in further comparison of public and private schools. His findings suggest that school organization, environment and structure are closely tied up with the performance of such schools. Since public and private schools have very different environments (public schools are characterized by political and authoritative control; private ones by market and competitive control), they provide an excellent setting for comparison. With private schools performing better, it is interesting to note that private schools have many of the qualities that reformers are pressing for public schools: attention to clients and markets, less control by unions, better, more experienced principals, and higher expectations.

While public school principals, according to the Chubb chapter, may look to promotion out of school, private school heads tend to see the school as their career. And private schools, as the Chubb survey shows, tend to require more stringent courses and a greater number of credits than public schools — which tend to focus on basic literacy and numeracy. Overall, Chubb found that staff in private schools had a clearer grasp of the mission of the school, and interestingly, were in closer agreement on school policy and procedures with their principals. The 'relative harmony' in private schools may be at the very heart, according to Chubb, of the success of private schools: 'Private schools do look more like teams'.

The future of compensatory education and reform, as seen by Chubb in his chapter, rests with instilling the 'attributes of effectiveness' in schools, attributes which resemble the qualities of private schools. But how can large, system-bound public schools be made to act like private ones, within their current educational framework?

Chubb argues that real reform requires a new, a different system, one where autonomy and professionalism flourish. He argues, as do Doyle and Cooper, that individual funding — vouchers, for example — is the best and perhaps the only way to break the deadlock and free schools to improve. Competition and choice, he says, are the best ingredients of school change, particularly for schools that serve the poorest and least prepared of the nation's students.

The three reactors, Savage, Rattaray and McLaughlin, brought dramatically different experiences to the conference. Savage was for a short time an employee of the National Institute of Education, and most recently the chief education correspondent for the *Los Angeles Times*. Rattaray, a Washingtonian, has worked widely with neighborhood self help groups and is the founder of The Institute of Independent Education, an organization devoted to helping minority private schools to begin and then flourish. McLaughlin, now of Stanford University, was for many years at the Rand Corporation where she earned a national reputation for her research and policy analysis.

Savage began with a sardonic comment:

> I ... read (the papers) and was so depressed at the end that I felt like going back upstairs and going back to sleep.

In a more optimistic vein, he went on to observe the general idea that Washington can't tie a lot of strings to the money; that 'schools and teachers are not puppets that can be pulled on strings'. But he went on to add that he disagreed with Cuban's emphasis that schools are 'almost independent entities' and the 'school boards and the federal government have no business trying to set goals'.

Savage went on to thread the needle of federal interests and the legitimacy of local control. Each party has interests that are real and well defined, and the error of the federal government 'is in trying to specify very narrowly' to see to it that the 'people in the schools do what the people in Washington would like them to'. He concluded with his conviction that accountability is both desirable and possible and asserted that progress can be measured and incentives and rewards for progress built into the system.

Joan Rattaray observed that the education of the poor is not well understood, and that she has little confidence that the schools as they are presently constituted will be able to respond to their needs. Her observations were based on work she is doing in schools at the present, and her conviction that in effective schools something is going on that has escaped the attention of most researchers:

> The sense of family, the sense of the relationship, the sense of commitment that I have seen in many of the schools that I have been involved with in the same neighborhood, says that there is something else going on that we need to look at.

Rattaray was also concerned about the cultural implications of the use of accountability measures that would impose the values of the dominant culture on youngsters from different backgrounds. She is convinced that 'the criterion for success is to be able to suppress one's culture'. Which, she adds, is a 'fundamentally flawed assumption'.

Milbrey McLaughlin was, by luck of the draw, the last respondent, and, as is her wont, rose to the occasion with comments that skillfully framed the issues before the conferees. She not only captured the essence of the papers in the concluding session, but wove them together with the papers and commentary from the earlier sessions. She framed her comments in the larger context of the school and the differences among schools across the nation, by way of introducing the issues of 'overregulation and standardization', room at the local level and autonomy, and the problem of 'displacing local innovation and local initiative with federal regulation'.

She observed that the problems were complex and multi-layered; for example, she noted that there is 'not a wave of innovation waiting to be unleashed out there'. The issue that this raises is

> what is the implementation response that on the one hand provides the autonomy to move, while on the other hand

recognizes the capacity issues and that there is not a wave of innovation out there...

The issue is important because the context of regulation is a school universe which is so varied that it is a system in name only. Describing field work by a colleague, McLaughlin observed that

> I can't even see a job description there. They aren't the same thing at all. Teaching in this New York City school is nothing like teaching in Los Angeles schools which is nothing like teaching at a school in San Francisco.

Her sense of variety and diversity in the schools, however, did not lead her to support Chubb's point of view. 'How do you get from there to a market system?' she asked. She attempted to answer her own question by listing a set of policy responses. First, she believed that 'reformulating' *Chapter 1* was a serious issue. She visualized a 'phase three' in the Federal role, beyond Paul Peterson's second phase. She recommended looking at such things as a technical assistance role for the Federal government, as well as more extensive evaluation and research. She agreed some decentralization was desirable, but that there had to be a 'central authority for inspection, for accountability and for observing the natural experiment'.

McLaughlin remained convinced, then, that a federal role remained, one that went beyond simply passing out funds. By way of illustration she described what happened when *Chapter 1* mandates were withdrawn: 'parent involvement went away overnight ... and evaluation didn't'. The lesson she draws from this is two-fold. Both were originally required by Washington, yet only one 'stuck'. The one that did did so because it turned out to be genuinely useful; the locals developed a taste for it. Parent involvement never engendered 'any authority at the local level'. When the federal authority left so too did parent advisory boards. McLaughlin's lesson, then, is that Washington can make a difference. The evidence is that it has.

Conclusion

Throughout the conference, and the papers that make up the chapters of this book, ran (and continues to run) a sense of political irony.

Washington supports education for the best of reasons: to improve the life chances of the poor and dispossessed. But the political logic of Washington's support for any program is some sense of *quid pro quo*; Washington expects to get something for the dollars it is spending. It is for this reason that revenue sharing was so vulnerable when the budget crunch came. Thus, the ideas advanced so persuasively by Larry Cuban and others — that what goes on in the school is most important, that there is little Washington can do beside 'putting the money on the stump and running', — flies in the face of the realities of Washington politics. Perhaps it is for this reason that Congress, over the years, has been more generous with operating funds than program evaluation or research and development funds. Particularly in the pork barrel, ignorance is bliss.

This book, then, provides both depth and richness, both description and analysis of the federal government's major 'lower' education program, *Chapter 1*, at a time when the Congress is reauthorizing it and educators and analysts are re-examining it. The range of perspectives in this volume is substantial, including those who support continuation of the program basically as is, with some mild refocusing, targeting, and sharpening, to those who see the need for dramatic change.

This book has valuable insights into the history and development of federal aid to education: Kirst traces it from regulation through the bully pulpit; Cuban goes back even further, to the very origin of federal, state, local relations, and the growth of the 'modern' school system.

Despite substantial differences, each chapter shares a commitment to serving those in society most in need. Each author accepts the concept of a Federal role to help the poor and disadvantaged; they divide on how best to accomplish so ambitious an undertaking. Some advocate more governmental control, more requirements in targeting, concentrating resources on schools; others express skepticism about the ability of institutions like the government and the schools as they are presently organized to help the poor, and would rather empower parents to help their own children through vouchers.

To some readers this diversity of viewpoint will make the book seem inconclusive. To others, it will make the book more valuable. There is no party line in this volume: this not a Democratic or Republican, Left or Right-wing book. It is not a set piece for a point of view. Because the authors are committed to *Chapter 1*, the book will be useful to those most concerned about running compensatory education programs.

This book may not change your mind about the future role of the Federal government in schools; if it makes you stop and think, however, we will have accomplished out objective.

This range of reaction and commentary reflects the success of those who fashioned *Title I* over two decades ago. Its durability is witness to its ability to accommodate private and public schools, supporters of local control and the interests of state and federal government. It is fitting that it should be so, for *Chapter 1* has taken its place as a symbol of what is functional and dysfunctional about a national government, in a Federal system, working with states and schools districts, on behalf of the least advantaged of our children.

Section 1:
The Federal Role

2
The Evolution of the Compensatory Education Program

Paul E. Peterson, Barry G. Rabe, and Kenneth K. Wong

Over time, compensatory education has become an increasingly institutionalized and effective Federal program. Although examples of bureaucratic ineptitude, concessions to special interests, and inefficient use of Federal resources persist, the dominant pattern is quite the opposite. Instead of conflict, one finds cooperation. Instead of Federal coercion, one finds mutual accommodation on the part of national, state, and local officials. Instead of misappropriation of Federal resources, one finds ready acquiescence to Federal guidelines at the state and local level. Above all, instead of a heavy Federal presence, one finds, for the most part, a cooperative system in which responsibility is shared among professional administrators at all levels of government.

Mutually accommodating intergovernmental relationships in compensatory education are founded on the reality that each participant needs the other. Federal agencies have crucial legal and fiscal resources; locals have the operational capacity without which nothing can be achieved. Cooperative relations are also facilitated by the fact that the program is the product of a broad social movement with both national and local adherents. Also, professional administrators at all levels of government identify with the goals of these new programs, have been recruited to direct them, and as a result have a stake in making them work.

Cooperative relationships in compensatory education emerged gradually. Between 1965, when legislation authorizing the program was enacted, and 1981, when Congress modified many of the law's statutory requirements, the program evolved through three distinct phases. Originally it was little more than a vague expression of a general Federal commitment to help educate those in poverty. By the early 1970s the program had acquired a well-defined set of rules and guidelines that many state and local officials had difficulty under-standing, to say nothing of implementing. Eventually, Federal, state, and local policymakers worked out their differences so that by the early 1980s a stable set of expectations concerning program operations emerged.

These conclusions are based upon a review of the existing literature and our own research on Federal-state-local relations in four urban areas: Baltimore, Dade Country, San Diego and Milwaukee. Field research, including documentary research and interviews with Federal, state and local officials, was conducted between 1980 and 1982; all unattributed quotations are from these interviews (see Peterson, Rabe and Wong, 1986 for a more complete description of this research).[1]

Phase One: High Expectations and Vague Requirements

In the first phase of a redistributive program the central government is bold in its expectations, unclear in its objectives, imprecise in its stipulations, and inept in its administrative actions. A bold preamble is sketched, a vague program framework is developed, and the funding sluice gates are opened. Details regarding costs and implementation procedures are treated as secondary concerns, dust that will settle once the legislation has been enacted. If the program develops problems, rational analysis can presumably solve them. In the exuberance of the moment such programs are seen as points of departure for future Federal action rather than definitive steps in the evolution of a social welfare state.

The expectations for compensatory education were especially high. The eminent sociologist Kenneth Clark (1966) spoke for a generation of scholars when he stated that 'providing more effective education in our public schools for the children of the poor, Negro and white, is the crucial battle in the overall war against poverty and will determine its eventual success or failure' (p. 175). President Lyndon Johnson concur-red and made compensatory education a cornerstone of the Great Society. After signing the legislation, he said, 'I will never do anything in my entire life, now or in the future, that excites me more, or benefits the nation I serve more, or makes the land and all of its people better and wiser and stronger, or anything that ... means more to freedom and justice in the world than what we have done with this education bill' (Johnson, 1966, p. 416). The program was expected to eradicate past inequities and was also perceived as a stepping stone to an American educational renaissance. Social psychologist Robert Havighurst reflected a widespread belief that compensatory education was only the beginning of a new movement that would change the nation's overall level of ability. He expected passage of the Elementary and Secondary Education Act of 1965 to be followed by an all-out effort to 'raise the average IQ of children from low-income families by ten points ... [and] clear out 50 to 75 per cent of the severe retardation in reading and arithmetic which now exists in elementary schools' (Havighurst, 1965, p. xi).

As extravagantly as these expectations were stated, the law itself was extremely vague as to how they were to be achieved. In part this was due to the fact that school officials opposed any Federal instruction on how the job was to be done. The legislation providing for compensatory education was shaped in part by the National Education Association, the Council of Chief State School Officers, the National School Boards Association, the American Association of School Administrators, the National Association of State Boards of Education, and the National Congress of Parents and Teachers. Widely known as the 'big six' in educational policy circles, these long-established and influential organizations shared 'an ideological preference for protecting local and state control of education and minimizing Federal interference' (Kirst and Jung, 1982, p. 130). The sole lobby group promoting categorical restrictions on the program was the National Catholic Welfare Board, which was interested in making certain that some of the monies were used in non-public schools.

Federal direction of compensatory education funds was thus initially limited. Requirements for fiscal control and accounting procedures 'as may be necessary to assure proper disbursement of, and accounting for, Federal funds' and requirements for adopting 'effective procedures' for program evaluation proved to be more exhortation than carefully crafted procedures with which local districts were expected to comply. Although the Federal government also required that funds be denied to local school districts if the state found that 'the combined fiscal effort ... of that agency and the state [was] ... less than [the] fiscal effort' (Elementary and Secondary Education Act of 1965, Title I, Section 207(c)(2), 79 Stat. 32) of the previous year, state and local expenditures for education were increasing rapidly enough during the inflationary period that the provision proved neither restrictive nor meaningful. Consequently localities sometimes used part of the Federal aid for local tax relief instead of using all of it to increase educational services. One econometric analysis discovered that in 1970, for every dollar in Federal aid they received, localities reduced their own local expenditures on education an average of twenty-eight cents (Feldstein, 1978).

Not only were Federal restrictions minimal, but the administrative staff to enforce them was small and inexperienced. The job of administering compensatory education programs, observed Stephen Bailey and Edith Mosher (1968) in their authoritative chronicle, 'fell to an agency with a long and pedestrian past'. The professional staff of the Office of Education averaged more than 50 years of age, they suffered from 'an almost pathological suspicion' of the Department of Health, Education, and Welfare, and they feared the change of Federal control in a way that had a 'crippling effect on initiative and leadership' (pp. 72 and 75). 'Instead of being oriented toward compliance, Federal administrators viewed themselves as professional educators; the idea of enforcing regulations was simply incompatible with their view of public education' (Murphy, 1971, p. 53). But even if Federal and state officials had been more zealous in their commitment to the objectives of compensatory education, there were simply too many districts and classrooms for any single method of implementation to become dominant. As late as 1976 the Office of Education employed only one hundred persons with administrative responsibilities in compensatory education to supervise a program operating in 14,000 local school districts. Commenting on early program experiences, Milbrey McLaughlin (1975) observed, 'The [Office of Education] does not "run" Title I. The design and content of the more than 30,000 Title I projects across the country are determined by [local school systems]. Consequently, the use of Title I dollars reflects multiple and diverse goals, which are not easily transformed into measurable, overarching objectives' (p. 117). Perhaps the situation was best summed up by Alice Rivlin (1971): 'No one really knew *how* to run a successful compensatory education program. There were hunches and theories, but few facts' (p. 80).

If Federal administrators had limited resources and experience, local administrators and teachers had only vague ideas of what a compensatory education program entailed. Indeed, it was this very vagueness that motivated some of the original supporters of the program. Testifying before the congressional committee considering the 1965 legislation, Robert Kennedy complained of having 'seen enough districts where there has been a lack of imagination, lack of initiative, and lack of interest in the problems of some of the deprived children' (cited in McLaughlin, 1975, p. 2). If that were the state of affairs when the legislation passed, schools could obviously not be redirected overnight. Among the four school systems included in our study, Baltimore was especially slow in developing a special focus for its compensatory education program. As late as 1975, according to a Baltimore administrator, 'Federal auditors came in and said there was no comparability [local spending on compensatory schools equal to that on other local schools]. We said, "What's new?" There was no deliberate effort on our part to deceive the feds. There was some ignorance, some things we just didn't know, and some things we didn't want to do.' Not only was there no comparability, but Baltimore, the most politicized of the four cities, was said to have allocated its funds according to politically defined criteria.

Inexperience, a small administrative staff, and ill-defined objectives combined to produce a diverse, inchoate program that failed to concentrate its fiscal resources on the population it was supposed to serve. Even several years after passage of the act it was easy to conclude that the program illustrated perfectly what a generation of analysts have come to criticize as a fundamental flaw of redistributive programs and of American federalism: 'The Federal system—with its dispersion of power and control not only permits but encourages the evasion and dilution of Federal reform, making it nearly impossible for the Federal administrator to impose program priorities; those not diluted by Congressional intervention can be ignored during state and local implementation' (Murphy, 1971, p. 60).

Phase Two: Imposing and Enforcing Regulations

The second phase in the evolution of a new intergovernmental program attempts to correct the problems and abuses experienced in the first phase. As evidence accumulates that funds for redistributive programs are being diverted from the populations they are supposed to be serving, the Federal government intensifies its oversight of local activities. New regulations are enacted to compel greater program unity, regulations that may be supported or even designed by organizations representing the program's intended recipients. Rather than continue to acquiesce in locally defined resource allocation, programs are adjusted to make the goals of Federal policy clear. As local officials chafe under the new regulations, intergovernmental conflict and confusion increase.

The experience of the compensatory education program illustrated this pattern of change. Before the 1981 deregulations introduced by the Reagan administration, Congress amended the original legislation on four occasions: 1968, 1970, 1974 and 1978. Each set of amendments resulted in new provisions that specified more clearly the congressional commitment to helping disadvantaged children from low-income families. The Office of Education developed its own increasingly elaborate set of regulations and guidelines, many of them stated in letters to specific school districts or in interpretations of specific decisions. Even if one looks at only the formal requirements, the number of Federal regulations added is astonishing. In 1965 the program had eight requirements; by 1980 it had fifty-nine.

To prove that they were concentrating services on the disadvantaged, local districts had to show that they were identifying as compensatory education schools those with the highest concentration of students in poverty, that they were contributing as many local resources to these schools as to any other school in the district, and that they were committing at least the same level of local resources as they had provided in previous years.

To help them achieve these objectives, the Federal government established a number of specific guidelines. Under maintenance of effort, districts' revenues from state and local sources could not be lower than those of the preceding year. Comparability ensured that locally funded services in every compensatory education school were at least at the average level of those provided to non-compensatory education schools in the same district. This concept was intended to prevent local districts from using Federal funds merely to provide the poor with services already available in other schools. A supplement, not supplant, provision, added in 1970, specified that school districts were to use Federal dollars 'to supplement, and to the extent practical, increase the levels of funds that would, in the absence of such Federal funds, be made available from non-Federal sources' (Amendments to the Elementary and Secondary Education Act of 1965, Title I, Section 109, 84 Stat. 124) for programs and projects for the educational disadvantaged. These funds were 'in no case' to be used to supplant such funds from non-Federal sources. This provision was clarified by the excess cost guideline, which stipulated that compensatory education dollars pay only the costs of supplementary services that exceeded normal instructional expense. Another provision required that all services provided to non-compensatory education students also be furnished to compensatory education children. Each provision was intended to make certain that disadvantaged children directly benefited from Federal dollars. Still other Federal provisions helped govern the design and operation of compensatory education at the local level. Under concentration of services, school districts were required to channel Federal aid to schools with a higher proportion of poor students before spending money on schools with a lower proportion. Needs assessment directed districts to identify all educationally dis-advantaged children in low-income areas and to formulate a program design on how to meet the needs of these children. To avoid program duplication, local authorities were encouraged to coordinate compensatory instruction with other Federal and state programs.

Federal enforcement activities also became more rigorous as audi-tors scrutinized state and local allocation practices and found many inconsistent with the new guidelines. The increased enforcement effort began in earnest during the early years of the Nixon administration. One key Federal bureaucrat recalled that before 1968 it had been politically risky to push for careful enforcement of Federal regulations on comparability and non-supplanting. But during the early Nixon years, Federal officials decided that the program was not working because states and localities failed to follow regulations. Thus, despite the administration's dislike of excessive paperwork, the Office of Education tightened Federal controls. As one Federal bureaucrat later admitted, 'A hell of a paperwork burden was imposed on the states and local districts for the sake of ensuring comparability.'

These changes were enthusiastically supported by a wave of new groups, such as the National Advisory Council for the Education of

Disadvantaged Children, the Lawyers Committee for Civil Rights Under Law, the Legal Standards and Education Project of the National Association for the Advancement of Colored People (NAACP), and the National Welfare Rights Organization. These organizations functioned as advocates for the low-income, low-achieving students compensatory education was designed to assist. Unlike the groups that had helped initiate the legislation in 1965, these organizations argued repeatedly that greater Federal specificity was needed in allocating funds and overseeing their use. In the process they provided reports and suggestions that influenced congressional thinking and were sometimes simply adopted in various amendments. The Children's Defense Fund and the NAACP, for example, were instrumental in gaining congressional support for the comparability and non-supplanting provisions. They compiled considerable evidence, much of it from previously unheralded Federal audits, that local districts were misusing Federal money. The publication of these findings in a 1969 report, entitled *Title I: Is It Helping Poor Children?*, prompted a major intensification of Federal oversight of the program (Martin and McClure, 1969).

During the 1970s such organizations became increasingly active and effective. For example, the Lawyers Committee for Civil Rights Under Law, a public interest law firm, was a constant thorn in the side of local educators and their organizational representative in Washington. The law firm not only published manuals advising citizens how to bring suit against districts believed to be in violation of Federal guidelines, but 'several of their recommendations for strengthening the program requirements [were] quite evident in the 1978 amendments' (Kirst and Jung, 1982, p. 132).

At the same time, Federal officials responsible for the compensatory education program became increasingly impatient as audit and other evaluation reports indicated considerable local divergence from Federal requirements and expectations. Ultimately, some districts were charged with outright misuse of Federal funds. Audits conducted in 1973, for instance, charged the Milwaukee school district with the misuse of $5.9 million of compensatory education funds between 1968 and 1973, through violations of the supplement, not supplant and comparability requirements. Federal dollars, the audits indicated, were used to pay for the salaries and related costs of many compensatory education teachers who had previously been paid from state and local sources. The audits also charged that some projects, such as an environmental education mobile laboratory and field trips to museums, served all students in certain grade levels (and not just the disadvantaged ones eligible for services). In 1980, after years of negotiations, Milwaukee returned $120,266 to the Federal government (Wisconsin Department of Public Instruction, 1982).[2]

The Baltimore school district was even more resistant to Federal restrictions of fund use. Baltimore officials mingled compensatory education dollars with the general school fund and often used the Federal funding to supplant general school expenditures. A 1978 Federal audit charged that the district had failed to fulfill its responsibilities to ensure that funds were spent in the Baltimore schools in conformity with Federal regulations (US Department of Education, 1980). From 1974 to 1978 the Baltimore school district allegedly misspent $14.6 million in Federal funds, one-fourth of the total Federal compensatory education allocation to the district during the period (Assistant Secretary for Elementary and Secondary Education, 1981). Most of the funds were allegedly used to cover general administrative costs and regular curricular activities that benefited all students. Although the leading state and local school officials contended that the allegations were inaccurate, many administrators and instructors with extensive experience in Baltimore's program agreed that the charges were generally legitimate. They concurred with audit findings that Baltimore had 'operated the program inefficiently, used a deficient accounting system', and paid scant attention to many program guidelines.

The rigorous regulatory and enforcement efforts of the early 1970s did serve to concentrate compensatory education services on the low-income, educationally disadvantaged student, however. By 1976 the program had acquired sufficient definition that only three per cent of the students who were neither poor nor educationally disadvantaged were participating in federally funded reading programs (Table 1). The Federal law, to be sure, did not give poor, disadvantaged students a right to compensatory services, so in fact only a third of the most eligible students actually were receiving them, a point often made by those calling for program expansion. But even though the program may have been smaller than advocates wished, poor, low-achieving students were eleven times more likely to be in the program than their better-off counterparts. Clearly Federal rules were by this time shaping policy implementation at the local level.

Table 1: Percentage of Children in Compensatory Reading Programs by Status and Program, 1976 *

Program	Poor low achievers**	Not poor, low achievers	Poor high achievers	Not poor, high achievers
Title I	32.7	20.4	4.9	2.7
Other compensatory services	14.4	14.9	8.1	6.3
Non-participants	52.9	64.7	87.0	90.9

*Columns may not total 100 per cent because of rounding.
**Bottom 50 per cent in reading.

Source: *Poverty Achievement and the Distribution of Compensatory Education Service* (First interim report of the National Assessment of Chapter 1), (p. 88) by Kennedy, MM, Jung, RK, and Orland, ME, (1986) Washington, DC, US Department of Education.

Phase Three: Toward More Mature Program Operation

Repeated conflicts over program regulations generate a third stage in the administration of redistributive programs. Federal bureaucrats, facing complaints from local leaders and from their legislative representatives, once again modify guidelines and procedures. A new tolerance of local diversity, a new recognition that no single program-matic thrust is clearly preferable, and an appreciation of the limits as to what can be directed from the center steadily emerges. Phase three is *not* a return to phase one: there is no dramatic oscillation from permissiveness to detailed regulation and back again. Instead phase three is more a synthesis, a discernment of the appropriate balance between what is desirable and what is possible. Since local administration of the program is now in the hands of experienced professionals and the basic redistributive goals of the program are understood and accepted by all levels of government, central government decision makers more readily accept that all programs must necessarily be modified as they are carried out in particular contexts. Unresolved issues remain, problems arise, and adjustments become necessary, but the dimensions of the debate are now contained within well-understood boundaries.

Pullouts

The increasing maturity in the operation of the compensatory education program is particularly evident from the way in which the 'pullout' issue evolved. During the program's second phase, Federal auditors often insisted on evidence that compensatory monies were being used exclusively for the benefit of educationally disadvantaged students, that is, that school systems were complying with supplement, not supplant regulations. 'Pullout' programming satisfied the auditors' expectations because the disadvantaged students were 'pulled out' of the classroom and given special instruction in reading and mathematics in small groups or tutorial sessions. The reading specialists and teacher aides who taught these special classes were paid for entirely with Federal monies, and their presence in the school was clearly an additional school activity. Pullout programming also became widespread because the practice helped legitimize the growing sub-professions in reading and learning disabilities, it justified recruiting teacher aides from the low-income community, and it reflected a respected, widely held view that socially disadvantaged students required special instructional techniques (Peterson, 1986). The practice became subject to increasing criticism in the late 1970s, however. Critics pointed out that separating the educationally disadvantaged from other students could undermine their self-confidence by stigmatizing them as 'dumb', that education in small groups conducted by teacher aides and less experienced reading specialists was not necessarily superior to that provided in the regular classroom, that shuffling children from one classroom to another disrupted the school day and reduced active learning time, and that the curricula of the regular classroom teacher and the compensatory educator were typically uncoordinated, thereby confusing students as to how and what they were expected to learn (*ibid*).

The pullout concept gradually came into disfavor after a comprehensive review of the compensatory education program was conducted in 1976 (Kenoyer, Cooper, Saxton, and Hoepfner, 1981). According to one influential interpretation of the findings, compensatory education had positive, long-term effects on student achievement when program design did not involve pullouts; it had no significant effects when the pullout arrangement was used (Cooley, 1981). By the 1980s, enthusiasm for the practice was on the wane, though the evidence as to its effectiveness or ineffectiveness remains open to further research and discussions (Archambault, 1986).

In response to these criticisms, Federal and state officials insisted that they had never required pullout programs, that many educational strategies were consistent with Federal guidelines, and that their only concern was to ensure that monies were used to serve the eligible population. After this, local officials felt greater freedom to explore such alternative strategies as the use of in-class aides, after school programs, and reduced class sizes. But the controversy caused by pullout programs continues. In 1986 one local official complained that the potential threat of a Federal or state audit prevented the implementation of alternative educational strategies. 'The greatest fear of [local educational] coordinators is a visit by the Inspector General's office. Time and again programs reviewed, approved, and monitored by [state educational] personnel are found to be illegal by the Inspector General's staff' (Rosica, 1986, pp. III-126–127). But this view was in the minority; as the evidence against use of the pullout practice mounted, most observers felt that Federal and state officials had relaxed their auditing requirements and a broader range of educational strategies was being explored (Jung and Kirst, 1986).

Federal-State Relations

The pullout dispute was only one example of the administrative issues that required discussion and resolution, but by the late 1970s, regulatory provisions that had once been ill defined and poorly understood had become a way of life. Federal officials gradually began to concentrate on collecting only that information necessary to determine local compliance. Of the five criteria initially thought necessary to assess compliance with the supplement, not supplant provision, for example, Federal officials settled on two. They decided that knowing the number of staff and the expenditures per child would be sufficient to tell them whether local and state funds were being equitably spent. After these requirements became well established, evidence suggested that compliance was nearly universal, and the organizations that had represented compensatory education recipients so assertively in the early 1970s ceased to cite non-compliance as a problem. Federal audits conducted in the late 1970s also found a steady decline in the misuse of Federal funds. The findings from these formal reviews were confirmed by more informal assessment in interview with Federal , state, and local officials.

As states developed a greater understanding of what was and was not permissible, they increasingly integrated the Federal program into their overall efforts. Compensatory education no longer seemed peripheral to their mission. Florida, for example, revised state achievement testing during the 1970s to measure the performance of children receiving compensatory services and of all other children. The state also combined auditing for the program with auditing for overall school expenditures, enabling it to trace each educational dollar to individual schools and class levels. While the combined audit initially caused some confusion, especially for districts such as Dade County, that had never examined the expenditure patterns of individual schools, it gradually became standardized and widely supported, in part because the new procedures enabled school principals to exercise greater latitude in allocating resources. Wisconsin developed a similar procedure for including audits of Federal program compliance into a computerized comprehensive school audit.

Such intermingling of Federal and state purposes also improved state and local relations. As states became increasingly adept at managing Federal regulations, they sought more collaboration with local school systems. Florida increasingly solicited suggestions from local educators before deciding on state guidelines, and state officials set up regional meetings to review draft copies of proposed compensatory education applications before their formal submission.

All four states in which our research was conducted further embraced the Federal program by enacting their own compensatory education programs. In 1981 Florida spent $34 million for its own program in addition to the $81 million it received from the Federal government. Both programs were monitored by the same bureau, and in both programs the state concentrated a disproportionate share of resources on students from kindergarten through grade three. Maryland also used Federal funds in conjunction with those for its own program and other state categorical monies. Since the Federal program served fewer than half of all eligible Maryland students, state funds were said to be concentrated on the rest. In 1981 Maryland added $5.5 million for program funding to $37 million of Federal funding. Compensatory education was thus increasingly assumed as a state responsibility, both through Maryland's considerable role in Federal program oversight and the emergence of its own comparable programs.

California probably did the most of the four states to take advantage of the new Federal flexibility. Like the others it combined the Federal compensatory education program with its state program in an attempt to create a comprehensive policy. In the late 1970s it also developed a consolidated form so that local districts could request money for a dozen different state and Federal programs in one application. This form encouraged local principals and school personnel to develop a more integrated approach to the use of various categorical program monies. Meanwhile, reviews of compensatory education programs were combined with those of other programs to create a comprehensive review process. This development furthered the integration of the various categorical programs and encouraged communication among local educators, inasmuch as program reviews in any given district were normally performed by local educators from other districts.

California's innovations initially encountered considerable difficulties with the Federal government. From Washington's perspective, the Federal program in California had become so well integrated with state programs that it practically lost its identity, and whether regulations on comparability and non-supplanting were being followed had become difficult to determine. Arguing that its procedures ensured comparability and non-supplanting, the state reached an uneasy truce with the Federal office for several years. The problem was resolved in the late 1970s when provisions for state programs were written into the 1978 amendments to the Federal law that facilitated the coordination of Federal and state compensatory programs. By 1981 several Federal officials whom we interviewed were enthusiastic about the high quality of California's local programs.

Professional Development

The administrative role in compensatory education developed a distinct identity in the two decades following the creation of the program. At all levels of government, those working in the field came to identify more with their program than with the governmental units that paid their salaries. In the perhaps exaggerated words of one fairly recent recruit to the Federal compensatory education staff, 'I'm always surprised when people ask if there's been any tension between us and the states. It's always been a cooperative professional relationship.'

This professional identity and expertise in compensatory education was fostered by a variety of Federal pressures. During the late 1960s and early 1970s local school officials were reprimanded by Federal and state officials for non-compliance. These reprimands, involving intensified Federal and state audits and the threat of loss of funding, influenced local school systems to encourage professional development in the operation of their compensatory education programs. One state compensatory education official said, 'While chief state school officers and superintendents might have publicly been saying, "We've done nothing wrong," they were saying to their staffs in private, "Let's not let this happen again"'. Baltimore decided to 'not let this happen again' with a major reorganization of its compensatory education office. The school district created a position of assistant superintendent for compensatory education and recruited a highly regarded administrator who instituted numerous changes. In Milwaukee, although most of the Federal money was initially used in questionable ways, the scale of the charges and the harassment they caused forced compensatory education administrators to be more careful in their subsequent use of Federal funds. After initial difficulties, 'everyone wanted to learn the regulations and be in compliance with them', explained a Federal administrator. 'States took pride in the fact that they knew the regulations and they wanted to show off their knowledge. They took pride in tightening their own enforcement of the program.'

The new commitment to redistributive objectives was not merely a function of Federal pressure, however. As compensatory education specialists became school principals and school system administrators, greater sensitivity and commitment to the program spread throughout the system. In Maryland and Wisconsin the directors of both the Federal and the companion state programs served from the inception of the program until their retirement in the early 1980s. Specially trained personnel were also being recruited to work directly with the children receiving the services. In Maryland 700 teachers specialized in reading in 1980 compared with only three before 1965. Many of these were involved in compensatory education or related efforts funded by the state. A Maryland Department of Education official observed that 'before the [Federal program], people did not believe that poor children could learn'. A former compensatory education official in Wisconsin agreed, noting that 'no one really believed that they had educationally disadvantaged children in their schools' before the Federal program. In short, the Federal compensatory education program encouraged new interest in and efforts on behalf of the disadvantaged.

The most notable program development took place in Dade County. A new superintendent, Johnny Jones, the first Black to hold the position, seized upon the compensatory education program in the late 1970s as a vehicle for providing innovative educational services to disadvantaged children. Instead of continuing the lackluster approach of dispatching aides and other resources to local schools while providing little program structure, a practice that had prevailed during the first decade of compensatory education in the county, Jones and leading aides developed a program that introduced the concept of the 'extended day'.

The program was designed to serve about half of all elementary students participating in compensatory education. Federal funds were used to hire outstanding district teachers to provide an extra hour of instruction in reading and mathematics after the students had completed a normal day of classes. Instruction was intended to complement regular classroom work and emphasize basic skills. 'Instead of six hours a day, we went to eight hours a day of instruction', explained an administrator active in the pilot program. 'Teachers who were selected had to be experienced, and they had to be believers in the program. Previously, we just hired extra staff and scattered them about.' Classes were kept relatively small, and participating teachers were rotated in and out of the program frequently to limit burnout. In addition to an extra stipend for their efforts they also received special training.

To be asked to teach in the extended day program was considered a recognition of high ability because the program sought out only the district's best teachers to participate. In the earlier period, program personnel lacked prestige and often certification: 'Now, you must be tops to be a Title I teacher', one leader of a local parent advisory council remarked. After students performed well on standardized tests and a public review of the pilot program was favorable, the school board accepted the extended day concept as a model for all district elementary schools receiving compensatory education funds.

Dade County's compensatory education program was thus transformed from a potpourri of uncoordinated activities into one of its most prominent and popular educational programs. One district administrator commented that 'Non-Title I parents used to say that Title I kids cannot learn and that any special programs for them were a waste of time and money. Now, many of them want [the program] for their own kids.'

Jones was instrumental in this transformation not only by encouraging the program's initial development but also by touting it as a creative use of Federal grant-in-aid funds. The program was cited in Congress as a model worthy of emulation on the national level, and Jones rode the crest of this support to national prominence as well, when his nomination to be the first secretary of education was suggested. 'Dade and its superintendent could do no wrong in the public eye, locally and nationally', recalled one administrator. 'We had a super situation, and everyone was interested' in the program.

The image of the Dade compensatory program was badly tarnished, however, when Jones was indicted on several counts of bribery, one of which involved kickbacks from a contract approved for purchases of instructional materials for the extended day program. His drawn-out, televised trial and his resulting conviction cost the program its most prominent and eloquent supporter as well as its once unquestioned public esteem. Moreover, test scores of participating students never increased as dramatically in subsequent years as they did during the first year of the program. Nonetheless, the extended day program continued to draw considerable professional and parental support in the district and was continued by the administration that succeeded Jones.

The increased cooperation among the central government and the four states and localities we observed seems to have reflected a national pattern. A major study by the National Institute of Education (NIE) found a significant decrease nationwide in reported instances of supplanting. The decrease, according to the NIE, was largely a function of less assiduous efforts by Federal officials to identify, report and verify supplanting. The report even implied that higher level education officials refused to accept as veritable the reports of supplanting submitted by members of their staff (National Institute of Education, 1977a). But long-term employees of the Office of Education interpreted the decline as an indication that local officials had acquired an understanding of Federal requirements and how to adapt to them. Certainly in the states we visited, efforts at greater compliance during the mid-1970s were described repeatedly. Perhaps both views can be accepted. Each component of the Federal system was learning to be less confrontational and more cooperative: local school officials learned how to comply, while Federal administrators learned that more was to be gained from accommodation than rigid rule enforcement. As one study reported, 'State conflicts with Federal programs did not exhibit the intensity we had expected from popular accounts'. Instead, 'administrative problems are overstated and inaccurately ascribed to Federal programs as their singular source' (Moore *et al*, 1983, pp. 11–12). According to another survey, 'local problem solving, Federal and state adjustments, and gradual local accommodations have generally reduced to a manageable level' the cost associated with implementing Federal education programs (Knapp, Stearns, Turnbull, David and Peterson, 1983, p. 159). The results of econometric studies have agreed with these findings. Instead of using Federal compensatory education monies as a substitute for local funds, states and localities were spending money over and above what they received from the Federal government. One study estimated the average additional expenditure to be twenty-two cents for every dollar received; another study estimated it as twenty-eight cents (Chubb, 1985; Craig and Inman, 1982).[3]

Program Effects

The long-term effects of the compensatory education program on educational attainment have not been precisely determined. The kind of evaluation required to assess conclusively the overall effectiveness of this large-scale, complex undertaking will probably never be conducted. Even the large-scale Sustaining Effects Study that attempted a formal evaluation in 1976 reached no definitive conclusions with respect to the overall, long-term impact of compensatory education. However, there are signs that differences in educational performance between minority and non-minority children have steadily narrowed since the early 1970s. A recent definitive review of the evidence concludes that eight of nine major studies 'showed a consistent and unambiguous narrowing of the gap between Black and non-minority students, leaving little doubt that this pattern is real and not an artifact of some aspects of the tests or groups tested'. The review also notes that 'differences between Black and non-minority students ... shrank more rapidly among elementary and junior-high students than among high-school students' (Congressional Budget Office, 1986, pp. 150 and 157).[4]

The causes of these gains are difficult to ascertain conclusively. They may primarily be due to broad social changes, including the passage of new civil right laws in the 1960s, improved minority educational and employment opportunities, and altered expectations of teachers, parents and students about the capacities of minorities to achieve. To the extent that the compensatory education program contributed to these general changes in perceptions and expectations, its most significant effects may have been intangible, indirect and symbolic. But a more direct, material contribution to minority educational gains cannot be ruled out. For one thing, gains in minority educational attainment have occurred despite the continued stagnation, and even deterioration, of minority well-being in other social spheres. The unemployment rate for young Black males has escalated since the 1960s, Black wages relative to those of Whites have shown little improvement, and Black families are even more likely to be headed by single parents than they were a generation ago when this problem first became a national issue. The one area of social life in which Blacks have made clear, identifiable gains has been within the educational system. What is more, those gains have been greatest during the elementary years, the very years minorities attended the schools that were the focus of compensatory education policies.

The Future of Compensatory Education

Changes Under Chapter 1

The changes in compensatory education under the Reagan administration have been much less than were anticipated in the summer of 1981 when legislative changes included in the Omnibus Budget and Reconciliation Act stripped most of the regulatory requirements from the law authorizing the program. The new law continued to declare that monies should be spent on the disadvantaged, but it no longer spelled out the way the money was to be dispersed within school districts and inside individual schools. In legislative terms, compensatory education had come full circle; the generalities contained in the law in 1981 looked more like the original 1965 legislation than any of the revised authorizations that had occurred in the intervening years.

Yet the legislative change of 1981 rendered few changes in administrative practice by 1986. Recent studies commissioned by the National Assessment of Chapter 1 are finding more continuity than change in program administration. The criteria for identifying schools and students within schools are similar to those used a decade ago; Federal monies are also still being used as a supplement to locally provided educational services. There is little evidence that the vague elements in the 1981 law are encouraging a dispersion and a diffusion of Federal funds such as had occurred in the first phase of the program inaugurated in 1965.

It may be that these studies are underestimating the effects of the 1981 legislation. Perhaps deregulation takes as long to have an effect as regulation does; perhaps an observer of compensatory education programs ten years from now will discover major changes that gradually accumulated over time. We should not repeat the mistake of early studies of compensatory education by concluding that one can observe within five years the full effects of a legislative change.

There is, nonetheless, good reason to believe that, in the absence of still further legislative revisions, compensatory education will continue in future years along much the same lines as it has evolved up until now. Much to the surprise of many policy analysts, the formal deregulation of the program under the Reagan administration has been greeted with a remarkable lack of enthusiasm by state and local officials. They complained that the new law and accompanying regulations were too vague. They preferred to keep in place the extra administrative work to which they had grown accustomed rather than risk being audited for non-compliance at some future date. Even Congress, in a bipartisan move, backed away from the deregulation of 1981, reinstituting requirements that had been deleted in the rush to deregulate. The law was amended in 1983 to restrict eligibility to schools in areas where at least 25 per cent of the families were of low income. The amendments also specified that evaluations be conducted every two years, data on participants be collected, and that schools hold annual parent forums. What's more, in a period of fiscal stringency, compensatory education received virtually as much funding in constant dollars in 1985 as it received in 1980 (see Table 2).

Allocation Formula

Congress continued past practices in one other important respect as well: the formula for allocating Federal funds among states and localities. The way in which the allocation formula shapes substantive

Table 2: *Federal Expenditures for Compensatory Education Programs Selected Fiscal Years, 1968-1985 (Millions of dollars)*

Expenditures

Year	Current Dollars	Constant Dollars*
1968	1,049.1	2,188.8
1972	1,507.4	2,724.7
1976	1,760.8	2,245.1
1980	3,005.6	2,528.1
1982	3,063.6	2,303.5
1984	3,501.4	2,450.2
1985	3,721.8**	2,513.0**

*1970 dollars
**Estimated

Sources: *Digest of Education Statistics* by National Center for Educational Statistics, 1982 and 1985, Washington, DC, US Department of Education. Block grants data from *Education Times*, 3 January 1983 and 28 October 1985.

compensatory education policy is little appreciated and therefore the issue is worth further consideration in this concluding section.

Continuing congressional interest in specifically designating the formula for allocating compensatory education (and other Federal) funds is easily explained. Members of the Senate and House of Representatives are chosen in ways that allow for direct, immediate representation of territorial interests. Because each member of Congress represents a specific state or district, each cares deeply about the effects of policies on his or her territory. Undisciplined by strong political parties of the kind prevalent in Europe, senators and representatives are as concerned about their own territories' interests as about broader political issues. It is at least as legitimate to vote one's constituency as to vote one's conscience, and territorial issues are especially likely to provoke constituency consciousness.

This concern for constituency interests is reflected in the explicitness with which Congress legislates on territorial questions. Senators and Representatives know that once a bill affecting territorial interests is passed, any remaining ambiguities will be resolved by executive departments less concerned than they are about precise territorial effects. Consequently, Congress seeks ways to restrict the discretion of administrative agencies on these questions.

The interest in the territorial effects of compensatory education funding was evident from its very beginning. In 1965 the formula for distributing the funds was based on two major considerations: the number of children from low-income families living within a school district and the average cost per pupil for education within the state. While the formula seemed consistent with the objective of serving disadvantaged children, Republican critics argued that some of the school districts that would receive the most resources were already well endowed. They proposed instead that the program offset existing inequalities in local fiscal resources. The Democratic majority prevailed, however, perhaps because the formula tended to favor large central cities and the rural south, the areas of greatest Democratic strength.

Within two years of the legislation's passage, efforts were begun to shift funding away from the highly industrialized north-east. In 1967 southern Congressmen demonstrated (by means of a computer simulation) that southern states, which spent relatively low amounts on education, would greatly benefit if the allocation formula were based on the average national cost per pupil instead of the state-wide average. Accordingly, Congress adjusted the formula. In 1970, after program evaluations revealed that wealthier districts were receiving more Federal funds, further changes were made that 'generally shifted the aid from wealthier urban states to the poorer, rural ones' ('Education Action Completed', 1974, p. 3423).

In 1974, debate centered on the weight that should be given to the number of children receiving public welfare assistance. Since wealthier, more industrialized states tended to have the least restrictive welfare practices, it was argued in Congress that 'the wealthier a state, the more likely it is that it will ... be able to add AFDC [Aid to Families with Dependent Children] children under Title I' ('Education Bill Debate', 1974, p. 701). While New York Representative Shirley Chisholm countered that reducing the weight of this provision of the formula represented a 'retreat' from the intent of Title I to assist those areas with large concentrations of needs, the distribution formula was further modified. Once Republicans gained greater strength at both ends of Pennsylvania Avenue, the arguments they originally made in 1965 became much more persuasive.

By 1978, when the program came up for reauthorization a third time, Democrats were once again in political ascendance, and new changes in the distribution formula were proposed. A study by the National Institute of Education had shown that little was to be gained

Table 3: Compensatory Education Program Allocations by Region and *Type of Community for Each School-Aged Child, 1975–76*

Type of Community	Northeast	North Central	South	West
Central city	58.24	38.02	40.81	31.58
Large	67.03	44.94	41.29	33.79
Other	37.11	24.97	40.12	26.83
Suburbs	17.77	14.22	26.42	22.80
Non-metropolitan	29.18	27.46	54.14	34.53

Source: *Title I Funds Allocation: The Current Formula* (p. 17) by the National Institute of Education, 1977, Washington, DC, US Department of Health, Education, and Welfare.

from, and great complexity would be introduced by, changing the formula so that funds were distributed among school districts according to the incidence of children whose educational performances were deficient instead of the incidence of children from low-income families (National Institute of Education, 1977b). Another study, well received in the new political climate, argued that 'the fiscal and educational needs of the high-expenditure metropolitan states and their major cities deserve greater consideration than they received from Congress' (Goettel, 1978, p. 192). As a result, in a formula that amendments had already made increasingly complicated, large cities regained some of their initial advantage. But even before the passage of these new amendments, which determine the current funding pattern, the distribution of funds had favored the north-eastern cities and southern rural areas, the original winners in the allocation contest (see Table 3).

Improving Compensatory Education Policy

These territorial interests of Congress in fact constitute one of the major obstacles to further improvement in the design of compensatory education programs. As currently structured, the program serves a widely dispersed constituency in countless numbers of schools in thousands of school districts scattered across every state and congressional district. It is well designed for obtaining maximum political support that every member of the House and Senate can appreciate.

This political support comes at some considerable cost in program effectiveness. The price that is paid is two-fold. First, to reach the target population the Federal government must write regulations insuring that funds are used for the educationally disadvantaged within schools. Otherwise the funds would be dispersed so widely that the target population would not be adequately served. To keep this from happening, local school districts must show that they designed programs especially for those children within a specific school who are performing below a particular standard. While this may ensure that the disadvantaged are being served, it also means that local schools are being asked to distinguish among children, stigmatizing some as needy. They are also being asked to fragment the school curriculum either by withdrawing some children from the classroom in order to receive special instruction or by using teacher aides to help low-performing children within the classroom. More generally, compliance takes precedence over pedagogy. Federal regulations are preventing local principals and teachers from using their resources in the way they think is best for the benefit of the local school. Compensatory education becomes subject to the complaint that it is more interested in rule-making than educational engagement.

The second price that is paid is that scarce monies are not reserved for those schools in which the greatest concentrations of poverty and educational disadvantage are to be found. According to the interim report of the National Assessment of Chapter 1, educational attainment is just as adversely affected by living in a poor neighborhood as by coming from a poor family. If both factors are combined (i.e., if a child comes from a poor family living in an impoverished neighborhood), the incidence of educational disadvantage is approximately twice as high as when neither factor is present (Kennedy, Jung, and Orland, 1986). In other words, compensatory education is especially needed in those communities where the incidence of poverty is very high. In these contexts all children have a lower chance of doing well in school, and those coming from poor families are particularly likely to suffer educational deprivation. A compensatory education program that has only limited resources should be carefully designed so that it is concentrated on schools in these neighborhoods. To do so within current fiscal constraints means that many fewer schools would become the recipients of compensatory education funds.

Congress could learn from its twenty years of experience with the compensatory education program if, in the future, it decided to target schools, not students. If monies were concentrated only on those schools located in the most impoverished neighborhoods, it would be reaching the population most in need. Since most students in these schools would be in need of help, the decisions as to how funds could best be used could be left to local educators, who could combine Federal, state and local funds for the maximum benefit of all children within the school. Federal regulations could be kept to a minimum, specifying only the ways in which schools would be selected and requiring only that Federal funds for the school be in addition to, not a substitution for, local resources. Quality programming, as well as equality of opportunity, could become an enduring feature of compensatory education.

To redesign compensatory education in these ways, Congress would have to exercise unusual political forbearance. In the interest of educational improvement, it would have to put to one side its desire to give a little Federal aid to each and every Congressional district. For twenty years, Congress has considered and reconsidered its formulas for aiding the education of the nation's poor. Each time it has found a solution that makes political sense. It is now time for Congress to choose a formula that makes educational sense as well.

Notes

1 The authors gratefully acknowledge support for this research from the National Institute of Education, Ford Foundation, and the Exxon Educational Foundation.
2 In 1983, 75 per cent of these funds were returned to the Milwaukee public schools as a compensatory education program 'grant back' ('Update on the News', 1982).
3 These are averages for the program during 1965–79 and 1967–77. Unfortunately, neither study analyzes the pattern year by year to ascertain whether the stimulative effects of federal compensatory education increased. However, one may infer this by comparing the results of these studies with those of Feldstein (1978) that relied exclusively on 1970 data. A review of studies of categorical grants reported that, in general, the grants seem to 'stimulate total local spending roughly equal to the grant [possibly] because they come with effective effort-maintenance provisions' (Gramlich, 1977, p. 234). Similar results from other studies are reported in Tsang and Levin (1982).
4 The study also reports that comparable gains are being made on the part of Hispanic students, although the data are sparser and less reliable. Also, see a similar review of the evidence in Peterson (1983).

References

ARCHAMBAULT, F. X., JR. (1986). 'Instructional setting: Key issue or bogus concern' in WILLIAMS, B. I. RICHMOND, P. A. and MASON, B. J. (Eds) *Designs for Compensatory Education: Conference Proceedings and Papers*, Washington, DC, Research and Evaluation Associates.

ASSISTANT SECRETARY FOR ELEMENTARY AND SECONDARY EDUCATION, (1981) Memorandum to David W. Hornbeck, Superintendent of Schools, State Department of Education, Maryland (Enclosure No. 1), 29 July.

BAILEY, S. K. AND MOSHER, E. K. (1968). *ESEA: The Office of Education Administers and Law*, Syracuse, NY, Syracuse University Press.

CHUBB, J. E. (1985) 'The political economy of federalism', *American Political Science Review*, **79**, pp. 994–1015.

CLARK, K. B. (1966) 'Education of the minority poor: The key to the war on poverty', *The Disadvantaged Poor: Education and Employment, Third Report of the Task Force on Economic Growth as Opportunity*, Washington, DC, Chamber of Commerce of the United States.

CONGRESSIONAL BUDGET OFFICE (1986) *Trends in Educational Achievement*, Washington, DC, US Government Printing Office.

COOLEY, W. W. (1981). 'Effectiveness of compensatory education', *Educational Leadership*, **3**, pp. 298–301.

CRAIG, S. G. AND INMAN, R. P. (1982). 'Federal aid and public education: An empirical look at the new fiscal federalism', *Review of Economics and Statistics*, **64**, pp. 541–52.

'Education action completed.' (1974) *Congressional Quarterly Weekly Report*, **32**, p. 3423, 28 December.

'Education bill debate begins.' (1974) *Congressional Quarterly Weekly Report*, **32**, p. 701, 16 March.

FELDSTEIN, M. (1978). 'The effect of a differential add-on grant: Title I and local education spending', *Journal of Human Resources*, **13**, pp. 443–58.

GOETTEL, R. J. (1978). 'Federal assistance to national target groups: The ESEA Title I experience' in TIMPANE, M. (Ed) *The Federal Interest in Financing Schooling*, Cambridge, MA, Ballinger.

GRAMLICH, E. M. (1977). 'Intergovernmental grants: A review of the empirical literature' in OATES, W. E. (Ed) *The Political Economy of Fiscal Federalism*, Lexington, MA, DC Heath.

HAVIGHURST, R. J. (1965). 'The elementary schools and the disadvantaged pupil' in BECK, J. M. AND SAXE, R. W. (Eds), *Teaching the Culturally Disadvantaged Pupil*, Springfield, IL, Charles C Thomas Press.

JOHNSON, L. (1966). 'Remarks to members of Congress at a reception marking the enactment of the education bill', *Public Papers of the Presidents: Lyndon Johnson, 1965*. Washington, DC, US Government Printing Office.

JUNG, R AND KIRST, M. (1986). 'Beyond mutual adaptation, into the bully pulpit: Recent research on the Federal role in education', *Educational Administration Quarterly*, **22**, 3, pp. 84–95.

KENNEDY, M. M., JUNG, R. K. AND ORLAND, M. E. (1986). *Poverty,*

Achievement and the Distribution of Compensatory Education Services (First interim report of the National Assessment of Chapter 1), Washington DC, US Department of Education.

KENOYER, C. E., COOPER, D. M., SAXTON, D. E. AND HOEPFNER, R. (1981) *The Effects of Discontinuing Compensatory Education Services* (Sustained Effects Study: Tech. Rep. No. 11). Santa Monica, CA, System Development Corporation.

KIRST, M. W. AND JUNG, R. (1982). 'The utility of a longitudinal approach in assessing implementation: A thirteen-year view of Title I, ESEA' in WILLIAMS, W., ELMORE, R. F., HALL, J. S., JUNG, R., KIRST, M., MACMANUS, S. A., NARVER, B., NATHAN, R. P. AND YIN, R. K. (Eds.), *Studying Implementation Methodological and Administrative Issues*, Chatham, NJ, Chatham House.

KNAPP, M. S., STEARNS, M. S., TURNBULL, B. J., DAVID, J. L. AND PETERSON, S. M. (1983) *Cumulative Effects of Federal Education Policies on Schools and Districts*, Menlo Park, CA, SRI International.

McLAUGHLIN, M. (1975). *Evaluation and Reform: The Elementary and Secondary Education Act of 1965, Title I.* Cambridge, MA, Ballinger.

MARTIN, R., AND McCLURE, P. (1969) *Title I of ESEA: Is It Helping Poor Children?* Washington, DC, Washington Research Project and NAACP Legal Defense and Educational Fund.

MOORE, M. T., GOERTZ, M. E., HARTLE, T. W., WINSLOW, H. R., DAVID, J. L., SJOGREN, J., TURNBULL, B., COLEY, R. J. AND HOLLAND, R. P. (1983) *The Interaction of Federal and Related State Education Programs: Executive Summary*, Princeton, NJ, Educational Testing Service.

MURPHY, J. T. (1971) 'Title I of ESEA: The politics of implementing Federal education reform', *Harvard Educational Review*, **41**, pp. 35–63.

NATIONAL INSTITUTE OF EDUCATION (1977a) *Administration of Compensatory Education*, Washington, DC, National Institute of Education.

NATIONAL INSTITUTE OF EDUCATION (1977b). *Title I Funds Allocation: The Current Formula.* Washington, DC, National Institute of Education.

PETERSON, P. E. (1983) 'Background paper', *Task Force on Federal Education Policy: Making the Grade*, New York, Twentieth Century Fund.

PETERSON, P. E., RABE, B. AND WONG, K. (1986) *When Federalism Works*, Washington, DC, Brookings Institution.

PETERSON, P. L. (1986). 'Selecting students and services for compensatory education: Lessons from aptitude-treatment interaction research' in WILLIAMS, B. I., RICHMOND, P. A. AND MASON, B. J. (Eds) *Designs for Compensatory Education: Conference Proceedings and Papers*, Washington, DC, Research and Evaluation Associates.

RIVLIN, A. M. (1971). *Systematic Thinking For Social Action*, Washington, DC, Brookings Institution.

ROSICA, T. C. (1986). 'Program and staffing structures: Reactions' in WILLIAMS, B. I., RICHMOND, P. A. AND MASON, B. J. (Eds) *Designs for Compensatory Education: Conference Proceedings and Papers*, Washington, DC, Research and Evaluation Associates.

TSANG, M. C. AND LEVIN, H. M. (1982) *The Impact of Intergovernmental Grants on Educational Spending*, Stanford, CA, Stanford University, School of Education.

'Update on the news' (1982) *Education Times*, p. 3, 24 May.

US DEPARTMENT OF EDUCATION. (1980) *The Audit Report on the Review of Comparability Data under Title I of the Elementary and Secondary Education Act of 1965: School District of Baltimore City for the Period July 1 1974 through June 30 1978*. Washington, DC, US Department of Education.

WISCONSIN DEPARTMENT OF PUBLIC INSTRUCTION (1982) *Information on the HEW Audit Agency Report of Audit 1968 through 1973: The Milwaukee Public School System*, Madison, WI, Wisconsin Department of Public Instruction.

3
Program Strategy and Design: Options for Federal Action in Education[1]

Paul T. Hill

Funding Individuals, Funding Organizations

This chapter analyzes design alternatives for Federal elementary and secondary education programs. It identifies the range of program strategies available and analyzes their strengths and weaknesses. My goal is not to identify the one best design for Federal education programs, but to provide a framework of options that policymakers can consider.

The theme of this chapter is that the proper design for any program depends on four factors:

- goals;
- the availability of Federal funding to pay for necessary services and administrative actions;
- accommodations necessary to enact the program and sustain its political support; and
- the capacity of the organizations that deliver services to beneficiaries.

I do not assume that all programs can have sharply defined goals or that simple administrative structures are always best. Some programs are established only because legislative brokers are able to fashion agreements that let contending groups hold different beliefs about who is supposed to benefit. Many programs are able to function only because potential opponents are coopted by arrangements that give them a stake in providing services. Under some circumstances, an elegant design (for example, unconstrained cash transfers to beneficiaries) could doom a program to failure by making its goals too sharp and its administrative structure too simple.

Program designs are not intrinsically good or bad, but they are better and worse suited to particular situations. I hope this chapter will help policymakers choose program designs based on a better understanding of the interplay among goals, available funding, legislative and bureaucratic politics, and the technical capacities of service delivery organizations.

The chapter has three parts: a review of the alternative designs available for Federal programs, an analysis of the design of Chapter 1/ Title I, and a comparison of alternative program designs according to several standard criteria.

Types of Programs

This section identifies the range of alternative program designs and selects three for further analysis. To identify the range of logical possibilities, we start with a simple classification scheme. A program design has three dimensions: source of funding, source of decision about the character of services to be delivered, and the source of the services. Each of the three dimensions can be divided as follows:

Who pays for the services
  State Educational Agency (SEA)/Local Educational Agency
  (LEA)
  Federal Government
  Mixture of SEA/LEA and Federal Government
Who chooses services
  LEA
  Client (i.e., beneficiary or proxy)
  Other (for example, courts or Federal officials)
Who delivers the services
  LEA
  State agency or institution
  Federal agency or institution
  Contractor or private organization

These factors provide a framework for the identification of pro-

Who Pays for Services

	SEA/LEA			Federal Government			Mix of SEA/LEA/Fed		
Who Delivers Services	Chooser of Services			Chooser of Services			Mix of SEA/LEA/Fed		
	LEA	Client	Other	LEA	Client	Other	LEA	Client	Other
LEA	1		2	3	4		5		
SEA									6
Federal agency					7				
Private or independent agency						8	9	10	11

KEY: 1 = Regular district instructional program
2 = Civil rights mandates
3 = Chapter 1 services
4 = Alum Rock-style vouchers
5 = Education for All Handicapped Children Act (P.L. 94-142)
6 = Education in state hospitals or custodial institutions
7 = Department of Defense Dependent Schools and other schools on Federal reservations
8 = Bureau of Indian Affairs Schools run by tribes or other independent agencies
9 = Title I 'by-pass' arrangements for services to nonpublic school students
10 = Unconstrained Chapter 1 voucher plan
11 = Special vendor services (for example, private placements) under P.L. 94-142

Figure 1:   Matrix of Program Characteristics

gram design alternatives. A matrix of the thirty-six cells defined by the intersections of all the above characteristics is presented in Figure 1. Each cell of the matrix describes a distinctive program design.

To give the matrix concrete meaning I have placed the principal public elementary and secondary education programs in the appropriate cells. The distribution of programs in the matrix and the pattern of empty cells show that some program designs are more likely to occur in the real world than others.

The reasons for large regions of empty cells are readily apparent.

The empty cells on the lower left side of the matrix reflect the fact that LEAs strongly prefer to deliver any services they pay for. The many empty cells in the second and third rows of the matrix reflect the fact that state governments and the US Department of Education seldom engage in direct delivery of educational services. (The exceptions are informative: the Federal and State Governments run custodial institutions for special needs populations, and regular schools in remote government reservations, for example Native American settlements and military bases.)

In general, our Federal system leaves the delivery of educational services to local governments or private organizations, and there is little reason to expect that to change.

The pattern of filled cells is also informative. The programs in the lower right-hand corner, in which private schools and agencies receive public money to deliver educational services, are funded at least in part by the Federal government. SEA/LEA programs seldom use private service vendors. Federal programs are slightly more likely to work through private organizations, but two of the four examples of private service delivery cover exceptional circumstances that arise in the implementation of much larger Federal programs (i.e., Title I 'by-pass' arrangements for services to non-public school students, and special private placements for handicapped children who cannot be served in regular LEA programs). The 'by-pass' concept may have wider applicability as a program concept, but the P.L. 94-142 special placements concept is suitable only for handling exceptional cases. (See Madey and Hill, 1982 for a discussion of the problems that would result from any effort to make the right to due process in student placement decisions more generally applicable.)

Client choice of services is exceedingly rare. It has occurred (or might occur in the future) under publicly funded voucher plans. It also occurs in programs for the handicapped, when parents think the LEA has placed a child incorrectly and convince a judge or hearing officer to order an alternative placement.

A relatively small set of realistic possibilities emerges from the matrix of conceivable program designs. They are:

(1) Programs run by LEAs with mixes of Federal, state, and local funds.
(2) Programs run by special institutions for populations distin-

guished by geographic remoteness or need for mixed educational and custodial services.

(3)   Programs run by contractors in lieu of LEAs.
(4)   Programs that give clients claims on government funding for services to meet demonstrably unusual needs.
(5)   Programs that give clients the initiative in finding and choosing educational services.

Of these, numbers (2) and (4) are essentially ways of making special accommodations for unusual groups and individuals. Only (1), (3) and (5) are feasible methods for serving all students or large, geographically distributed sub-groups. They are, therefore, the main design alternatives that will be examined in the rest of this chapter.

Design of Chapter 1/Title I

This is a highly telegraphic description of Chapter 1, meant only to state basic facts for analysis. I assume that readers know Chapter 1's design, so I won't belabor the description. By starting with a well known program, I hope to familiarize readers with the vocabulary and analytical methods used in the rest of the chapter.

What Chapter 1 Is

Goals

Deliver supplementary services for educationally disadvantaged (low-achieving students) in low-income schools. Concentrate on basic skills services; deliver directly to the most needy students and upgrade the general educational quality of schools with high concentrations of disadvantaged students. Within schools, beneficiaries are selected under criteria set by the local system according to general state and Federal guidelines. Eligible students in non-public schools may receive services. Eligibility is contingent on residence: no student is personally entitled to services.

Funding

Federal funds are allocated to counties based on a statutory formula that emphasizes census-based poverty measures. SEA allocates Federal funds to LEAs using a sub-county allocation formula that it may choose, but which must be based on some measures of poverty. Funds are spent by LEA central administration, and services purchased are allocated to eligible schools. LEA must preserve an audit trail on funds to allow state and Federal governments to verify maintenance of effort and non-supplantation.

Choice of services

The LEA delivers Chapter 1 services under a plan that is submitted annually to the SEA. SEA reviews the plan for adherence to fiscal regulations and broad curricular guidelines: LEA discretion is considerable. LEA allocates program funds for teacher salaries, equipment, and other service components. Principals of eligible schools choose services from a limited menu offered by school district Chapter 1 office.

Service delivery

Most services are delivered in program-eligible schools during regular school hours. Services must demonstrably add to regular instructional program. Chapter 1 services are managed inside the school by the principal. Parents of recipient children may organize and maintain a loose advisory relationship with LEA program administrators. Eligible non-public school children receive services under special arrangements created by the LEA. Few are served in their own schools, most are served off the school site. Instructional programs and results may be evaluated by SEAs and Federal agencies; district must do its own evaluation and make results public. Program administrators are encouraged to share ideas via inter-district meetings, publications, state and Federal networking efforts.

Explanation for the Features of Title I/Chapter 1

The foregoing complex description is only a tip-of-the-iceberg account of the funding and administrative arrangements for Chapter 1. Why is it so complicated, and how did it get that way? I shall try briefly to answer those questions in light of the political constraints that faced legislative supporters of the original Title I, and the limits of organizational capacity that faced the Federal officials who were assigned to implement it.

Goals

Title I had one overarching goal — to induce public school systems to attach higher priority to the education of poor and racial minority children. But the entrepreneurs who developed Title I (i.e., President Johnson, his staff, and his congressional collaborators) had important subsidiary goals: they wanted to establish the principles that the Federal government could aid in the funding of elementary and secondary education, and that local education agencies were no longer immune to influence from the national government.

Funding

Johnson *et al* wanted Title I grants to be attractive to state and local education agencies, but they also wanted to get credit for the program's achievements. They made the program attractive in two ways: by writing funding formulas that guaranteed grants to virtually all jurisdictions and by establishing funding levels high enough to make a real difference in state and local budgets. Because poverty levels differ enormously from one locality to another, they allowed school districts to determine eligibility thresholds for schools and students; they knew that such provisions would create cross-district horizontal inequities, making identical students eligible for Title I in one district and ineligible in another.

Political constraints

Johnson and his legislative allies needed to avoid creating alarm about Federal intrusion into an area traditionally reserved for state and local governments. They coopted state and local officials by making their education agencies the channels for distribution of Title I funds and services. They coopted teacher organizations by providing that most Title I services would be delivered by certified teachers in regular school sites.

67

The support of Catholic Congressmen was essential, but to get it the entrepreneurs had to provide some benefits for parochial school students. On the other hand, Federal aid to education could not survive a squabble about church and state issues. Sam Halperin and others invented the 'child benefit theory' to emphasize that aid to nonpublic school students would benefit the children as individuals, rather than the schools that they attended.

In the program's early years civil rights groups became convinced that LEAs were not using Title I funds to help poor children. A coalition of civil rights advocates, liberal Congressmen, and journalists arose to insist that LEA compliance be forced via program audits and enforcement actions. The US Office of Education created an enforcement machinery and a rich body of concepts and theories to demonstrate that Title I funds led to service improvements for eligible children. To ensure that national Democratic politicians could take credit for program successes, they required Title I services to be delivered in ways that made them readily identifiable.

Organizational capacity

Though the decision to run Title I through state and local education agencies was a result of Johnson's basic goals, it was further reinforced by the fact that no other organizations had any ability to provide the desired services. If public school systems had neglected the needs of the disadvantaged, they were not alone. Schools of education had only just been awakened by Benjamin Bloom's call for compensatory education, and few private institutions had developed relevant expertise. So public school systems seemed to be the only feasible delivery system.

The entrepreneurs assumed correctly that a major new funding program would stimulate research and program development in the area. But they were not willing to wait for market forces to work. They permitted SEAs and LEAs to divert parts of their grant funds to research, demonstrations, curriculum development, dissemination, and teacher training. The US Office of Education also funded separate research and development grant programs to stimulate the schools of education, and funded new research centers dedicated to the education of the disadvantaged. The evaluation requirements proposed by Robert Kennedy provided further funding and stimulation for the academic community's involvement in Title I.

Finally, the entrepreneurs hoped that the beneficiaries (or their parents) would become an organized constituency that public school systems could no longer ignore. But they knew that poor people were not well organized for educational advocacy, and that parents generally did not have a good understanding of their children's needs. So the program design included a mandate for Title I parents to take part in local program decision-making and to receive training on educational issues.

Conclusion

The foregoing shows how different considerations interact to make a program complex. It is meant to suggest that program designs must meet a range of criteria, few of which support an emphasis on simplicity of design. Due to multiple goals, political constraints, and organizational capacity considerations, many effective Federal programs are highly complex and distribute benefits to many groups in addition to the principal beneficiaries. (For these reasons the Education for All Handicapped Children Act is even more complicated than Chapter 1: see Hill and Marks, 1982.)

Program designs should be evaluated for workability in a world of multiple goals, political constraints, and organizational limitations, rather than in vacuums.

Strengths and Weaknesses of Alternative Program Designs

This section analyzes the special strengths and weaknesses of three broad classes of program designs. They are:

(1) subsidies to assist (or induce) state and local public school systems to change their service delivery patterns;
(2) contracts with nongovernmental organizations to deliver certain services or serve designated groups; and
(3) transfers of purchasing power to students or their parents.

We shall assess each class of services according to its suitability for particular goals, requirements for Federal funding, potential for gaining and keeping political support, and the organizational capacities it requires.

Subsidy to State and Local Agencies

Goals

Subsidy to state and local agencies is particularly appropriate for programs intended to enhance the quality or quantity of existing services. Subsidy is also the obvious design for programs that require close coordination between a special federally supported enrichment program and the beneficiaries' regular schooling.

Subsidy is an ideal choice whenever the goal is to create leverage, i.e., effects on educational activities other than the ones directly supported by Federal funds. If the program is meant to influence broader educational practice, it should operate in close proximity to regular school programs. If it is meant to change local habits and priorities so that the desired activities will continue even after the Federal program has expired, it should be run by local school district employees who will ultimately filter back into standard teacher and administrator roles.

By these criteria, Title I and the Education for All Handicapped Children Act (EHA) were both properly based on subsidy. They both were meant to change local priorities and capabilities on behalf of particular beneficiary groups. As I have argued elsewhere (Hill, 1979; Hill and Marks, 1982), both Title I and EHA have created and institutionalized the desired changes in local practice.

Funding

Subsidy is possible only when Congress and the executive branch are willing to spend the money necessary for major intergovernmental transfers. Costs can be moderated if SEAs and LEAs can be induced to provide complementary services, and administrative costs can be treated as marginal. New conditions in the form of unfunded mandates can be imposed on subsidy programs that SEAs and LEAs have come to depend on. (But such mandates are often funded by reducing services for beneficiaries of the original subsidy program: see Kimbrough and Hill, 1981; Madey and Hill, 1982.)

But the minimum costs of a subsidy program are inevitably high, especially if it is to operate, as most Federal programs must, in many school districts.

Political constraints

The overwhelming political advantage of a subsidy-based program is that it attracts support from those people at the state and local level who are normally most interested in education, for example, members of state legislative education committees, senior SEA officials, school boards, principals and teachers. If those groups' continued support is essential for program success, subsidy is the obvious program design approach. (The regulatory apparatus and unfunded mandates that become attached to the subsidy may become controversial, but the subsidy itself is usually unpopular only with the advocates of governmental economy.)

Subsidy of established public education agencies has additional important political advantages. It embeds the Federal program in an organization that is clearly accountable to the courts and the public for its adherence to a variety of civil rights laws, public employee protections, and financial propriety rules. These laws and rules ensure that beneficiary groups have channels of access to their service providers, and they spare Federal officials the need to intervene in routine local disputes. Subsidy also makes the flow of Federal benefits to local jurisdictions completely transparent. This appeals to members of Congress, who like to call attention to Federal benefits brought to their districts.

Running programs through state and local agencies imposes real limitations on what the Federal government can accomplish. As the implementation literature documents so thoroughly, local officials' conceptions of their jobs must be reckoned with. Federal programs that seriously challenge local preferences are seldom implemented faithfully. Enforcement programs and efforts to strengthen the local political clout of program beneficiaries may work in the long run, but progress is slow and the costs are high (see Berman and McLaughlin, 1975; Hill and Marks, 1982). Even when Federal programs do not impose alien values and procedures, local agencies are likely to compete with Federal officials for influence over program design, and to require side

71

payments in the form of support for all associated administrative costs, whether or not they were previously borne locally.

Organizational capacity

Public school systems have well-established access to teacher recruits, instructional materials, consultants, and other resources necessary to develop and deliver services. They have established administrative and accounting procedures and some capacity to fit new instructional activities into students' daily routine. They are also experienced at fulfilling the ancillary requirements of Federal programs (for example due process in hiring, evaluation, and consultation with beneficiaries).

On the negative side, local agencies are constrained by their obligation to provide regular instructional services, by the limited length of the school day, by teachers' civil service protections and union contracts, and by local political forces. Some also have reputations that would interfere with the hiring of new groups of highly trained teachers. For these reasons, some public school systems may have very little capacity to manage new programs.

Contracts with Non-governmental Organizations

Goals

Contracting is a means of by-passing public school systems in order to obtain services from another provider. The motivations for such a by-pass are mainly organizational and political. If public systems refuse to deliver a class of service or determinedly neglect a group of students, contracting is a way to get the services delivered or the students served. If particular school systems are unable to recruit the teachers needed to deliver a program (due to local political constraints or bad agency reputation), contracting is a promising alternative.

Contracting could become a practical necessity if a private organization had a proprietary curriculum that it would not let others deliver. But in the real world firms can make more money selling books and materials to public school systems than by delivering services directly.

In the late 1960s contracting was seen as a way of introducing profit incentives to education. Though the results of 'performance contracting' were disappointing, the prospects of applying business methods to education make contracting attractive.

Contracting is also an excellent way of trying out a program concept while preventing it from taking root in the local educational bureaucracy. In this respect contracting's advantages are the mirror image of those discussed under subsidy: the practices of contracted programs are unlikely to influence regular classroom instruction or continue after Federal funding stops.

Funding

Contracting is likely to cost the Federal government more on a per pupil basis than would the traditional programs based on subsidies to SEAs and LEAs. Federal funds would have to pay all the costs of service delivery and administration. Contractors cannot embed their adminis trative costs in other ongoing activities, and public school systems are very unlikely to help the Federal government by subsidizing a private contractor.

The Federal government may be able to bear such costs for an experimental program or emergency intervention in a few sites. But a nationwide program based on formula allocation to beneficiaries would probably be much more expensive than a program of subsidies to SEAs and LEAs.

Political constraints

Most of the political advantages and disadvantages of contracting are the mirror images of those noted under subsidy. Contracting lets the Federal government run a program that flies in the face of local public educators' preferences. Contracting is relatively invulnerable to vetoes and diversion of benefits by local public officials and interest groups.

On the negative side, a contracting program would have to survive the opposition of school boards, principals, teachers' unions, and general government leaders. Beneficiary groups may also feel that they lack access to contractor personnel and that their civil rights are less directly enforceable. Contractors' customary freedom from the public sector's need for fiscal propriety may prove a further liability: scandals about fiscal or service delivery problems could promptly destroy a contracting-based program.

73

Organizational capacity

Though there are many proprietary educational institutions, few deliver services on anything like the scale required for a Federal program in a large school system. Contractors may have grave difficulty scaling up their operations. Though they may be less constrained than LEAs by teacher certification requirements and hiring rules, contractors may have trouble recruiting good enough personnel in large enough numbers.

The Federal government's organizational capacity for a major contracting program is also questionable. Its ability to let and monitor the hundreds of separate contracts required for a nationwide program is doubtful. The Department of Education would almost certainly need to arrange for licensing and technical inspection of contractor services — a major organizational problem and a political liability.

Contracting is probably feasible as a way of running an experimental program or of disciplining a recalcitrant local education agency. But the organizational challenges are probably too great for a major multi-district high enrollment program.

Transfers to Beneficiaries[2]

Goals

Transfer of purchasing power is meant to give students and their parents control over the selection of educational services. Such programs are based on one or both of two assumptions: first, that beneficiaries understand their own needs better than do service providers, and can therefore make more appropriate choices of services; and second, that competition for students will force schools to offer higher quality services.

The first assumption reflects the enthusiasm for income transfers that characterized the Federal government's 'war on poverty' after 1968. The economists who dominated antipoverty thinking in the Nixon-era Office of Economic Opportunity argued that the most direct way to improve a person's welfare was to increase his income, i.e., by transferring purchasing power instead of by providing a specific service. Income transfer programs were proposed at that time for education, health care, housing, and food assistance. The proposed income transfer programs were either unconditional (for example, welfare income supplements, which could be used for any purchase the recipient chose to make) or linked to the purchase of a specific class of service (for example, housing allowances or education vouchers). In general, conditional transfers were offered in areas in which the public interest required that the recipients consume a high minimum level of the service.

The second assumption reflects a desire to impose market disciplines on public service bureaucracies. Under this assumption, increases in beneficiaries' purchasing power are means to another end, which is to increase the quality and diversity of services offered. The recipients may or may not make astute choices among services; but the need to compete for patronage would force service delivery organizations to operate more efficiently and offer more attractive products.

Two present-day education proposals reflect different mixes of the two assumptions. Education tax credit plans generally emphasize the value of consumer choice, and education voucher proposals emphasize the importance of market discipline on providers.

Funding

Transfer programs in education can cover a wide or narrow range of services, and Federal payments can either be open-ended (for example, for a voucher to pay whatever a particular service costs) or controlled (for example, a fixed allowance that the beneficiary may supplement).

But like contract-based programs, transfers force the sponsor to bear high per unit costs. State and local governments are unlikely to share costs unless program services are limited to ones they deliver. Existing non-public schools may charge only marginal costs for services purchased via voucher plans, but they could not greatly expand their capacity. A Federal program that increased demand for privately delivered educational services would require investments in new plant, equipment and salaries, and the vast majority of those costs would have to be paid directly. Services provided by parochial schools in particular would be much more costly if they were forced to pay market-rate wages to large numbers of new teachers.

Political constraints

Like contracting, transfers are attractive to those who distrust public bureaucracies. But such programs must do without the support from state and local education agencies and teachers' unions that have been the main political foundations for Federal education programs since Title I. Parents of beneficiary students may, or may not, be an important alternative source of support: it depends on how good the services are and how hard they are to obtain.

Support, based on the attractiveness of income transfers in principle, may not be enough to sustain a program in the long run. support for 'good government' theories is typically broad but shallow, and activists are likely to shift their attention from education to other fields if interesting opportunities arise. But opposition from the 'bureaucrats' who are by-passed or disciplined by transfer programs will be consistent and strong. Those who hope competition will spur innovation may be disappointed first, if they discover that competition leads providers to cluster together near the middle of the spectrum of current educational practice, in hopes of attracting the very large numbers of students whose parents have no taste for educational innovation. (I hope I have not butchered Elmore's point here.)

Finally, the enduring public need to educate the young will ultimately lead courts and legislatures to treat service delivery organizations as quasi-governmental bodies. As transfer programs acquire the trappings of public accountability, they are almost certain to become less flexible and distinctive.

Organizational capacity

Most income transfer programs presume that the market can respond to an increase in demand. That assumption is clearly warranted in the case of food stamps and medical care (though in the latter case price increases may soak up a major share of transfer payments). But it may not be so justified when service delivery requires substantial front end investment (for example, housing) or when the capacity of the private market is small (for example, education). The greatest unanswered question about the feasibility of large-scale transfer programs for elementary and secondary education is the capacity of the private market to respond.

Subsidiary questions concern the ability of public agencies to certify the quality of privately provided services. As Elmore argues, government cannot escape its responsibility for ensuring that children get the necessary amounts and qualities of educational services. As is the case for other privately provided services, government retains the responsibility to license providers, set minimum service standards, protect consumers against providers who make false claims, prevent racial or sex discrimination in delivery of services, and guard against misuse of public funds. These functions will ultimately require an extensive licensing and enforcement bureaucracy — one that could become as large and intrusive as the one that manages Chapter 1, programs for handicapped children, and the civil rights laws. That bureaucracy might not need to be all Federal, but there is reason to doubt whether state and local education agencies would be willing to enforce the terms of a program that was intended to bypass them

Conclusion

Each of the three basic program designs discussed above has its distinctive strengths and weaknesses. Because none is superior for all cases, the Federal government should be prepared to use them all in combinations.

The traditional concept of subsidy emerges from my analysis as the one with the broadest applicability. On grounds of costs, political support, and institutional capacity, programs of subsidy to state and local education agencies are the only plausible method for delivering federally-funded services to large numbers of students nationwide.

The other two basic program strategies, contracts with non-governmental organizations and direct transfers to beneficiaries, have more limited applications. One very important use is to fill the interstices in major subsidy programs — providing service alternatives in states and school districts whose public education agencies will not or cannot serve all the intended beneficiaries. Contracts and direct transfers may also supplement subsidy programs by providing service alternatives for beneficiary children who need rare or costly services. Vouchers might, for example, be ways of permitting the parents of severely handicapped children to select services directly, while limiting the government's total cost.

Another highly promising use of contracts and direct transfers is for the development and demonstration of new ideas. Transfer programs could be run temporarily in a few sites as a way of stimulating private sector innovations — new ways to serve needy populations and services that may be attractive to special interest groups. Contracts could be used temporarily in particular sites to demonstrate or test new methods for administering or regulating Federal program services. Pretesting such mandates would help prevent the application of ill-advised new mandates to ongoing subsidy programs.

Notes

1   The views expressed in this chapter are the author's and may not reflect the opinions of the Rand Corporation or its sponsors.
2   An excellent article by Richard Elmore (in press) has greatly influenced my thinking on this topic. The analysis that follows is mine, and I take full responsibility for it. But much of what is good comes at least indirectly from Elmore.

References

BERMAN, P. and MCLAUGHLIN, M. (1975). *Federal Programs Supporting Educational Change: Vol. IV. The Findings in Review*, Santa Monica, CA, Rand Corporation.

ELMORE, R. F. (in press) *Options for Choice in Education*, Santa Monica, CA, Rand Corporation.

HILL, P. T. (1979) *Do Federal Programs Interfere With One Another?* Santa Monica, CA, Rand Corporation.

HILL P. T. and MARKS E. (1982). *Federal Influence Over State and Local Government: The Case of Non-discrimination in Education*, Santa Monica, CA, Rand Corporation.

KIMBROUGH, J., and HILL P. T. (1981) *The Aggregate Effects of Federal Education Programs*, Santa Monica, CA, Rand Corporation.

MADEY, D. L. and HILL P. T. (1982). *Educational Policymaking Through the Civil Justice System*, Santa Monica, CA, Rand Corporation.

4
Increased State Capacity and Aid to the Disadvantaged

Susan Fuhrman

The capacity and willingness of states to provide for public education have increased markedly in recent years. State government has modernized and matured; the wide-ranging programmatic and fiscal reforms enacted since the early 1980s dramatically demonstrate state interest in education. However, an important question is the extent to which this expanded state activity will benefit the educationally disadvantaged. Historically, the states have not served this constituency particularly well, defining such service as part of the Federal government's role. There are also troublesome concerns about the effects of recent reforms on at-risk youngsters. On the other hand, elements of the new reform movement bring significantly expanded services for the low achievers, and it is likely that future developments may benefit them as well. On balance, the recent reforms and proposals next on the state agenda may cause the scales to tip in favor of children with special educational needs for the first time in recent state history.

State Capacity and Education

Over the twenty to twenty-five-year period prior to the recent state reform movement, states vastly modernized and improved their capacity to take the lead in educational policymaking. Once called the 'fallen arches' of the Federal system, states were broadly criticized for their unrepresentative, antiquated governance systems. They had outdated constitutions, weak governors, and malapportioned and cumbersome legislatures. Their tax systems were regressive and inadequate. All that has changed. With revised constitutions, modified revenue bases, gubernatorial offices strengthened by longer terms and improved veto power, and professionalized legislatures, states have become capable of domestic policy leadership.

States now have the improved fiscal capacity necessary to support an expanded policy role. State revenues have consistently grown as a per cent of total public sector receipts since the late 1960s, in contrast to both Federal and local revenues. State aid to local government has quadrupled since 1969. The growth was made possible by a steady strengthening and diversification of state tax systems; between 1959 and 1977, thirteen states adopted an income tax and twelve states adopted a sales tax. In the same period, states developed several fiscal discipline measures to assist with budget management: 'rainy day funds', statutory or constitutional expenditure limitations and guber-natorial line item veto (Advisory Commission on Intergovernmental Relations, 1984).

At the same time states were strengthening their fiscal bases, they were improving the institutions of governance. Governors' offices have become considerably more capable of policy initiation. Since the 1960s state planning and development offices have been created as staff for the governors in all but five states. While the average staff size of the governor's office was four in 1956, by 1979 the average staff size was thirty-four (Sabato, 1983). In medium and larger states the staff tend to be specialized by policy area; it is not unusual to find three to four staffers working on education policy. In addition, executive branches have been reorganized, and the majority of states have created a cabinet system, with the cabinet serving as the problem-solving group for the governor (Doyle and Hartle 1985).

Nowhere has the change in composition and functioning been more dramatic than in the case of the state legislature. Legislatures not only became more representative as a consequence of reapportionment, they became increasingly professional as well. Legislators began to spend much more time at their jobs, extending session time and working during the interim in addition. As requirements for financial disclosure became stricter and as legislative duties began to take up more and more time, fewer citizen legislators — lawyers, in particular — ran for office and more full-time politicians took their place. Professional politicians are politically ambitious; they see legislative service as advancing future political careers, and, consequently, value responsiveness to constituents above all else. They have improved the physical setting in which they spend so much time serving their constituents, providing offices and sophisticated electronic equipment for themselves. They have also vastly augmented their staffs. The great growth in legislative staffs was during the late 1960s and early 1970s. It has been estimated that professional staffing increased 30 per cent between 1968 and 1974 (Rosenthal, 1981). In the last few years, the total number of staff has been relatively stable. However, the staff is becoming increasingly fragmented, with fewer staff placed in central research agencies or committees and more staff going to individual legislators for constituent service.

The improved information flow about local conditions, the incentives and capacity to respond to constituent demand, and the long-term political ambitions that lie at the heart of the improvements in capacity all make for a more aggressive legislature. Today's legislatures are flexing their muscles; they believe themselves capable of leadership and are exerting it wherever they can. They are seizing a leadership role in more and more areas, particularly in the case of policy issues where political costs are small. It is not likely they will lead in establishing a position on abortion or in cutting budgets, but they will take the lead on drug education and economic development, where there is widespread support for action.

The muscle-flexing and credit-claiming posture has undoubtedly contributed to the extensive educational policymaking activities of state legislatures. Education is, after all, the largest single item in state budgets. Legislative interest in education grew throughout the 1970s in tandem with the growth in legislative strength. School finance was the education issue that legislators had always cared about the most, because of their budgetary responsibility. As activist courts and sophisticated issue networks pushed school finance reform into prominence as *the* education issue of the seventies, the assumption of a leadership role by legislatures was accelerated. By the end of the decade, legislators were the predominant education policymakers in many states (Rosenthal and Fuhrman, 1981).

By the start of the 1980s, legislatures and modernized governors' offices were poised for an expansion into more programmatic education concerns. State aid to education had doubled in the course of school finance reform. The infusion of so much new money created the demand for enhanced accountability controls. Policymakers were already noting public concern about declining test scores and warnings about shortages of qualified teachers. State leaders were turning their scrutiny to curriculum issues and teacher quality when *A Nation at Risk* and other reform reports came along to lend momentum to their efforts.

State Education Reforms

Between 1982 and 1986 states enacted a set of education reforms that are extraordinary in scope and nature. In that period, virtually every state addressed at least three of the following substantive areas of education reform:

- teacher certification and training — including scholarship and loan programs, entrance and exit testing, and teacher education requirements;
- teacher compensation and career structure — including minimum or across the board salary increases, career ladder plans, and other incentive programs;
- governance and finance — including formula revisions and changes in governance structures at the state, local, or intermediate levels;
- school attendance, calendar, and class size — including revisions in the compulsory school age and in attendance policy, longer instructional days and years, and special early education programs;
- graduation standards — including new course requirements and exit-testing policies; and
- curriculum and testing — including more widespread assessments, promotional gates, and model curricula.

To pay for these initiatives, states increased real revenues devoted to education by $2 billion during the 1982/83 school year; $0.9 billion in 1983/84; $3.5 billion in 1984/85; and $3 billion in 1985/86. The state share of education spending rose from 48.9 per cent at the start of the decade to 50.1 per cent in 1986 (Dougherty, 1986).

Several aspects of the reform movement make it quite unique and remarkable. First, with many of the reforms, state government entered into areas of schooling previously left to the education establishment and to locals. Legislators and governors made unprecedented decisions about what shall be taught, in what manner, by whom and at what level of compensation. For example, even in states where the local bargaining process still determines salary scales, legislatures have provided aid for new minimum salaries and incentives for the development of differentiated pay scales.

Second, the reforms spread through the states with unprecedented rapidity. Historically, policies without specific Federal incentives or sanctions have taken as long as four years to reach half the states. School finance reform reached half the states within six years, but many elements of the recent reform movement, such as the increase in graduation requirements, spread at nearly twice that rate.

Third, a number of states — including Arkansas, California, Florida, Georgia, North Carolina, South Carolina and Tennessee — enacted reform packages that were much more comprehensive than any previous state education laws. Several of the new reforms included 100 discrete changes. The 1985 Georgia reform, the Quality Basic Education Act (QBE), incorporated a major overhaul of school finance, extensive new testing programs, an information management system, incentives for district reorganization, training for administrators and school boards, and a teacher career ladder, to name just some of its elements. The comprehensive approach to educational change is a noted departure from the much more incremental tack generally taken. Even legislatures noted for their activity in education have tended to address one or two important educational issues each year or session, rather than parcelling so many together at once.

Why were such far-reaching, comprehensive reforms enacted with such speed at that particular moment in history? The perceived decline in educational quality was not the immediate impetus; conditions had in fact bottomed out. The decline in student achievement that began in the late sixties was already reversing by the time of the reforms (Peterson, 1983). Certainly among the explanations was the fact that states were recovering from the recession and by 1983 experienced more fiscal flexibility. Also important was the fact that there was virtually no opposition to the school reform movement. The business community, the foremost opponent to increased education taxing and spending in the past, was now among reform's most active supporters because it recognized the link between education and a healthy economy. Educational interest groups, which opposed many of the reforms because they threatened local autonomy or appeared to define local educators as part of the problem, were neutralized in their opposition because they also realized that this was the first opportunity in a long time to gain major funding increases for education. The public pressure for reform, indicated by intensifying criticism of the public schools and a simultaneous willingness to support increased taxes if they led to improvement, provided another incentive. The national reform reports set out a reform agenda and garnered so much press coverage that educational reform could hardly be avoided (McDonnell and Fuhrman, 1986).

It is the juxtaposition of these factors — fiscal slack, weak opposition, mounting public demand, pressure by business elites, and the presence of a reform agenda — with the ever-growing search for leadership on the part of increasingly aggressive legislators and governors that accounts for the nature and extent of the reform movement. The importance of legislators and governors in shaping and promoting reform is critical to an understanding of the reform movement. Even more significantly in this context, the implications of the reform movement for disadvantaged youth hinge on the support for special needs from legislators and governors. In the past, there was reason to question that commitment.

States and the Disadvantaged: A Historical Perspective

Traditionally, states have not taken a strong role in supporting programs for the disadvantaged. A survey of states in 1979/80 found that twenty-three states provided funding for compensatory education (Winslow and Peterson, 1981). Many states had funding formulas similar or identical to Title I and included requirements and restrictions to assure the expenditure of funds on the supplementary instructional programs for the appropriate students. In fact, the majority of the state programs appear to have been deliberately patterned on Title I and reflect state response to a Federal initiative, rather than state leadership (McQuire, 1982).

Perhaps the Federal stimulus explains why state commitment to disadvantaged programs has never been very strong. Total funding for these programs never exceeded 1 per cent of total state funding for education. In some cases the presence of state compensatory aid did not necessarily mean that disadvantaged children were actually receiving program services. Some programs were established merely as political side payments to urban interests to gain their support of other state goals and were never intended to subsidize special programs. In other cases, the state intended districts to provide programs but was hampered in providing direction by low state agency capacity or traditional deference to local control (McDonnell and McLaughlin, 1982a). Only those programs most tied to Title I were likely to receive substantial state supervision (Milne and Moskowitz, 1983).

Furthermore, when budgets were tight, compensatory programs were often among the first to suffer. In the early 1980s, fiscally hard-pressed states yielded to pressures for maintenance of general aid support at the expense of special need programs (Wolf, 1981). For example, in 1981/82, Minnesota made a 6.5 per cent cut in general education support funds, but a 9 per cent cut in categorical programs. In the same year Utah cut compensatory and bilingual aid by 30 per cent and increased support for the general program by 10 per cent (Milne and Moskowitz, 1983).

State compensatory programs also changed over time to be less compensatory, in the sense of making up for poverty-related educational deficits, and more remedial. Although most programs were initially created in the image of Title I, in some states achievement was always a sole criterion for selecting both eligible schools and students. New York's compensatory program, for example, targeted funds at low achievers not served with Title I funds. Over time, more states moved to an achievement focus, and away from an income definition of disadvantage. For example, in 1982, Connecticut determined to abolish its income-based program and to shift the funding to a remediation program. State leaders proclaimed support for achievement-based remediation rather than surrogate action through funding of low-income children. The metamorphosis toward a focus on basic skills remediation indicates that compensatory programs increasingly became differentiated to reflect state goals, rather than Federal goals (Milne and Moskowitz, 1983; Winslow and Peterson, 1982).

Analysts posit that weak political support accounts for the rather discouraging state commitment to the disadvantaged. Proponents of compensatory services have never organized very effectively at the state level, in comparison to the Federal level. Legislatures and governors are responsive to the larger constituency; to the extent that education is a political issue, they win or lose elections based on the success of the general program, not on support for specialized programs. They are likely to subordinate special needs programs to more general educational goals (McDonnell and McLaughlin, 1982b). A study of state special need programs in six states showed that governors indicated a propensity to fold special need programs in with the more general education program, for example, by consolidating a set of categorical programs into block grants and letting local districts sort out service priorities (Milne and Moskowitz, 1983).

The low priority accorded to disadvantaged programs in the past by legislators and governors offers reason to doubt that the current reform movement they fashioned provides an improved outlook. In fact, it is feared that the emphasis on excellence will divert attention from equity goals and further disadvantage low-achieving students.

Education Reform and the At-Risk Youth

Many concerned educators are convinced that the reform movement does not augur well for educationally disadvantaged youth. They worry about the impact of graduation tests on marginal students. Those who are substantially behind at high school entry will not have time to close two- and three-year learning gaps and will fail or drop out rather than attempt what seems like an impossible task. Critics also question the imposition of additional course requirements for graduation when low-achieving students are barely making it through existing course loads. New requirements for advanced math and science classes can fill up the school day, leaving no time for remediation or career preparation. Concern also focuses on efforts to extend the school day or year without corresponding attention to the quality of learning opportunities for all students during existing school hours. Finally, a number of critics doubt that all students will have equal access to recent improvements. For example, new academic courses taught to disadvantaged students, particularly those in poor or isolated schools that have difficulty attracting high quality teachers, may be watered down or taught by teachers without the appropriate training. The trend toward the development of career ladders for teachers may not mean the same for all students. Master teachers may be concentrated in elite schools or districts unless career ladder programs have explicit provisions to assure distributional equity (Levin, 1985; Brown and Haycock, 1984).

It is too early to tell whether the dire predictions about the deleterious effects of reform will be borne out in practice. It is true that the failure rate on new competency tests has been much higher in urban areas and among minority students. For example, 35 per cent of urban students failed the reading portion of the 1986 High School Proficiency Test in New Jersey, as compared to 10 per cent of students in non-urban districts. There was an even larger difference in the passage rates on the mathematics portion of the test. Even though there has been considerable improvement in the passage rates of urban school children over the three years the test has been administered, the gap between urban and non-urban performance is substantial and disturbing.

However, there is another side to the argument about the impact of reform. New standards may not result in further disadvantage. After all, the concept of standards is based on sound educational philosophy. High standards represent high expectations which in turn are strongly associated with effective schooling. High standards can also be supported by research on the 'opportunity to learn'. Students learn more when exposed to more content. In addition, there is some evidence to show that increasing standards may benefit all students, disadvantaged and more advantaged. Preliminary data from the High School and Beyond Study suggest that even students with low prior achievement may learn more from more academic courses (Clune, 1985).

Some evidence exists to indicate that the recent reforms — or at least the climate and public attention surrounding the reforms, which are still in their infancy — benefit lower achieving students. A recent study of course enrollment patterns in twenty California high schools conducted by Policy Analysis for California Education (PACE) shows that schools with children of lower socioeconomic status (SES) experienced sizeable increases in academic course offerings between 1982/83 and 1984/85. Schools below the mean in SES had a 32 per cent increase in the number of science sections while schools above the mean had only an 8 per cent increase (Grossman, Kirst, Negash and Schmidt-Posner, 1986). In the same state, most data sources suggest test score improvement in inner-city schools and no evidence of increased dropping out (Haycock, 1986). Early reports from South Carolina indicate that low-achieving students made substantial progress since the enactment of comprehensive reform in 1983. For example, the percentage of fourth grade students scoring in the lower quartile on basic skills tests declined by 12 per cent between 1983 and 1985 (Peterson and Strassler, 1986).

The impact of the reforms on the disadvantaged remains an empirical issue, particularly as new higher standards have yet to be fully implemented. State oversight efforts should track the differential effects of course requirements, testing and curricular changes over time. The questions of access to improvements and the impact of reform on marginal students are among the most important any assessment of reform must answer. However, the reforms' effects depend not only on how new standards or teacher policies work out in practice but also on the success of a number of new programs specifically addressed at low-achieving youth. In many states, the reform movement incorporated special initiatives for at-risk youngsters along with higher standards and other general program improvements.

Recent Trends in Programs for the Disadvantaged

The recent state reforms employ a number of approaches to programming for at-risk youth. First, there have been modest increases in spending on existing state compensatory programs. States such as New Jersey and New York, which have long had compensatory education programs, increased funding for those efforts. Second, states that never had compensatory programs developed significant new services.

South Carolina is a case in point. The state that now has the highest per capita funded compensatory and remedial basic skills program in the country had no state disadvantaged program before its reform legislation in 1983. At that time it established a $55 million remediation and compensatory basic skills program in reading and math in elementary schools and in those two subjects plus writing in secondary schools. Compensatory services are guaranteed to children scoring below the twenty-fifth percentile; approximately 117,000 children are served through this program which requires daily services, is fairly tightly regulated and is closely tied to Chapter 1. In most grades, those students who score above the bottom quartile but still need help are provided remedial services.

Remedial services are more flexible; districts may choose from a number of different models, including directed teaching, computer-assisted instruction, independent study and tutoring. If appropriate score gains are not shown within two years, a district is required to redesign its model. The program is proving to be a major success with achievement gains of two to three times above the expected outcomes.

Pennsylvania also has a new remediation effort as part of its Testing for Essential Learning and Literacy Skills (TELLS) program. TELLS was established in 1984 as part of Governor Richard Thornburgh's 'Turning the Tide' reform agenda. TELLS tests measure reading and math skills in third, fifth and eighth grades. Thirty-eight million dollars are provided for remedial programs for those scoring below the cut-off level; the major portion of the funding is a direct categorical program that flows directly to the low-achieving child's district. Almost 30 per cent of the states' children were targeted for remedial aid through the 1986 round of tests. About half of those needed help in both reading and math.

Georgia is an example of a state that offered compensatory education before its 1985 reform, but expanded and revised its programming concurrently with changes in the general education program. The previous compensatory program served children in grades one through eight who failed to achieve fifteen of twenty objectives on the fourth grade reading portion of the state criterion-referenced test. However, according to the Governor's commission that developed the 1985 comprehensive reform package, the program lacked standard eligibility criteria, focus and coordination. Quality Basic Education includes a new remedial program that serves students in more grade levels and is supported by the revised general aid formula. Eligible pupils — those in grades 2 to 5 who score a half year or more below grade level on a state-approved standardized test or below the twenty-fifth percentile on a norm-referenced test in reading or math; ninth graders who achieve at one or more years below grade level in reading or in math on a standardized test and those in grades 10 through 12 who fail the state basic skills test — are weighted in the determination of formula aid. Local districts design programs that are subject to state board monitoring and evaluation.

Another new approach states are taking to services for the educationally disadvantaged is the provision of targeted early childhood programs. Encouraged by research on the long-term positive effects of high-quality pre-school programs for at-risk youth (Schweinhart, Berrueta-Clements, Barnett, Epstein and Weikart, 1985), several states have established or expanded early childhood services. For example, in 1985 Illinois adopted a pre-school program targeted to at-risk 3 to 5-year-olds. It serves 7400 children in 234 districts and permits non-profit agencies as well as school districts to provide the services. Louisiana, Michigan, Texas and Washington State also have pre-school programs that target the at-risk or disadvantaged. For example, Washington uses Head Start eligibility as a criterion for its program for 4-year-olds and supplies funds to both Head Start agencies or schools, with priority given to districts with the most at-risk children. Massachusetts, Maine and Rhode Island have expanded Head Start programming with their own revenues (Grubb, in press).

South Carolina's reforms included early childhood programs as well. A half-day state-funded program for at-risk 4-year-olds will eventually be supported at a level of $10m a year. Eligible children, deemed not ready to start school, are identified through a referral system with the cooperation of various state and local agencies. The schools screen the children who are placed in child development centers with very small pupil-teacher ratios. By 1988/89, the state intends that its program and Head Start together will serve all at-risk 4-year-olds, an estimated 25 to 30 per cent of the 4-year-old population.

A second component of South Carolina's approach to early childhood education is mandatory attendance in kindergarten. After discovering that first grade children who had not attended kindergarten were significantly behind their peers (32 per cent of low-income children without kindergarten were likely to repeat first grade as compared to 12 per cent of low-income children with kindergarten), the state determined to lower the compulsory school age by requiring kindergarten and supporting it with state funding. South Carolina is one of three states with mandatory kindergarten attendance (McDonald, 1986).

Finally, there are a growing number of programs aimed at specific problems strongly associated with educational disadvantage, for example, teenage pregnancy, substance abuse and truancy. The most extensive developments are in the area of dropout prevention programs. The Education Commission of the States estimates that up to fifteen states have recently initiated dropout programs; a number of others are planning such efforts. The programs vary considerably, but state activity is characterized by better recordkeeping on dropout statistics, support of local programs and dissemination of promising practices, and efforts to encourage cross-agency cooperation. California's program, which has a goal of reducing the high school dropout rate 25 per cent by 1990, includes support of special counseling services and a media campaign to encourage potential dropouts to stay in school. Wisconsin's new 'Children At Risk' law mandates that districts develop plans for meeting the employment, education, personal and health needs of at-risk children, defined as teen parents, dropouts, truants, and those in trouble with the law. Washington state supports educational clinics that diagnose a child's needs and produce an individualized program for each potential dropout (*ibid*).

These efforts — new or expanded remedial programs; early childhood programs for at-risk students and dropout programs — represent an impressive array of state action. They indicate a commitment to those who are not likely to benefit from the general educational reform movement without additional help. In South Carolina, the compensatory/remedial and early childhood programs were explicitly coupled to the other 'excellence reforms' that included promotion standards and exit testing. The Governors' office, which was instrumental in developing the reform package, and other leading actors recognized that it would be unfair to raise standards without giving everyone a fair shot to meet them. This point of view was clearly and broadly articulated. As a result, the ensuing reform package embodied an explicit trade between the business community that was strongly pushing exit testing and other performance standards and the educators and minority leaders who particularly supported programs for the disadvantaged.

The coupling of general program improvements and disadvantaged programs indicates that the highest levels of state leadership are speaking out for at-risk students at the same time they are making significant changes in the general program. The juncture bodes well for disadvantaged youth. Even though programs for at-risk students are relatively small in many states, their inclusion in larger reform packages and their acknowledged importance to the success of the state's overall educational efforts mean state leaders are including programs for the disadvantaged squarely within their scope of activities. Legislators, governors, and the business community that urged political leaders to pursue reform are defining at-risk youth as an important constituency for the receipt of state services, not as a marginal group that the Federal government will take care of, perhaps with some limited state add-on. Tying these programs to the general reforms in operation and in new legislation — remediation is triggered by new statewide tests introduced as part of the reform — further integrates them with the general program. The remedial programs emerging out of the reform continue the trend for state compensatory programs to move from imitations of Title I to achievement-driven programs that reflect state needs. The achievement emphasis integrates them with the regular program and thus makes them more likely to sustain general political support.

Integration of at-risk programs with the general reform offers encouragement for the long-term support of such programs by political leaders. Nonetheless, the many new at-risk programs are relatively small in funding, compared to the dollars going into other aspects of reform, and largely categorical in nature. It is also true that services for the disadvantaged, while tied to the larger reforms rhetorically, were arrived at somewhat late in the reform process. A survey of state excellence commissions in 1984 found only 14 per cent addressing dropout prevention. The concern for dropouts has come more recently, in some states only after critics pointed out the potentially damaging effects of reform on marginal students.

The small, categorical programs for at-risk youth are not likely to satisfy the critics who worry about the impact of new standards, tests and course requirements. They would argue that side programs are too little, too late; that remedial programs that are not well integrated into the entire school day have little promise of really making a difference for at-risk children; and that what is needed is an early and continuous effort to make the entire school experience effective for all learners.

Making the entire school experience more effective is a key goal of a new set of reform proposals that encompass reform's 'Second Wave'. State leaders are now deliberating how to address the recommendations of several recent education reform reports. The reports of the Carnegie Forums on Education and the Economy Task Force on Teaching and The Holmes Group envision a vastly different school, a 'restructured' school where teachers diagnose and respond to individual student needs, rigid ability tracking is a thing of the past, and the self-contained classroom is only one of many instructional models. In such a school, say the reports' authors, the teacher as a revitalized professional can structure curriculum and instruction to the benefit of all types of learners.

The *1991 Report: A Time for Results* released by the nation's governors, reiterates the call for a restructured learning environment; in addition, it includes other recommendations, such as encouraging choice among public schools, that could have important ramifications for students who are unsuccessful in traditional school settings. Included in the governors' list of priorities are early childhood programs and other programs for at-risk students. In fact, one of the seven task forces that contributed to the report concentrated on school readiness issues. The *1991 Report* is remarkable in that it pledges the support of the highest state political leadership for educational improvement. Collectively the governors promise to stick with education reform for at least five years, to publicize their recommendations and to monitor and report on implementation by individual states.

The second wave of reform will be a long, slow and expensive undertaking, one that will be very problematic in the many states experiencing fiscal distress. It will be characterized by difficult political negotiating, for example, balancing the demand for increased teacher leadership with the concerns of school principals. The vision of a restructured school has yet to take concrete shape. However, if the governors are true to their promise to keep working at education reform and if those reforms do revitalize schools, at-risk students certainly stand to benefit.

Summary

States have undoubtedly assumed the leadership role in education policy implied by their constitutional responsibility for education but never truly exercised before the 1980s. In the recent reform movement, state legislators and governors made policy in a number of areas that had been largely delegated to local school districts. States also stopped playing follow-the-leader to the Federal government, as exhibited by their creation of remedial programs that move state disadvantaged programs away from the Federal model and integrate them with the state general program. The fact that the new programs for disadvantaged children were coupled with general school improvement initiatives, supported by top state leadership, and developed out of state needs rather than in response to a Federal stimulus indicates a new, stronger level of state commitment than in the past. The proposed second generation of reforms may bring even more substantial benefits to at-risk children. In the interim, educators and citizens will be tracking the impact of the first wave of reforms, particularly those imposing higher standards on at-risk youth.

References

ADVISORY COMMISSION ON INTERGOVERNMENTAL RELATIONS (1984) *Significant Features of Fiscal Federalism*. Washington, DC, Author.

BROWN, P. R. AND HAYCOCK, K. (1984) *Excellence For Whom?* Oakland, CA, The Achievement Council.

CLUNE, W. H. (1985) *New Standards for High School Students: Technical Application*, New Brunswick, NJ, Rutgers University, Center for Policy Research in Education.

DOUGHERTY, V. (1986) *Funding State Education Reforms*, Denver, CO, The Education Commission of the States.

DOYLE, D. AND HARTLE, T. (1985) *Excellence in Education: The States Take Charge*, Washington, DC, American Enterprise Institute.

GROSSMAN, P., KIRST, M. W., NEGASH, W. AND SCHMIDT-POSNER, J. (1986) *Curricular Change in California Comprehensive High Schools*, Berkeley, CA, Policy Analysis for California Education.

GRUBB, N. W. (in press). *Young Children Face the States: Issues and Options for Early Childhood Programs*, New Brunswick, NJ, Rutgers University, Center for Policy Research in Education.

HAYCOCK, K. (1986) *The Impact of Reform on Minorities*, paper presented at the annual meeting of the American Educational Research Association, San Francisco, April.

LEVIN, H. M. (1985) *The Educationally Disadvantaged: A National Crisis*, Philadelphia, PA, Public/Private Ventures.

MCDONALD, J. G. (1986) 'Readiness for the educational standards', *Time for Results: The Governors' 1991 Report on Education*, Washington, DC, The National Governors Association, Task Force on Readiness.

MCDONNELL, L. M. AND FUHRMAN, S. (1986). 'The political context of school reform' in MUELLER, V. AND MCKEOWN, M. (Eds) *The Fiscal, Legal, and Political Aspects of State Reform of Elementary and Secondary Education*, Cambridge MA, Ballinger Press.

MCDONNELL, L. M. AND MCLAUGHLIN, M. W. (1982a) *Education Policy and the Role of the States*, Santa Monica, CA, The Rand Corporation.

MCDONNELL, L. M. AND MCLAUGHLIN, M. W. (1982b) 'The states' commitment to special need students', in SHERMAN, J., KUTNER, M. AND SMALL, K. (Eds) *New Dimensions on the Federal-state Partnership in Education*, Washington, DC, Institute for Educational Leadership.

MCQUIRE, K. (1982) *State and Federal Programs for Special Populations*, Denver, CO, The Education Commission of the States.

MILNE, A. M. AND MOSKOWITZ, J. (1983) *Serving Special Needs Children: The State Approach*, Washington, DC, Decision Resources.

PETERSON, P. E. (1983). 'Did the education commissions say anything?', *Brookings Review*, Winter, pp. 3–11.

PETERSON, T. K. AND STRASSLER, G. M. (1986). *The Impact of Recent Educational Reforms on Minority and All Low Achieving Students and on Minority and All High Achieving Students*, paper presented at the annual meeting of the American Educational Research Association, San Francisco, April.

ROSENTHAL, A. (1981) *Legislative Life*. New York, Harper and Row.

ROSENTHAL, A. AND FUHRMAN, S. (1981) *Legislative Education Leadership in the States*, Washington, DC, The Institute for Educational Leadership.

SABATO, L. (1983) *Goodbye to Good-time Charlie* (2nd edn) Lexington, MA, Lexington Books.

SCHWEINHART, L. J., BERRUETA-CLEMENTS, J. R., BARNETT, W. S., EPSTEIN, A. S. AND WEIKART, D. P. (1985) 'The promise of early childhood education', *Phi Delta Kappan*, **66**, pp. 548–53.

WINSLOW, H. R. AND PETERSON, S. M. (1981) *State Initiatives for Special Needs Populations*, Palo Alto, CA, Bay Area Research Group.

WINSLOW, H. R. AND PETERSON, S. M. (1982) 'State initiatives for special needs students' in SHERMAN, J., KUTNER, M. AND SMALL, K. (Eds) *New Dimensions on the Federal-state Partnership in Education*, Washington, DC, Institute for Educational Leadership.

WOLF, A. (1981) *State Spending on Education and Levels of Educational Services*, Washington, DC, The Urban Institute.

5
The Federal Role and Chapter 1: Rethinking Some Basic Assumptions

Michael W. Kirst

It is over twenty years since the major Federal program for the disadvantaged began, but surprisingly little has changed from its original vision. Regulations and targeting of aid have been tightened and loosened, while parents have come and gone as major policy participants. But the various amendments have been incremental around the same themes of a special program for special needs students that is separate and additional to the 'regular program'. A fundamental assumption was that something different (termed special services) was needed for the disadvantaged than the normal educational fare in terms of content and teaching methods. In parts of the country, however, disadvantaged children were hardly receiving any instruction at all in the early 1960s (Committee on Education and Labor, US House of Representatives, 1985).

The writer was the first program assistant hired by the 1965 Title I Director, John F Hughes, and has also participated in administration of the program as President of the California State Board of Education. I believe that it is now time to question some of the basic Chapter 1 policies in view of the change in conceptions about the Federal role and the recent state and local education reform movement. But there is a danger that radical Chapter 1 surgery will vitiate the established program base that stands out for its fidelity to those original 1965 legislative objectives. In effect, a high risk, high gain strategy would be to merge Chapter 1 closer to the 'regular academic core' program and focus on avoiding *educational supplanting* rather than fiscal compliance. The Federal role would feature curricular content that these special needs pupils should and do study, as well as effective classroom instructional strategies and practices. The historic Chapter 1 concern has been policing *fiscal supplanting* in order to prevent leakage of funds from the most needy children to their more fortunate classmates. The easiest administrative method to do this was by setting up special Title I classes and remedial teachers that received children 'pulled out' of their classes for a period of time.

If educational supplanting becomes a key concern, then the Federal role will change from fiscal audits and regulatory concern that now preserve a separate identifiable program. The new Federal role would focus on technical assistance, research, and the use of the bully pulpit to stimulate and disseminate linkages with the regular core academic program. The Federal role would not be prescriptive and regulatory in the areas of curriculum and instruction, but rather lead through exhortation, assistance and teacher training.

In sum, a strategic change in the Federal role should be implemented. Before turning to this issue, we need to review the evolution of the strategies used to advance the current Federal role. The chapter will conclude with several alternatives as a basis for thinking about future policy directions. A persistent theme will be that more needs to be done to improve the education of disadvantaged children than revisions in fiscal regulations and special classes. The Federal role must include providing better regular classroom teachers who have the resources to make a difference and need not rely on pullout specialists. The chapter will not address the appropriate level of Chapter 1 funding, but it is noteworthy that only 30 per cent of the eligible children are now served.

Modes of Federal Influence

There have been basically six alternative modes of Federal action for public schools.

1 *General aid*
Provide no-strings aid to state and local education agencies or minimal earmarks such as teacher salaries. A modified form of general aid has been proposed by President Reagan. He would consolidate numerous categories into a single block grant for local education purposes. A

tuition tax credit or voucher program is also a form of general aid. No general aid bill has ever been approved by the Congress.

2   *Stimulate through differential funding*

Earmark categories of aid, provide financial incentives through matching grants, fund demonstration projects, and purchase specific services. This is the approach of the Elementary and Secondary Education Act (ESEA) and Chapter 1. This chapter will not cover the problems of reallocating Chapter 1 funds among schools and districts to reach the most needy pupils. New funding allocations per se do not change the mode used in the Federal role.

3   *Regulate*

Legally specify behavior, impose standards, certify and license, enforce accountability procedures. The bilingual regulations proposed by the Carter administration (and rescinded by President Reagan) are a good example. Chapter 1 has extensive regulations and merges strategies two and three.

4   *Discover knowledge and make it available*

Have research performed; gather and make other statistical data available. The Office of Educational Research and Improvement (OERI) performs the first function and the National Center for Education Statistics the second.

5   *Provide technical assistance and build capacity at other levels of government or the private sector*

Furnish technical assistance and consultants in specialized areas or curricular subjects. The Federal Office of Civil Rights will advise school districts who design voluntary desegregation plans. Chapter 1 builds a strong evaluation capacity in state education agencies (SEAs).

6   *Exert moral suasion through use of the bully pulpit*

Develop vision and question assumptions through publications, speeches, and a carefully orchestrated media campaign by top officials. For example, Secretary Bennett has frequently called for more attention to the education role of parents.

The Reagan administration promotes the following basic changes in the Federal educational policy of the 1965–1980 era:

(1)   from minimal support of private education to significant support;

(2)   from a prime concern with equity to more concern with efficiency and state and local freedom to choose;

(3) from a larger and more influential Federal role to a mitigated Federal role;

(4) from mistrust of the motives and capacity of state and local educators to a renewed faith in governing units outside of Washington;

(5) from categorical grants to more unrestricted types of financial aid; and

(6) from detailed and prescriptive regulations to deregulation.

Despite the recent Reagan emphasis, however, the poorly defined value of promoting equal educational opportunity has been the most pervasive theme of Federal education policy. Its most obvious expression is through numerous categorical grants targeted to students not adequately served by state and local programs (for example, disadvantaged or handicapped). The Federal Government has also attempted to stimulate educational reform through the Teacher Corps or demonstration programs such as women's equity and career education. The Reagan administration has scaled back aggressive Federal innovations in such areas. The categorical interest groups that are the major recipients of Federal policy will resist his basic policies, but the key will be whether they can form coalitions. The findings by Mosher, Hastings and Wagoner (1981) are not optimistic for such alliances among these categorical groups:

> There is little evidence of common effort among the groups; the various categories of need tend to be strictly compartmented when demands are made for political remedies.
>   ... All of the interest groups have demonstrated, from time to time, effectiveness and sophistication in political maneuvering, a sophistication evident in their success at concentrating as much influence as possible, at the appropriate time, in a variety of policy arenas: the courts, particular state legislatures, the Congress, Federal agencies, and so on. (pp. 46–7)

The last comment indicates that the objectives of categorical interests such as the handicapped may lose out at one level of government only to succeed at another. It also suggests that the legions of Title I specialists built up over the years will politically resist attempts to amalgamate them with the core curriculum.

The Evolution of the Federal Role

In 1950, when the US Office of Education (USOE) was transferred to the Federal Security Agency, forerunner to the Department of Health, Education and Welfare (HEW), it had a staff of 300 to spend $40m. Growth was slow and largely unrecognized. In 1963, forty-two departments, agencies, and bureaus of the government were involved in education to some degree. The Department of Defense and the Veterans Administration spent more on educational programs than the USOE and National Science Foundation combined. The Office of Education appointed personnel who were specialists and consultants in such areas as mathematics, libraries, school buses; these specialists identified primarily with the National Education Association (NEA). Grant programs operated through deference to state priorities and judgments. State administrators were regarded by USOE as colleagues who should have the maximum decision-making discretion permitted by categorical laws.

While the era of 1963–1972 brought dramatic increases in Federal activity, the essential mode of delivering services for USOE changed gradually. The differential funding route was the key mode, seeking bigger and bolder categorical programs and demonstration programs. The delivery system for these categories continued to stress the superior ability of state departments of education to review local projects. Indeed, the current collection of overlapping and complex categorical aids evolved as a mode of Federal action that a number of otherwise dissenting educational interests could agree on. It was not the result of any rational plan for Federal intervention but rather an outcome of political bargaining and coalition formation. Former USOE head Harold Howe (1967) expressed its essence this way:

> Whatever its limitations, the categorical aid approach gives the states and local communities a great deal of leeway in designing educational programs to meet various needs. In essence, the Federal government says to the states (and cities) 'Here is some money to solve this particular program; you figure out how to do it ...' But whatever the criticisms which can in justice be leveled against categorical aid to education, I believe that we must stick with it, rather than electing general aid as an alternative. The postwar period has radically altered the

demands we place on our schools; a purely local and state viewpoint of education cannot produce an educational system that will serve national interest in addition to more localized concerns.

An incremental shift in the style of USOE administration also came with expanded categories. The traditional provision of specialized consultants and the employment of subject-matter specialists were ended in favor of managers and generalists who had public administration rather than professional education backgrounds. The states emulated the Federal model and decimated their capacity to provide leadership in curriculum content and teaching. These newer Federal and state administrators became more aggresive regulators and created a political backlash against Federal regulation that Ronald Reagan was able to highlight in his 1980 campaign. These managers were not experts in instructional strategies and rarely cognizant of the overall curriculum that disadvantaged children experience in classrooms.

Centrality of the Bully Pulpit Role Under the Reagan Administration

Previous administrators have used moral suasion or the bully pulpit to reinforce more direct regulatory, funding, and service efforts. For example, Commissioner of Education Sidney Marland's 1970 advocacy of career education was backed by a new grant program. However, the Reagan administration has featured this tactic of speeches, commissions, and advocacy by the Secretary and President as a primary mode of action. Although a relatively inexpensive strategy, significant personnel and financial resources have been targeted toward influencing public opinion and thereby impacting policy. In a self-assessment of his first term, President Reagan (1984) wrote:

> If I were asked to single out the proudest achievement of my administration's first three and one-half years in office, what we've done to define the issues and promote the great national debate in education would rank right up near the top of the list. (p. 2)

The Reagan administration's use of the bully pulpit in education is consistent with its new federalism philosophy that the state and local authorities and citizens are the proper and most effective means of action and change. Mr. Reagan has deliberately rerouted much of the responsibility for governing away from Washington. In that process, his use of the bully pulpit has been integral not only to promote devolution of authority but also to advocate 'excellence' including discipline, merit pay, and prayer in the classroom.

In accord with the new federalism philosophy, a major goal of the administration has been to deregulate the myriad categorical programs that began in 1965. Reagan campaigned on a promise to dismantle the Department of Education in an effort to symbolize this decentralization of power. Likewise, in an interview with *Educational Record*, former Secretary of the Department of Education, Terrell Bell (1981), stated that he hoped, if nothing else, to be remembered as one who reversed the relentless trend toward Federal education control.

Ironically, it was the Democratic administration that enlarged the national education pulpit from which Education Secretaries Bell and Bennett have spoken. Shortly after the creation of the US Department of Education, an optimistic former Democratic Commissioner Harold Howe (1980) stated. 'A Cabinet-level department lends importance to the Secretary's voice, which will influence the thinking of many persons about education's goals, practices, results, governance, and costs' (p. 446). However, there is still no overall Federal education policy spokesperson because education programs remain scattered throughout the government. For instance, there are major education initiatives in the National Science Foundation, the National Institutes of Health, the Veterans Administration, and the Educational Programs for Youth in the Department of Labor.

Certainly the most graphic example of this bully pulpit strategy has been the report of the National Commission on Excellence in Education (NCEE) and subsequent follow-up activities. The Commission's report, *A Nation at Risk*, sold 70,000 copies during its first year, the Government Printing Office's best seller in recent years. The Department of Education estimates that approximately seven times that number, 500,000 copies, were distributed within a year of the report's release. Extensive excerpts in national and regional periodicals, such as the *New York Times*, the *Washington Post*, and *The Oregonian*, provided millions direct access to the report. The *New York Times* ran fifty articles mentioning the Commission's report within the first few months of its release.

The NCEE findings, as well as those of similar task forces and individuals, clearly captured the attention of Americans concerned about education. Whether the administration realized the potential of the Commission's work at its inception is unclear. However, once NCEE had established the tone, the President and the Secretary took full advantage of this rhetorical opportunity to advance their agenda. While at an obvious level the issue was one of return to quality, the 'excellence movement' also has provided a vehicle for the administration to push the onus of responsibility for education back to the state, local and parental levels.

President Reagan had a high level of involvement with the introduction of the report and subsequent activities. Among other things, the President visited schools around the country, participated in two regional forums, and addressed a plenary session of the National Forum on Excellence in Education, with consistent themes stressing quality, discipline, merit pay and the virtues of homework.

The Department of Education scheduled various activities to maintain the momentum fostered by the reports and to encourage action at the state and local levels. The Department sponsored twelve regional forums and a National Forum on Excellence in Education. Secretary Bell designated most of his discretionary fund toward that effort and stated that a major portion of the budget was to be spent on the problems and priorities addressed by the Commission report.

Upon the first anniversary of the release of *A Nation at Risk*, the Department disseminated a follow-up, *The Nation Responds: Recent Efforts to Improve Education*. The publication was at once an assessment and another push for continued action at the state and local levels. The report cited glowing stories and statistics about the 'tidal wave of school reform'. After only a year, researchers were aware of 275 state level task forces on education, stimulated in part by NCCE. Forty-eight of fifty-one states and jurisdictions had adopted or were considering new high school graduation requirements.

The prevalence of the bully strategy is evident from a review of speeches, operational statements, and budgetary considerations. Other efforts have included the very visible 'Wall Chart' (comparing resources and college entrance scores across states), *Becoming a Nation of Readers, What Works,* and *First Lessons.* Secretary Bennett (1985) described the role of the bully pulpit in promoting the work of American education as follows:

> The work is principally the American people's work, not the
> Federal government's. We, in Washington, can talk about these
> matters, comment on them, provide intellectual resources, and,
> when appropriate, limited fiscal resources, but the responsibility
> is the people's.

Assistant Secretary Finn (1986) wrote in the *National Review*:

> Third, and perhaps most remarkably in the 'war of ideas' about
> education, the Federal Government is beginning to look like an
> asset rather than a liability. Washington is not promoting new
> programs or promulgating new regulations. It is amplifying the
> voice of common sense, taking issue with establishment folly,
> and emitting a steady stream of ideas and suggestions, facts and
> analyses, examples and interpretations that help arm state and
> local educators for the battle they are fighting.
>
> ... To be sure it would be good to deregulate bilingual
> education, to convert the big Chapter 1 compensatory educa-
> tion program into an optional voucher, and to effect a handful
> of other changes in Federal Government policy. But leadership,
> backed by sound understanding and solid information, may be
> more important (p. 36).

Finn goes on to emphasize that solid research is needed to overcome the
'accumulated dopiness' of the educational establishment. Such research
findings 'need to be heralded with all the legitimacy of scientific
research and all the amplification that a President and Cabinet Secretary
can supply'.

Issuance of the Wall Chart that compared state education outcomes
exemplifies the Reagan administration's use of the bully pulpit strategy.
'The publication of the "wall chart" brought to the forefront the issue of
state-to-state comparisons', wrote the report's authors. 'On a political
level, the attention given to the Secretary's wall chart makes inevitable
future state-to-state comparisons on outcome measures'. In a dramatic
reversal, the Council of Chief State School Officers (CCSSO) approved
a plan to conduct regular comparisons of the educational performance
of the states rather than permit the Federal government to preempt
interstate performance comparisons. While initially opposed strongly to
such techniques, the CCSSO is now determined to influence the sorts

of performance measures used, including a de-emphasis on Scholastic
Aptitude Test (SAT) comparisons. The CCSSO's new attitude about
interstate comparisons suggests they would not resist as strongly in
1987 Federal leadership in curriculum and instruction as they did in
1965. Such Federal curricular leadership must be permissive and
decentralized in the spirit of the bully pulpit role.

Assessing the Impact of the Bully Pulpit

Although the administration's use of the bully pulpit has been its
centerpiece of education policy, there is almost no research on its
effectiveness. An Educational Resources Information Center (ERIC)
search revealed one piece which focused on the impact of task forces
during previous administrations. A bully pulpit type strategy can have
substantial impact on changing policymakers' assumptions or viewpoint about policy priorities. Such activities are effective in agenda
setting and percolate indirectly into the policy process by changing
assumptions and how people view a problem.

The Department of Education's assessment of the bully pulpit's
impact has been handled more in a public relations vein than a scholarly
one. The Department published *The Nation Responds*, but its primary
purpose was to reinforce the administration's message of optimism and
to encourage continued state and local effort. The following quotation
is indicative of the report's tone: 'deep public concern about the
Nation's future created a tidal wave of school reform which promises to
renew American education'. Research on the impact of symbolism like
'excellence' for guiding the policy agenda suggests the bully pulpit
could be quite effective (see Jung and Kirst, 1986).

Not only does the bully pulpit strategy seem to have impact upon
the early stages of policymaking, but it also has an impact upon
education research priorities and trends through indirect means. More
federally funded research has been directed at curricular content,
academic standards, parent choice, and the excellence agenda as exemp-
lified by the Federal regulations on the OERI Center competition. The
same strategy could be employed to rethink the instructional and
curricular assumptions surrounding Chapter 1.

Implications for Chapter 1

The Chapter 1 program has reflected this gradual shift in strategies for carrying out the Federal role. The program was the centerpiece of the equal opportunity focus and assumed that state and local educators could not be trusted to target scarce Federal dollars to the disadvantaged. The Federal view was that local political concerns frequently would lead to diversion of Chapter 1 funds to less needy children. Therefore, the major Federal mode of delivery was through detailed regulation backed by field audits. There was a deep fear from 1965 to 1986 that some Title I money might spill over to the non-Title I kids in the class. Consequently, a separate administrative apparatus was created and sustained, composed of state and local Title I coordinators whose allegiance was antithetical to the core curriculum and the regular classroom teacher delivering Title I/Chapter 1 services. Chapter 1 coordinators have their own professional association and identities and meet separately from most classroom teachers in state and national conventions. Technical assistance and provision of services such as curricular models was abandoned by the late 1960s. The managers and auditors became the key Federal players and curriculum or teaching experts were shunted to other Federal divisions. Federal research efforts focused on regulations and compliance, with scant attention to the commonplaces of education — teaching, curriculum, and learning strategies.

This regulatory and distinct categorical Federal role was reinforced by a view that Chapter 1 was working and it was unwise and risky to shake up success. It was assumed that acceptable levels of compliance with Chapter 1 targeting and special services requirements were linked to achievement gains in the early grades among Southern Blacks. Indeed, a careful administrator could follow the Federal bully pulpit surrounding Chapter 1 in the 1970–1985 period and hear nothing about curricular content or how to teach these children. There was a Federal assumption that something educationally different needed to be done for these children, but the Federal government transmitted no clear message on what or how.

At a recent conference sponsored by the congressionally mandated study, several learning theorists proposed a 180 degree turn from the traditional Title I view — the new viewpoint is that nothing much different needed to be done for disadvantaged children in terms of instructional strategy and tactics. Harry Passow (1986) puts the research debate this way:

> Considering the controversy concerning the significance of cultural, language, and linguistic experiences of low-income and racial/ethnic minority children in beginning reading and other instructional areas, the omission of this literature could imply that these reviewers do not think that those differences make a difference with regard to curriculum and instruction of disadvantaged students. There are educators who believe that good reading instruction for middle-class standard English speakers (whatever that may encompass) is good reading instruction for all students regardless of mother tongue or dialect or family culture. There are educators who believe that there is such a thing as 'dialect interference' and conflict between communication systems and those who view this notion as irrelevant in designing instruction. The equivocal nature of much of the research on grouping, both between-class and within-class, results in drawing very different conclusions about the outcomes of such practices. (pp. IV-250–251)

Despite this controversy, experts agree that we do know a lot more about instruction now than when most Chapter 1 programs were designed. Passow (1986) cites a paper written by Robert Calfee concerning reading which states, 'Tracking, pullout programs, reliance on paraprofessionals to monitor remedial learning serve as barriers rather than facilitators to improving the curriculum of literacy for youngsters at risk' (p. IV-248). Calfee contends that Chapter 1 should be aimed at improving schools as educational organizations instead of programs targeted to the individual student. For instance, low-income students receive Chapter 1 services that differ from the regular curriculum and are less likely to develop literacy. Chapter 1 teachers place a stress on decoding and a neglect of comprehension, and ask students to sound out words rather than make informed guesses. According to Calfee, there are rare requests to justify an answer or provide appropriate feedback that is balanced between support and correction using appropriate pacing. Calfee (1986) hypothesizes that 'if the curriculum was more straightforward ... the amount of differentiation between children from lower- and middle-class backgrounds might be relatively small' (pp. IV-247–248).

The Federal role needs to catch up with recent research on curriculum and instruction that has increased our knowledge greatly in such areas as reading. Chapter 1 programs I observed spend too much time on sounding out words and too little on reading interesting passages. This does not mean that all pullout programs are bad and this strategy cannot be improved. Until regular classroom teachers are retrained, there will be a need for pullout strategies. The point is that both pullout and regular class teachers need a new vision of Chapter 1 curriculum content and improved instructional techniques. Too much time is spent in drill and practice approaches, and some pullout programs do a better job at higher order skills than regular class techniques.

Bill Honig (1986), California's Chief State School Officer, put the Federal administrative issues surrounding this reconceptualized learning approach in this way:

Every student is entitled to a full, balanced curriculum. The Chapter 1 program should enrich the delivery of the instruction of this curriculum to eligible students. Instead, Chapter 1 is often operated as a separate remedial program, substituting a narrow, repetitious curriculum for a well-balanced core curriculum. Students eligible for categorical programs need the remedial instruction afforded them. It is important, however, that the students receiving needed remedial instruction do not miss the core curriculum. Otherwise they will only be exposed to a limited curriculum and experience another type of educational disadvantage. There is a need for some development work in this area to train teachers to help eligible students to master the base curriculum and to provide integrated learning experiences.

... School effectiveness research reveals that poor, low achieving students benefit greatly from going to effective schools. Yet the participation of Chapter 1 students and staff in activities characteristic of effective schools is unnecessarily restricted by law. The isolation of Chapter 1 students and service providers undermines efforts to attain academic excellence in school. Planning for the use of Chapter 1 funds should be at the school level and constitute an integral part of the schools' total program. Classroom teachers and school leaders should be empowered to play the central role, with parents of eligible students involved as a safeguard against the misuse of funds. If we enhance school effectiveness at the same time we are addressing the needs of eligible students, every student will benefit from going to a better school. Current Chapter 1 provisions for schoolwide projects have proven to be too restrictive in this regard. Once a designated, reasonable percentage of a school population has been determined to be eligible for Chapter 1, the school should be allowed to co-ordinate all remedial resources, under an approved plan, in a manner which will uplift the entire school.

The 1983–86 education reform movement has featured a renewed emphasis on a core academic curriculum that emphasizes the more traditional subjects and higher order skills. This academic core has been deemed as essential for all pupils and relies on a continuity of skills and content. The Chapter 1 pullout and special services approach has not been featured as a necessary separate entity. An urgent necessity is blending Chapter 1 with this revitalized core, but it is difficult to do this with the separate cultural and administrative structure that has been institutionalized. Chapter 1 Technical Assistance Centers are mostly useless for this task because they focus on aggregate test data that is not useful for local education agencies (LEAs). At the end of this chapter I suggest that these current Technical Assistance Centers be replaced with new units that stress curricular content and instructional strategies. There is an urgent need to retrain Chapter 1 classroom teachers in the approaches recommended by Calfee and Passow. There needs to be much more attention to the curricular content that disadvantaged pupils receive.

The Either/Or Curriculum Policy Syndrome

Curricular discussions in the United States have a disturbing tendency to oscillate between polar extremes. At one point we create new math and then revert to rote drill and practice. For a while there is a push for open classrooms, and then the topic drops off the policy agenda almost completely. High schools are urged to become shopping malls with a broad curriculum with many options, only to be pushed back to a required core of traditional subjects. The current re-examination of Chapter 1 pullout programs and classroom instructional strategies should not proceed from a naive belief that the current core curriculum for disadvantaged kids is just fine, and that they are primarily losing academic ground because they are missing some of it. Hank Levin (1986) points out that even in the regular class the traditional notion is that 'educationally needy students should be placed in slow, repetitive, remedial programs. Not only do these programs bore students, but they reinforce students' negative self-images' (p. 1). A Federal role that focuses on these types of instructional issues is quite different from one that is keyed to fiscal audit trails. Core curriculum instruction needs to be more fast paced for Chapter 1.

What many disadvantaged pupils are missing is first-class, rapid-paced instruction from teachers who have confidence that such pupils can learn. This cannot be provided by simply reorganizing classroom structures or exhortation from the Federal bully pulpit. Jane David (1981) analyzes the current need in this way:

> What we need are ways of implementing what we know — ways of getting support for smaller classes and for putting some of the best teachers with these students. We need teachers who have high expectations, excellent diagnostic skills, and enough understanding of the knowledge and experience ... But abandoning all targeting and fiscal controls, especially in today's social and political climate, would translate into general aid, and lose the whole point of the program.

In other words, there is a need to reorient the Federal role from routine fiscal monitoring and data collection without obliterating the special services basis of Chapter 1 for a particular group of children. But rethinking the impact of fiscal controls on curriculum and instruction is only a starting point. Accountability needs to be reconstructed in a different manner that does not rely so heavily on aggregate achievement scores and separate audit trails. Chapter 1 is a marginal program in the local setting and provides a very small percentage of school funding. The Federal Chapter 1 role needs a new strategy for attracting and retaining good teachers and influencing teaching strategies, curricular content, and classroom behavior. Moreover, a revival of the summer programs that were featured in the 1960s would mitigate summer learning loss and provide a setting for more intensive and fast-paced instructional strategies during the regular academic year.

Implications for the Federal Role

In keeping with the new emphasis on the bully pulpit, a first approach could be for the Federal leadership to orchestrate a large-scale media campaign to change state and local orientations towards Chapter 1. This strategy would not rely on large increases in funds. It could include the specific core curriculum themes that Honig recommends, as well as research findings on how to integrate compensatory education within the regular classroom. The bully pulpit probably needs to be preceded by a major research synthesis as well as additional field studies. Federally funded research would focus on math, English, science, and other subject fields in terms of the special needs of disadvantaged children. It is doubtful that such curricular integration and teaching strategies can be enhanced greatly by detailed regulations or new categorical funding earmarks. This level of Federal regulation within the classroom would be resisted strongly by state and local educators.

The initial Federal bully pulpit role needs to be backed up by a widespread technical assistance and network building focus that provides consultants to SEAs and LEAs. These technical assistance providers should be experts in curricular content as well as methods. They can be in regional centers and not necessarily Federal employees. Federal grants could be given to SEAs to develop better technical assistance capacity for instructional leadership. This would entail a switchback to the pre-1965 role of USOE subject matter specialists who are national leaders in their curricular and instructional fields. Part of Chapter 2 could be earmarked for increased state instructional leadership capacity. These new units would create locally based networks, coordinate field services, and produce curriculum handbooks for local consideration.

Still another component would include the Chapter 1 SEA program review strategies that carefully link the Federal categoricals with academic content and instructional strategies within the regular classes and core curriculum. The Federal government would design model ways to use Chapter 1 for schoolwide improvement plans. Federal policy should fund a major effort to retrain classroom teachers to improve techniques for the disadvantaged rather than leaving them to rely on pullout remedial specialists. This strategy does not change Chapter 1 allocations and thereby create winners and losers who might oppose it on redistribution grounds. We do have several examples of teacher inservice projects that have been successful such as the California Writing Project.

This first strategy assumes a straight-line extrapolation of the current Federal role under Reagan without large funding increases. An alternative could be a return to the 1965–1980 approach of more regulations, field audits, and new earmarked subcategories. For example, a new compensatory education categorical could focus on the dark continent of educational policy — the junior high school. Separate funds could be provided for summer school for junior high pupils so that they can catch up in an accelerated setting. Almost all of Chapter 1 funds are spent in the elementary grades, but achievement begins to fall most dramatically in the middle grades. A new Federal initiative could focus on these transitional years where schools become departmentalized so that the pullout concept is not as major a problem in terms of content continuity. An alternative to junior highs as a separate categorical focus could be a drastic revision in the allocations among school districts to focus on the most needy, as suggested by Smith (1986). With an increased funding base, more districts could move funds into the junior high grades.

Still another option would be to continue primary reliance on the current Chapter 1 fiscal regulatory approach. This keeps in place the administrative structure of state and local Chapter 1 coordinators as a key force for preserving the separateness of the program. Most of the current Chapter 1 coordinators are not subject matter or pedagogical experts, but are more attuned to administrative compliance issues. They would probably not be strong allies in the first option of a closer merger of Chapter 1 with the regular classroom teacher and academic core curriculum. The coordinator's entire professional socialization has been towards a need to safeguard Chapter 1's distinct identification. A possible compromise is: current fiscal accountability could be preserved *between* schools (including comparability), but *within* schools with very high concentrations of disadvantaged children the fiscal restrictions on schoolwide services would be dropped.

The Reagan administration's proposal for a Chapter 1 voucher has never received a serious hearing in the Congress, and the 1986 election makes it even less likely. This is a novel proposal that combines some aspects of the general aid role with a categorical approach. It is most likely, however, that the future Federal role in Chapter 1 will not involve a radical transformation, but rather will be an incremental move. The much heralded 1981 Act, in effect, merely repealed much of the regulatory underbrush that had built up from 1966 to 1980. It did not change any of the basic assumptions underlying the 1965 Act.

The time seems propitious now to reconsider some of the basic program assumptions. It will not be easy to blend a core curriculum approach, teacher training, and school improvement with financial accountability and targeting to the neediest pupils. Perhaps, this is the time to renew our search for differential treatment of states and localities, depending on whether they use the type of overall school site improvement strategy outlined by Odden (in press). States that develop an integrated curricular approach could have some of the strict fiscal tracking rules waived by the Education Department, and thereby merge their compensatory education strategy more closely with the core curriculum. LEAs that have very high concentrations of disadvantaged children could have different and less restrictive criteria for using Chapter 1 to reinforce the core curriculum, and more easily merge the problem in the regular classroom. States could be encouraged to submit alternative plans for targeting Chapter 1, but with much closer relationships to state reform programs.

References

BELL, T. H. (1981) 'T. H. Bell' (interview), *Education Record*, **62**, pp. 5–7.
BENNETT, W. J. (1985) *Address to the National Press Club*, Washington, DC, 27 March.
COMMITTEE ON EDUCATION AND LABOR, US HOUSE OF REPRESENTATIVES (1985) *A Compilation of Papers on the Twentieth Anniversary of the Elementary and Secondary Education Act of 1965* (Serial No. 99-D), Washington, DC, US Government Printing Office.
DAVID, J. (1981) Personal communication, 18 August.
FINN, C. E., JR. (1986) Interview, *National Review*, August, p. 36.
HONIG, B. (1986) Letter to Secretary Bennett, 5 August.
HOWE, H. (1967) *National Policy for American Education*, speech to the seventy-first annual convention of the National Congress of Parents and Teachers, Minneapolis, MN, 22 May.

HOWE, H. II (1980) 'Two views of the new Department of Education and its first secretary', *Phi Delta Kappan*, **61**, pp. 446–7.

JUNG, R. and KIRST, M. (1986) 'Beyond mutual adaptation into the bully pulpit: Recent research on the Federal role in education', *Educational Administration Quarterly*, **22**, 3, pp. 80–109.

LEVIN, H. (1986) quoted in *Stanford Daily*, 3 October, p. 1.

MOSHER, E. K., HASTINGS, A. H. and WAGONER, J. L., JR. (1981) 'Beyond the breaking point? A comparative analysis of the new activists for educational equality', *Educational Evaluation and Policy Analysis*, **3**, 1, pp. 41–53.

ODDEN, A. (in press). *How Fiscal Accountability and Program Integrity Can Be Insured for Chapter 1*, Berkeley, CA, Policy Analysis for California Education.

PASSOW, A. H. (1986) 'Curriculum and instruction: Reactions' in WILLIAMS, B. I., RICHMOND, P. A. and MASON, B. J. (Eds.), *Designs for Compensatory Education: Conference Proceedings and Papers*, Washington, DC, Research and Evaluation Associates.

REAGAN, R. (1984) 'Overview of education reform issues' in MARSHNER, C. (Ed.) *A Blueprint for Education Reform*, Washington, DC, Free Congress Research and Education Foundation.

SMITH, M. S., (1986) 'Selecting students and services for Chapter 1: Reactions' in WILLIAMS, B. I., RICHMOND, P. A. and MASON, B. J. (Eds.) *Designs for Compensatory Education: Conference Proceedings and Papers*, Washington, DC, Research and Evaluation Associates.

Section 2: Selected Issues of Access and Accountability

6
Selecting Students and Services for Chapter 1 [1]

Marshall S. Smith

This chapter addresses two central questions in the design of the program of Chapter 1 of the Educational Consolidation and Improvement Act: How should students be selected to receive services; and what kinds of services should be delivered by the program? As part of the discussion of these questions, a few comments are made about the two excellent papers prepared for the session 'Poverty, Achievement and the Distribution of Compensatory Education Services' by Kennedy, Jung and Orland and 'Selecting Students and Services for Compensatory Education: Lessons from Aptitude-Treatment Interaction Research' by Peterson.

This chapter argues for two major changes in the selection of students and in the way that services are delivered in the Chapter 1 program. The first change would target Chapter 1 funds only to schools with very high proportions of children whose families live in poverty. The second change would encourage the use of Chapter 1 funds in schoolwide programs to augment and improve the quality of the regular school program in these high poverty schools. Each of the changes can be generated through alterations in the Chapter 1 legislation. Although a compelling case can be made for both sets of changes, each would spark considerable political and substantive debate partly because each alters the distribution of resources.

There are four sections to this chapter. The first sketches general premises which help lead to the two sets of recommendations. The second considers the question of who should be served and the third section addresses what kinds of services should be offered. The final section summarizes the key recommendations and the rationales for the recommendations.

Premises

Six general and interrelated premises influence my thinking about Chapter 1. They are summarized below along with some of their implications for the program.

1 For twenty years Chapter 1 and its predecessor, Title I of the Elementary and Secondary Education Act (ESEA) of 1965, have served as a powerful symbol of the intent of the Federal government and the nation as a whole to provide equal educational opportunity to poor children (Smith, 1984; Kaestle and Smith, 1982). This argues that it would be a major mistake to eliminate or even reduce the program.

2 Chapter 1 programs have been implemented primarily at the elementary school level in grades K-6. The overwhelming percentage of the programs have focused on improving the reading and mathematics achievement of low-achieving students. Clear data from a number of sources show that Chapter 1 programs, on the average, have had only modest short-term and no long-term sustained effects on the reading and mathematics achievement of targeted students (Kennedy, Jung and Orland, 1986; Kaestle and Smith, 1982; Wang, Bear, Conklin and Hoepfner, 1981; Kenoyer, Cooper, Saxton and Hoepfner, 1981; Hoepfner, 1981; Rogers, Landers and Hoepfner, 1982). Over the years Chapter 1 has changed in a variety of marginal ways, yet the general conclusions about overall effectiveness have not changed. These findings suggest that further tinkering at the margins of the program will have little likelihood of producing major improvement in its overall effectiveness. Major changes in the program might be necessary to measurably improve its performance.

3 Our understanding of how to deliver effective educational services to poor children has changed dramatically since 1965 when Title I was first authorized and since 1972–1976 when the legislative framework was fully established. We have new knowledge about how students learn, about the nature and

content of effective instruction, about the characteristics of effective schools, and about the implementation of educational reform. This new understanding has important implications for the selection of students and the delivery of services (Peterson, 1986; Romberg, 1986; Calfee, 1986; Hallinan, 1986; Brophy, 1986). In a substantial number of ways Chapter 1 rules and regulations make it difficult to put this new knowledge into use. There are clear directions for major changes in the program, and there is considerable promise for improving the way that Chapter 1/Title I programs are delivered and implemented.

4   Poverty has a substantial and pervasive effect on the individuals in poverty and on the society as a whole. Although many children in poverty do very well in school, there is a robust relationship between the achievement of a child and the level of resources that the child's family can afford. This relationship is especially strong for children in families which are in poverty over substantial periods of time. Moreover, there appears to be an independent and negative effect on a student's achievement of a high density of poor children in the student's neighborhood and school. Finally, the number of poor children in the nation is increasing, poor children are found in disproportionate numbers in minority groups which continue to suffer from significant discrimination in the society, and there seems to be an increasing concentration of poor and minority group children in the inner cities of the United States (Kennedy *et al*, 1986; Kaestle and Smith, 1982; Levin, 1985 and 1986). There is a special need for Chapter 1 funding in districts and schools with very high densities of poor children. These are typically inner-city and poor rural areas.

5   Over the past fifteen years there has been some improvement in the reading and mathematics achievement of minority and poor students relative to the achievement of middle-income youngsters. By some estimates the gap between the two groups in the elementary and middle grades has closed by upwards of 25 per cent. This very encouraging sign suggests that further attention to the problem will yield benefits. Yet, the gap has closed by less in the later grades, and there appears to be some decline on measures of higher order academic skills. The effect on early achievement may be due in part to the symbolic effect of

Chapter 1 but does not seem to be directly due to the effects of the program (Kennedy *et al*, 1986; Peterson, 1986). Alternative, plausible reasons are the effects of desegregation (particularly in the south) and the multiple attempts at school reform in the cities — reform which has operated independently of Title I (Koretz, 1986; Levin, 1986).[2] The lack of a clear achievement effect in later grades is mirrored by depressingly high (upwards of 40 to 50 per cent) and, by some reports, increasing dropout rates (since 1974) for poor and especially Black and Hispanic groups in the cities.[3] This effect may be related to the relative degree of inattention given to the middle and high school years by education reformers in the 1970s and early 1980s, to the increasing degree of inequality of family incomes in the society within the Black and White populations which is reflected in an increasing concentration of the poor in the cities, and to the lack of clear rewards (such as jobs) that would result to poor and minority students as a consequence of their graduating from high school (Kennedy *et al*, 1986; Levin, 1985 and 1986).[4] Thus, Chapter 1, if changed in a way that would promote positive effects, could be especially useful in middle and secondary schools as well as elementary schools.

6   The status of the poor and minorities in the society and the quality and equality of the educational opportunities of their children will not be fully resolved by changes to the educational system — increased job opportunities and public commitment to the eradication of poverty are required. Yet recent data indicate that the quality of education has a substantial impact on the life chances of students.[5] It appears clear from past data summarized above, that marginal changes in the quality of education will not have a great effect on the opportunities of poor and minority students. Major, systematic change to our educational programs for the poor is necessary to meet a social goal of equal educational opportunity.

Who Should Be Served by Chapter 1?

A substantial part of the Kennedy *et al* paper deals with the technical and substantive sides of this question. It does not consider, however, the normative and political sides of the issue. Congress decides who should receive the services of Chapter 1 after members have reviewed data on the past successes and failures of the program, weighed information about the needs of students and educational systems throughout the nation and about ways of improving educational opportunity and quality, and made political judgments based on their own experiences and sets of values and the pressures brought to bear on them by their political friends and enemies.

The weight of this process is heavy on the side of making few significant changes in existing legislation even when the data show that the program has only minor overall effects. Major change generally creates a situation where some of the present 'winners' lose resources unless the overall pool of resources is dramatically increased, an unlikely prospect. Since those presently receiving resources know they have a stake, they mount pressure to justify the present system and suppress significant change. Local constituent groups make cogent arguments based on the facts that, if there were to be major change, many effective programs would lose funding and considerable educational and personal disruption would occur. With literally tens of thousands of separate Chapter 1 programs in schools, there are hundreds of very productive ones, even though the average effect of all of the programs is minuscule.

Another force that protects programs is a coalition of dedicated staff of Congress, the executive branch, and the educational associations based in Washington. For Chapter 1, this group is reinforced by many of the civil rights organizations. A great number of the people in these organizations have fought for the rights of children for twenty years and see any suggestion of change in Chapter 1 as a direct attack on the concept of equal educational opportunity.[6]

A major goal of many of these groups in the past has been to reduce the chances for significant change to occur in this twenty-year-old, relatively stable, and now, unthreatening program. It may be, however, that the accumulation of new knowledge about effective educational practice and the present spirit of educational reform have altered the odds for major change in the way the Federal government and the nation as a whole provides educational services for poor children. It should be possible to change direction in a program if it can be cogently shown that the present system is ineffective and inefficient and that there are plausible alternative approaches that promise greater effectiveness and efficiency. The first section of this chapter touched on the issue of the effectiveness of the current program and argued that its value was largely in its symbolism. The argument that effectiveness can be improved is addressed in the next section of this chapter in the discussion of the nature of the services. In the remainder of this section I consider the issue of efficiency. I will argue that the present allocation system necessarily leads to an inefficient distribution of resources to meet the needs of poor, low-achieving students and that the data presented by Kennedy *et al* document this inefficiency and suggest a more efficient allocation system.

In their paper Kennedy *et al* review the legislative intent and the current legislation and regulations that guide the Federal, state, local, and school-level allocation of resources. They also review data on the relationship between poverty (individual and collective) and achievement as part of their assessment of the validity of the framework. To develop an argument for altering the present allocation strategy, it is necessary to review both the present framework and the evidence amassed by Kennedy and her colleagues.

The legislative declaration of policy that has driven Chapter 1 for two decades 'recognizes the special educational needs of children from low-income families and the impact that concentrations of low-income families have on the ability of local educational agencies to support adequate educational programs' and calls for it to be a 'policy of the United States to provide financial assistance to local educational agencies serving areas with concentrations of children from low-income families to expand and improve their educational programs by various means which contribute particularly to meeting the special educational needs of educationally deprived children'.[7] To meet this policy, Congress over the years has developed and occasionally modified a variety of more explicit legislative language. In response to the language of the law, the administrative branch of the government (first the Department of Health, Education, and Welfare and now the Department of Education) has developed extensive regulations and other administrative, sub-regulatory guidance for states and local education agencies. In brief, Chapter 1 funds[8] are allocated in the following fashion:

- The total appropriation for the basic grants program is distributed among states and then within states to counties proportionally to the number of youth aged 5–17 who are in families that fall under the poverty guidelines. The number of poor youth in the various counties (and hence aggregated to states) is estimated using the most recent census. There is some adjustment made for the number of youth in families receiving Aid to Families with Dependent Children.[9]

- Within counties, funds are distributed to local education agencies generally in proportion to the number of poverty students, usually measured by eligibility for free lunch.
- Within local education agencies (LEAs), funds are distributed to schools according to a flexible set of guidelines. In general, LEAs have the authority to select grade levels to be targeted and to specify the goals and magnitude of programs within the following kinds of constraints: schools must be selected in order on the basis of their percentages of poverty students (free lunch eligibility is usually used as the poverty measure) with the greatest poverty schools within a district receiving first priority; at least half of all schools within a district and any school that has a poverty percentage of at least 25 per cent is eligible. After the selection of grade levels, schools are often stratified into elementary, middle and secondary before the other rules are applied.[10]
- After a school has been selected and the nature of the program and grade levels decided on, students are chosen to participate in the program. The legislation and regulations require that the lowest achieving students be selected. Most school and LEAs use standardized achievement tests (and often other means) to assess potentially eligible students in appropriate areas, such as reading or mathematics. The number of students selected depends on the size and nature of the Chapter 1 program, though in general the regulations require that the poorest schools have the largest programs.

The Kennedy *et al* paper presents a variety of interesting data that generally support two basic assumptions of the legislation and that are reflected to some degree in the allocation system: that family poverty, especially long-term poverty, is clearly associated with low student achievement, and that schools and communities with strong concentrations of poverty have an added negative effect on student achievement above and beyond the student's individual family status.[11] *A major contribution of their paper is to document the argument that students from low-income families who live in areas with a high concentration of other poor families have a double dose of disadvantage*: their families are unable to give them certain advantages that other students have, and their schools, for a variety of reasons, are not as able to aid them in achieving academic success as schools with an affluent student body. Moreover, poor students in these areas (the inner cities and poor rural areas) are more likely to be in families which are in long-term poverty; these students are more likely to be low achievers than students who are only temporarily in poverty and are more likely to require long-term attention.

Yet, while the legislation and regulations generally reflect this logic, the data on the distribution of Chapter 1 resources indicate that there is a lot of slippage.[12] With a small exception, little special treatment is given in the legislation or the regulations to areas with a high concentration of poor children; in the distribution of over 90 per cent of the funds a poor child in an affluent LEA counts as much in the allocation system as a poor child in the inner city or in the poorest county of Kentucky.[13] And, no special provision is made for children in long-term poverty. The provisions that allocate the funds to states and to counties and finally to LEAs spread the money very thinly to almost all of the 14,000 separate local educational agencies in the nation. Thus, in almost all school districts with only one school in total or only one elementary and one secondary school, there is a Chapter 1 program serving elementary pupils. In larger districts, the regulations allow the Chapter 1 program to serve at least 50 per cent of the schools serving the selected grade levels. In most communities the politics of the distribution of resources requires the administrators and school board to spread the funds out as much as possible. Overall, Kennedy *et al* estimate that 70 per cent of all elementary schools in the nation have a Chapter 1 program. This is tragically inadequate targeting for a program intended to reach low-scoring students in *high* poverty schools.

The actual application of the rules and regulations also leads to situations which clearly go against the philosophy of the program. Let me give two not extreme examples. In Madison, Wisconsin, a city that spends over $5000 per pupil and has an average elementary class size of under twenty-three students, there are Chapter 1 programs in schools which are in the 70th achievement percentile of all schools in the nation. Contrast the need in these schools with that in the hundreds of inner-city middle and secondary schools that average in the bottom quartile of achievement and that graduate under 60 per cent of their students but do not have a Chapter 1 program because there are insufficient funds in these cities to serve middle and secondary schools. In suburban systems throughout the nation there are schools with 10 per cent or less of the student body in poverty receiving funds because they are in the top half of the schools in their system in poverty percentage, while in city schools throughout the nation there are schools with considerably more than 15 per cent poverty that are ineligible because they are below the district average (Kennedy *et al*, 1986).

Kennedy *et al* present extensive data that show these problems in another way. Using data from the Sustaining Effects Study (SES), they show that substantial numbers of children served by Chapter 1/Title I in fact are neither in poverty nor score in the bottom 50 per cent of standardized achievement tests. They also show the other side of the coin — to wit that there are substantial numbers of poor and low-scoring children who are not served by the program. Using data gathered just on elementary school children, they estimate that Chapter 1 does *not* serve 68.6 per cent of poor students, 64.9 per cent of students achieving below the 25 percentile in achievement, 57.9 per cent of poor *and* low-achieving students, and even 55.1 per cent of poor and low-achieving students who are in Chapter 1 schools.[14]

These are not surprising figures when we consider the allocation mechanism for Chapter 1 funds. The distribution of funds to almost all LEAs and to over 70 per cent of the elementary schools of the nation means that many affluent schools with relative high-scoring children receive Chapter 1 funding. Moreover, unless the appropriation level is dramatically increased, this distribution guarantees that the funds are spread hopelessly thin; programs in many of the poorest schools with very low-scoring children are far too small to serve even a major percentage of the needy students.

What should be done to make Chapter 1 targeting more efficient? A typical response to this question has been to advocate tightened fiscal accountability regulations on the distribution of funds within schools without changing the fundamental distribution system. This approach cannot succeed. If funds continue to go to 14,000 LEAs and 70 per cent of the elementary schools in the nation, no tightening of within school criteria will change the fact that many of those students deepest in poverty will never have a chance to receive Chapter 1 services while many relative affluent and high-scoring students will be served by the program.

The alternative seems clear from the data presented in the Kennedy *et al* paper. To increase efficiency in the allocation of funds to the nation's neediest students, the targeting must be improved. *We must expand the level of allocation to schools with high concentrations of poverty students. To accomplish this in a time of constrained resources, funds must go to fewer LEAs and to fewer schools within the LEAs.* The concentration of funds cannot be minor — to make a significant change in educational opportunity for our neediest children, the resources brought to bear on the problems of schools in our inner cities and poorest rural areas must be considerable. The final section of this chapter suggests a practical approach to the targeting problem.[15]

What Services Should Be Offered by Chapter 1?

One aspect of the allocation system was not considered in the preceding section. I did not discuss how students within schools would be selected to participate in Chapter 1 programs. The reason is that this issue is intimately tied to the issue of services to be offered.

In the present system students within a school are identified as eligible to receive Chapter 1 services because they give evidence of low achievement through achievement tests and teacher judgment. In over 75 per cent of Chapter 1 schools, students are 'pulled out' of their regular classrooms to receive compensatory instruction. In upwards of 50 per cent of Chapter 1 programs the students are actually pulled out of their regular reading or mathematics class and placed in another setting for their compensatory instruction in the same subject. The Peterson paper at the conference offered a succinct critique of the pullout approach. She and others found that it has a number of inherent flaws that influence its effectiveness.[16] These include:

- Students are *stigmatized* by identification as Chapter 1 students who need special attention. They are labelled as 'slow', or 'dumb', or worse, by other students, by their parents, by teachers, by themselves, and in their permanent records.
- The instructional program for these students is *fragmented.*[17]

The regular and Chapter 1 staff are often physically and administratively separated in schools. They often use different textbooks and pedagogical strategies. For many Chapter 1 students, their 'regular' teacher does not instruct them during the time when they are supposed to be learning one or more of the core subjects of elementary school (math or reading). Yet reading and mathematics are 'taught' all day long by most effective elementary school teachers — in instances where a child is pulled out for reading or math the 'regular' teacher has no way of knowing the child's needs. Across years there is fragmentation within the Chapter 1 program. Students who succeed in the program by improving their scores sufficiently are not allowed to stay in the program while others are newly placed in the program. A certain amount of this movement happens simply due to the unreliability of the tests and the 'regression to the mean' phenomenon.

● Pulling the student out removes the *responsibility* for the education of the student from the 'regular' teacher. The fragmentation of responsibility makes it impossible to hold anyone accountable.

The reason that the pullout instructional model became the dominant approach in Chapter 1 stems from a record of early abuses of Title I funds — funds were spent for activities and resources unrelated to the purposes of the program. To tighten accountability, Congress instituted a set of fiscal requirements in the late 1960s and early 1970s. [18] A substantial number of these requirements operate at the building level. They require the LEA to insure that Chapter 1 schools receive the level of resources from sources other than Chapter 1 that they would have received had there not been Chapter 1 *and* this level be at least comparable to the level received by non-Chapter 1 schools in the same LEA.

One fiscal requirement operates on the expenditure of resources within schools. This requirement is generally called the supplement, not supplant provision. It is interpreted as stipulating that Chapter 1 funds cannot be used to pay for anything within the school that would otherwise be paid for by another source. A second provision, the excess cost requirement, stipulates that Chapter 1 funds can only be used to pay for the excess cost of services used exclusively by Chapter 1 students. Thus, for example, Chapter 1 funds cannot be used for teacher in-service programs which include teachers who are not Chapter 1 teachers, nor can they be used to pay the salary of a teacher who teaches some non-Chapter 1 students. For years, they could not be used for Chapter 1 paid teachers to assist regular teachers to oversee students in the halls or the playgrounds, if the duty included monitoring some non-Chapter 1 students.

In their attempt to implement this requirement, the US Office of Education and state departments of education (SEAs) issued regulations, guidelines, and other non-regulatory guidance and provided technical assistance to LEAs to help them design delivery mechanisms which were legal. The dominant choice to create a 'clean' fiscal trail was to create, in effect, a separate system within the school. Their goals were to keep the Chapter 1 teachers as separate as possible from the core program of the school, deliver Chapter 1 services in separate settings, and have separate technical assistance and reporting lines. By and large they succeeded.

Over the years, as Gaffney (1986) points out, there have been changes in the regulations and in the legislation which should influence the way that the fiscal requirements are interpreted. Existing Chapter 1 law (and Congressional language in the 1978 Amendments) even explicitly states that pullouts are not required by Chapter 1. And in 1981 Congress repealed the excess cost amendment. Pullouts never were required, but the simple fact is that responsible people in state and local agencies believed that it was certainly the easiest, and to some the only, way to meet the law. The District Practices Study carried out in 1983 with Department of Education funds found that the central reasons given by district administrators for using a pullout design were that: (a) it was easier to demonstrate compliance with Chapter 1 accounting requirements (73 per cent) and (b) that the state Chapter 1 office recommended its use (50 per cent). *Only 18 per cent of district administrators who used a pullout design indicated they believed it was educationally superior to any other mode of delivery.*

The primary alternative to pulling students out for Chapter 1 services is to deliver services within the classrooms. According to the District Practices Study a substantial number of districts (30 per cent) report using this design often as well as the pullout model. Gaffney discusses this Chapter 1 option in his analysis of the flexibility of the regulations. In a related paper presented at the conference, Archambault

(1986)[19] considered the evidence of in-class Chapter 1 practices and concluded that in-class strategies also suffer from problems of stigmatization and fragmentation. Although many find this surprising, the reasons seem obvious on reflection. The Chapter 1 fiscal trail also reaches into the regular classroom to influence instructional strategy. Within classroom approaches require that children be identified and that separate instruction be administered, generally by Chapter 1 teachers rather than the regular teachers. The forces to label, to reduce the continuity and organization of instruction, and to relieve the regular teacher of responsibility for the outcomes operate in this model just as in the pullout model. And the same restrictions on whole school activities such as in-service training to coordinate instruction apply for the within classroom models.

There is little wonder that data indicate, on average (a) that Chapter 1 has little short-term and no sustaining effects; and (b) that there is little systematic difference in the effectiveness of pullout and in-class models.[20] Because both models suffer from clear shortcomings, it is not surprising that Archambault concluded that instructional setting does little to determine the effectiveness of Chapter 1 programs. It seems clear that it is not useful to continue research that contrasts in-class and pullout instructional models in Chapter 1, each of which is required to identify and instruct children separately. So long as the supplement, not supplant provision operates in Chapter 1, research directed at improving compensatory education, as Archambault insists, should be on the content and instructional strategies used in the Chapter 1 programs.[21]

Can anything be done to overcome the problems created by the fiscal tracking of funds down to the level of the student? Suppose that the supplement, not supplant provision did not exist.[22] Suppose that in Chapter 1 schools there were no specific students identified as eligible for Chapter 1 and, instead, all students in the school were seen as 'at risk' academically. Under this approach funds from Chapter 1 could be used to upgrade the quality of the entire school. Following the discussion of effective teaching strategies in Peterson and the extensive research on effective schools, the Chapter 1 funds could be employed in ways that have a substantial backing in the literature.[23] Chapter 1 funds could be used to lower class size, to assist teachers in improving the curriculum of the school, to provide schoolwide in-service training, and to establish constructive programs with students' parents. Following the guide of the literature, the teachers and administrators within the schools could be responsible for the development of strategies to maximize the achievement of the neediest students. This would give the entire staff control over the nature and content of the instructional program, a condition which is related to the efficacy of the staff and hence to the effectiveness of the program (Good and Brophy, 1986; Purkey and Smith, 1983).[24]

This is not a new proposal. Three sets of arguments are generally raised to respond to it. The first is that by spreading the Chapter 1 funds throughout the school they would be too diluted to have much effect. After all, in many Chapter 1 schools there are not many poor and low-achieving students and, if the little Chapter 1 funds received by the school are not targeted to the level of the child, they will not be useful. One part of the answer to this argument is that Chapter 1 funds should only go to schools with high densities of poverty children for all of the reasons given in the early part of this chapter. In schools with very high densities of poverty children *all* of the children are at risk. The percentage of *long-term* poverty children is high in these schools. And the percentage of very low-achieving students is greater than would be expected on the basis of the poverty percentage itself. Moreover, substantial numbers of children will be at the margin on achievement measures; in schools with fewer problems and greater resources these students might accomplish far more. It makes great sense to approach the overall problems and quality of schools of this sort rather than to fund programs of dubious value that are deliberately on the margins of the school.[25]

A second part of the answer is that schools with high densities of poor children should receive substantial levels of Chapter 1 funds; the funds should not be thinly spread. For example, a 1000-student elementary school with 40 per cent poverty might receive an allocation of $200,000 ($500 per student for 400 students). Such a school might have a staff of forty. A Chapter 1 allocation of this magnitude might be used to reduce class size in the early grades by three to four students, *and* to put the entire staff through an intensive summer workshop on ways of improving their curriculum and teaching, *and* to purchase new materials to aid teachers in teaching problem solving and critical thinking, *and* to pay for a part-time coordinator to encourage parents to work with their children, *and* other programs. The point is that the overall quality of the school, its climate, curriculum, relationships with parents, and the expectations of its teachers could be influenced by

Chapter 1 *if* the funds were targeted to high poverty schools and used to influence the program of the entire school.[26]

A second argument used against this proposal is that accountability is lost if the dollars are not tracked and that the funds will be spent on frivolous things unrelated to the needs of the poor and low-achieving students. There are two ways of addressing this important issue. The first is to shift the discussion of accountability from *resources* to *outcomes*. At the present time the central way that we *know* that Chapter 1 is aiding poor and low-scoring students is to follow the dollar trail so that we are able to identify specific services paid for by Chapter 1 that are received by prespecified children. Although there are often carefully carried out evaluations of Chapter 1 programs, the local school or the local school system are not held accountable if the results of the evaluations are negative.[27] They are only held accountable if the funds are not spent in the prescribed fashions to meet the fiscal requirements. The alternative is to require in Chapter 1 that the local school and the LEA establish a set of outcome goals that are monitored by the state education agency and, perhaps, ultimately, by the Federal government. At the elementary school level these goals would be expressed in terms of reading and mathematics test achievement gains for the entire school and for the lowest scoring in the school. At the middle and secondary level achievement and attainment goals might be established. The key is that they are schoolwide goals involving the effort of all of the teachers and other staff within the schools. Within boundaries the teachers and staff of the school would be responsible for setting the goals.

But so what, you say. Suppose that goals are set and then not met. Where is the exercise of accountability? Wouldn't we be in the same situation as we are presently, without a means for exercising any clout? This leads to the second way of addressing the accountability problem. It would have four parts:

1   Schools would be expected to establish schoolwide outcome goals (within certain constraints established by legislation). The goals would cover a three to five-year period.
2   The school staff would develop a schoolwide instructional plan to reach the goals which would be reviewed and approved by the SEA.
3   Outcome assessments would be carried out by the LEA on a yearly basis and reported to the SEA and to the public. As part

of its application for Chapter 1 funds the LEA would be expected to establish incentives for schools which reach their goals.

4   If, after three years, the school was not reaching its goals, it would be required to modify its instructional plan in a significant fashion. If after a second three-year period the goals were still not being met, the LEA would be required to go to the SEA with a new plan to change the administrative and instructional staff and pedagogy of the school so that it met the needs of its students.

There are lots of other possible schemes for insuring some accountability. This particular one has three desirable components: outcome goals and plans developed by the staff for achieving the goals; incentives for reaching the goals; and a graduated set of procedures for improving the school if the goals were not met.

The third argument that will be used against this approach has a variety of components: one is that we have no assurance that it will 'work'; another is that it will eliminate lots of good existing programs; and still another is that it has already been tried in Chapter 1 legislation as an option and that local agencies did not make much use of it. This line of argument may have some truth to it in each component, and each should be addressed. First, certainly the new approach will not always work. But we do have substantial evidence referenced earlier and reviewed by Peterson and others at the conference that suggested that it will 'work' better than the present approach. The evidence is clear that the problems of the very poor and low achieving must be seen as belonging to the entire school rather than only being the responsibility of the Chapter 1 teachers. The literature on school management, in-service training, discipline and order in the schools, the quality of the curriculum, and school climate and culture all point in the direction of establishing clear goals, high expectations, and whole school planning efforts engaged in by the entire staff (Purkey and Smith, 1983). Moreover, this approach gives a clear system for establishing accountability for the key unit that the central administration of a school system must deal with — the school itself. School administrators and teachers are given the authority to define their programs to meet the needs of the poor and low achieving and, simultaneously, held accountable for meeting student outcome goals to which they have agreed.

The second part of this criticism is that there would be lots of disruption and many good existing programs would be destroyed. There seem to me to be three responses. First, without question there would be disruption both in communities and schools that would lose Chapter 1 funding because of more efficient targeting and in communities and schools where the programs would be enhanced. But productive change always entails some disruption. If this kind of disruption looms large even in the face of the evidence about the lack of efficiency and effectiveness of the program, we will never improve the education of the very poor in the nation. Second, though some strong programs will no longer receive funding, on the basis of the evidence there would be as many or more weak programs put in jeopardy and overall there will be a net gain. Third, it would be reasonable to let some of the present strong programs continue to exist in schools that continue to receive funding *if* the schools met the other conditions of developing a systematic set of goals and plans.

The third part of the argument is that the approach has already been tried in Chapter 1 and was neither successful nor widely tried by local schools. It is accurate that an approach of this sort was put into legislation in 1978 and subsequently tried by a number of school districts. The reasons for the few attempts by local districts to try the approach, however, is probably not because they disliked it. Rather the Federal legislation was far too restrictive and costly for the local agencies to carry out broad implementation. The legislation carried two major disincentives, a requirement that at least 75 per cent of the students be in poverty and a requirement that the LEA augment the amount of money that Chapter 1 provided by a substantial amount over and beyond the normal LEA allocation to the school. Yet even though the nation was entering economic hard times in 1979 and 1980 when this provision came into effect, a number of communities tried to implement the provision. In his paper for the conference, Archambault mentioned the experiences in Los Angeles and Austin where programs had to eventually be terminated because of cost. In Austin, the program was much more effective than a pullout model; students in the schoolwide programs gained an average of 2.5 months more in language arts, 2.1 months more in reading, and 2.2 months more in mathematics over a one-year program.

There is little question but that the cost per school would be greater in a whole school strategy. There would also be a smaller number of schools because of better targeting. The question for policymakers is whether they are willing to give up the broad-based program touching all of the LEAs and a large majority of the elementary schools and challenge the conventional approach to delivering instruction in return for an approach that has some substantial promise of improving the education of the very poor.

Summary of Proposal for ECIA, Chapter 1

In general, retain the present purposes and Federal/state/local structure for Chapter 1 *but* propose major, realistic amendments within that structure to improve the efficiency and effectiveness of the program.

1 *Efficiency: Improve the targeting of funds*: Target funds only to local education agencies with high concentrations of poverty and to schools within them with very high percentages of poverty children. These schools are primarily in inner cities and poor rural areas.

   Rationale: Poor students who attend high poverty schools are doubly disadvantaged. Data indicate that their families and schools are less able to help them achieve than are well-to-do families and schools with affluent populations. At present, Chapter 1 funds are spread out to over 95 per cent of America's 14,000 LEAs and over 70 per cent of our elementary schools. Low-scoring students in affluent communities have multiple opportunities outside of Chapter 1 to receive special attention. Thousands of much less fortunate schools in inner cities have far higher poverty levels, far lower achievement levels, and far fewer resources and are not served by Chapter 1 because the funds are inefficiently distributed.

2 *Effectiveness: Let good educational practice rather than accounting practice shape Chapter 1 programs*: In schools with high levels of poverty (say twice the national average), let the fiscal trail for Chapter 1 funds stop at the school building door and the funds be used to upgrade the quality of the entire school. For these schools, waive the supplement, not supplant requirement in Chapter 1. In return for the waiver the school should be

required to meet an accountability provision as described below.

Rationale: At the present time children are identified within school buildings as being in Chapter 1 and, generally, are pulled out of their regular classroom for 'supplemental' instruction. In many instances they are pulled out of reading or math classes to be given reading or math instruction by a Chapter 1 teacher. If they are not pulled out they are identified within their classroom as eligible for compensatory services. This form of program stigmatizes the child, leads to a lack of coordination within the school, and, according to the best available data, has no sustained positive effect on the achievement of the student. Considerable recent evidence on effective schools indicates that we know a lot about ways of improving achievement that would be appropriate if the funds were available for use in the whole school.

3   *Effectiveness: Establish systems of output accountability for Chapter 1 schools*: Develop incentives for schools that work toward specific goals.

Rationale: At present, there is no accountability system and there are no incentives for superior performance in Chapter 1. Schools receiving Chapter 1 funds should be required to establish clear goals and plans relating to improved academic outcomes and then be rewarded if the goals are reached. (Presently, if a school is too successful it loses its Chapter 1 funds.) If schools are not successful in attaining their goals, they would have to modify their plans in a significant fashion; if they are not successful for back-to-back three-year periods, the LEA would be required to take specific action or lose funds. Care must be taken to stimulate achievement goals that are not too narrow or too tied to a particular test. The key should be to challenge students with a greater range and depth of content. Recent evidence indicates that low-income and minority students in high poverty areas receive such a watered down curriculum that they are guaranteed to fail.

4   *Efficiency and Effectiveness: Encourage Chapter 1 funding of middle and secondary schools*: Establish incentives for low-income

students to graduate, perhaps by using school-business part-nerships.

Rationale: At present almost all of the Chapter 1 funds are used at the elementary school level. If funds were more tightly targeted to very high poverty schools, some funds would be available for especially needy schools beyond the elementary level. The outcome goals for these schools could include lowering the dropout rates as well as raising achievement. Information about student dropouts indicates that they often believe that there is no incentive for staying in school. If Chapter 1 funds were directed toward improving the entire school, they could be used to work with the local business community to establish incentives such as guaranteed jobs for graduates, as well as for efforts to improve the school curriculum and for tutorial programs.

Notes

1 This paper originally appeared in Williams, B. I., Richmond, P. A. and Mason, B. J. (Eds.) (1986) *Designs for Compensatory Education: Conference Proceedings and Papers*, Washington, DC, Research and Evaluation Associates. All references in the original to papers presented at the Conference on the Effects of Alternative Designs in Compensatory Education are shown as chapters in the book, *Designs for Compensatory Education: Conference Proceedings and Papers*.
2 See Koretz (1986) for a recent and interesting overall discussion of changes in achievement test scores over the past few decades. Koretz examines test score changes by birth cohort, an approach which leads to a different set of conclusions than those reached by other analysts.
3 See Natriello (1986) which deals with the dropout issue. Also see Levin (1986).
4 Also see publications from the Boston Compact, Boston School Department, and the *New York Times* article (6 July 1986) on the efforts that Boston and New York City are making to give students a clear incentive for graduating from high school.
5 One source of evidence comes from the effective schools literature. See, for example, Purkey and Smith (1983). Another literature has to do with the relationship between life chances and educational attainment. See Jencks *et al* (1979).
6 One way the desire to maintain the status quo is expressed is by reference

to the 'legal framework' — a constructed, internally consistent system of rules and regulations which is argued by its advocates to be inseparable from the intent of program itself. Thus, the justification goes, if the logic of the system of rules and regulations is violated, the violator must have values that are antithetical to the purposes of the program. Michael J. Gaffney's paper for the conference, 'Chapter 1: The Choices for Educators', is an example of this tradition. Gaffney describes the 'legal framework' for the program and argues that the legislation and regulations both insure that the program meets legislative intent and give great freedom to the local school system. As a variety of people at the Conference pointed out, the paper ignores existing knowledge about program implementation and the damaging effects of misunderstood and externally imposed regulations on the quality of services in reaching its benign conclusions about the real and potential effects of the legislative, regulatory, and sub-regulatory (administrative) guidelines. Gaffney supplies a careful critique of a set of three substantive papers in his session of the Conference. The touchstone for his critique, however, is always the existing 'legal framework' (for example, 'These proposals [for school-wide staff development] *must* be assessed in light of the legal framework' [emphasis added]) rather than the potential positive effect of such proposals for the achievement of poor and low-achieving students. There is an eerie sense of 'natural order' here. Gaffney's paper and its references are useful for students of the regulatory structure of Chapter 1 and its predecessor, Title I. The discussion in this section of this paper of the ways that funds are presently allocated in the Chapter 1 may be augmented by the Gaffney paper.

7 These quotes are taken directly from Sec. 101 of Title I of the Elementary and Secondary Education Act of 1965 as reported in 'A Report on the Education Amendments of 1978', H. R. 15, House of Representatives, 95th Congress, 2nd Session, Report No. 95-1137, 11 May, 1978.

8 See the Kennedy *et al* (1986) and the Gaffney (1986) papers for more detail and for references which supply more detail. The focus here is on the allocation of funds in the general compensatory education program. This discussion does not deal with the special programs for migrants and the handicapped.

9 This description is generally right. For a precise description see the Chapter 1 legislation.

10 The LEA has some options based on provisions in the regulations — for example, funding must go to schools in order of poverty intensity in the schools but if there is very low achievement in a particular school the order may be changed. Overall, however, the basic provisions listed in the text dominate the selection process. See the Kennedy *et al* (1986) paper, the papers from the first National Institute of Education Title I study which are referenced in the Kennedy *et al* paper and the paper by Gaffney (1986) prepared for the conference.

11 In keeping with one role of this paper (as a critique of the major papers of

the session) I have a variety of methodological quibbles with the Kennedy *et al* paper though I agree with the general conclusions. William Cooley (1986) cited a number of criticisms in his discussion of the papers at the Conference. Especially important are his points regarding the effect on correlations of changing the unit of analysis from the individual to the school. On the general issue of the relationship between poverty and achievement, the argument in the Kennedy *et al* paper about which of the measures of social status has the strongest relationship to achievement is not useful. The different relationships depend on many things, including how the independent variables are defined, the variation in the population, and the age and grades of the students. The K R White paper (1982) is misleading at best on these issues. It is difficult to judge some of the other methodological issues in the Kennedy *et al* paper since its methodological section (Appendix D) was not attached to the paper.

12   See Kennedy *et al* (1986) for more detail on these issues.

13   There is a concentration provision in Chapter 1 that would allow funds to be targeted to the 50 per cent or so of the 'poorest' counties in the nation. The provision was advocated by the Carter administration and passed by Congress in the 1978 Amendments to Title I of ESEA. The logic behind the development of the provision was similar to the logic of this paper's discussion of the issue, though Carter's analysts did not have the benefit of the kind of analysis that Kennedy *et al* have carried out in their paper. The concentration provision can be used only for 'new' money (above a current appropriation) and has not proved popular at appropriations time in Congress; it contains less than 10 per cent of the Chapter 1 funding for the basic program.

14   This position can be supported by a relatively conservative view of the Federal role in education. The argument would go something like the following:

- States have a responsibility to provide a high quality general education to all of their students. The Federal role should be marginal.
- Because of problems of the national economy and historical accident which transcend state policies, some states and localities within states have particularly high populations of students from poor families.
- As long as we evaluate students' achievement with measuring instruments that differentiate among and rank them, some will achieve relatively well and some relatively badly.
- Students from poor families, especially those in high poverty communities and schools, are very likely to achieve at a low level on our measuring instruments. Because the problems are so great in these schools, these students will receive less assistance and, therefore, less high quality education than both affluent and poor children in low poverty communities and schools.
- The Federal government has a responsibility from a variety of legislative acts to promote equal educational opportunity.
- A compensatory education program targeted on the highest poverty

schools in the nation would be focused clearly on an extraordinary and marginal role directed at meeting a national need that states may not have the resources to meet.

15   Other authors making the same kinds of arguments are Glass and Smith (1977), Archambault (1986), Smith (1984), Kaestle and Smith (1982) and Kimbrough and Hill (1981).

16   Peterson (1986) has a thoughtful discussion of the fragmentation issue on pages II-24 through II-28 of her paper for the conference. She sees the problem as especially acute for low-achieving students and finds that pullouts may lead to a fragmentation of content and to less emphasis on teaching higher order skills.

17   The evolution of these requirements is recounted in the Gaffney (1986) paper presented at the conference and in its references. See also Kaestle and Smith (1982).

18   This is an interesting and comprehensive review of the literature on instructional settings in Chapter 1.

19   The SES data cited earlier provide the overall evidence of effectiveness. A recent article summarizing these data is Carter (1984). The Archambault paper (1986) also reviews some of this literature. One legitimate question might be about why Chapter 1 has any short-term effect at all given the criticisms mounted against it. There are two answers: The first is that both settings, on average, probably provide a somewhat more intensive instructional setting than does the regular classroom which has not received any extra resources; the second is that a lot of the instructional content of Chapter 1 programs is oriented toward the short-term goal of increasing test scores. As Peterson (1986) suggests this second orientation may distort the instructional programs away from important longer term goals having to do, for example, with comprehension in reading and problem solving in mathematics.

20   In a provocative paper presented at the conference, Donald Moore (1986) contrasted the degree of coordination and the nature of the fragmentation of the curriculum in Chapter 1 and non-Chapter 1 schools and found that there was little difference. In effect, he found that Chapter 1 did not contribute to a generally low level of coordination and a high level of fragmentation. One conclusion from his presentation is that it does not matter whether the Chapter 1 program has a supplement, not supplant requirement, for no matter what happens the curriculum will be uncoordinated and fragmented. Another conclusion is that it will take a great deal of effort to improve the schools and, while removing the impediments to coordination created by Chapter 1, it will not solve all of the problems, but it might be one place to start. Many of Moore's comments were based on his experiences in Chicago which may have less coordinated and more fragmented schools than some other communities.

21   There would continue to be fiscal requirements if this strategy were adopted. 'Comparability', which requires that Chapter 1 schools receive at least the same levels of resources from other sources as do non-Chapter

1 schools, would be maintained. And 'maintenance of effort', which requires that Chapter 1 schools receive at least the same level of resources as they did in prior years, would also be maintained.

22 Peterson's conference paper (1986) reviews much of the literature on effective strategies for instruction and some of the literature on effective schools. For more extensive reviews of the literature on effective schools, see Purkey and Smith (1983) and Good and Brophy (1986). For a more extensive review of the teaching literature see Brophy and Good (1986).

23 Much of this literature focuses on the importance of the environment of the school and the level of expectation of the faculty for the achievement of students.

24 Politically, it may be impossible to fund only the very neediest schools. If schools with small percentages of poverty and low-scoring children which receive few resources continued to be funded by Chapter 1, it would be prudent to allow programs targeted toward low-achieving students. Perhaps a cutoff of 40 per cent poverty in the school would be reasonable: above that level (which is double the national average) the program would be schoolwide; below that level other approaches which would entail targeting students would be used. It is not obvious to me that, even in the lower poverty schools, the rigidities of the supplement, not supplant requirements are the only way of ensuring that the purposes of Chapter 1 are met.

25 See Kennedy *et al* (1986) for a discussion of the poverty-achievement relationship. See Purkey and Smith (1983) and Good and Brophy (1986) for discussions of the importance of school-based approaches. See Peterson (1986) for a discussion of the importance of higher order and critical thinking skills and their absence from the Chapter 1 curriculum. The figure $500 is not arbitrary; it is approximately what is spent in Chapter 1 programs on each Chapter 1 child. The 40 per cent poverty figure is not unusually high for most inner-city and poor rural area schools.

26 Local education agencies are urged to use the results of the evaluations to help improve their Chapter 1 programs, but again they are not held accountable for a failure either to perform well or to engage in active improvement.

27 A very important consideration here would be to ensure that local schools and LEAs did not choose too narrow a set of achievement measures and that at least the forms of the measures changed from year to year so that the teachers did not focus on instruction designed solely to improve student scores on a particular test. In my view the schools and LEAs should be accountable for outcome results at one time during the elementary years, the end of fifth grade. For students to do well on most standardized tests at the end of fifth grade in reading and mathematics, they need a firm and fairly broad grounding in basic and problem solving skills. They need to be able to read and comprehend text beyond simple sentences and paragraphs, to gather information in context areas from textbooks while working alone, to draw and make inferences from text,

to carry out the basic arithmetic operations and to solve word problems in mathematics that require selecting and accurately using the right arithmetic operation. The LEAs should and generally do require lots of other tests at earlier grade levels to monitor progress. At the middle and secondary levels similar kinds of standards could be defined.

References

ARCHAMBAULT, F. X. (1986) 'Instructional setting: Key issue or bogus concern' in WILLIAMS, B. I., RICHMOND, P. A. AND MASON, B. J. (Eds.) *Designs for Compensatory Education: Conference Proceedings and Papers*, Washington, DC, Research and Evaluation Associates.

BROPHY, J. (1986) 'Research linking teacher behavior to student achievement: Potential implications for instruction of Chapter 1 students' in WILLIAMS, B. I., RICHMOND, P. A. AND MASON, B. J. (Eds) *Designs for Compensatory Education: Conference Proceedings and Papers*, Washington, DC, Research and Evaluation Associates.

BROPHY, J. E. AND GOOD, T. I. (1986) 'Teacher behavior and student achievement' in WITTROCK, M. C. (Ed) *Handbook of Research on Teaching* (3rd edn) New York, Macmillan, pp. 328–75.

CALFEE, R. (1986) 'Curriculum and instruction: Reading' in WILLIAMS, B. I., RICHMOND, P. A. AND MASON, B. J. (Eds.), *Designs for Compensatory Education: Conference Proceedings and Papers*, Washington, DC, Research and Evaluation Associates.

CARTER, L. F. (1984) 'The Sustaining Effects Study of compensatory and elementary education', *Educational Researcher*, **13**, 7, pp. 4–13.

COOLEY, W. W. (1986) 'Selecting students and services: Reactions' in WILLIAMS, B. I., RICHMOND, P. A. AND MASON, B. J. (Eds) *Designs for Compensatory Education: Conference Proceedings and Papers*, Washington, DC, Research and Evaluation Associates.

GAFFNEY, M. J. (1986) 'Chapter 1: the choices for educators' in WILLIAMS, B. I., RICHMOND, P. A. AND MASON, B. J. (Eds) *Designs for Compensatory Education: Conference Proceedings and Papers*, Washington, DC, Research and Evaluation Associates.

GLASS, G. V. AND SMITH, M. L. (1977) *'Pullouts' in Compensatory Education*, unpublished manuscript, University of Colorado.

GOOD, T. L. AND BROPHY, J. E. (1986) 'School effects' in WITTROCK, M. C. (Ed.), *Handbook of Research on Teaching* (3rd edn) New York, Macmillan, pp. 570–604.

HALLINAN, M. T. (1986) 'Chapter 1 and student achievement: A conceptual model' in WILLIAMS, B. I., RICHMOND, P. A. AND MASON, B. J. (Eds)

Designs for Compensatory Education: Conference Proceedings and Papers, Washington, DC, Research and Evaluation Associates.

HOEPFNER, R. (Ed) (1981) *Substudies on Allocation and Targeting of Funds and Services, Assessment of Student Growth, and Effects of Attrition*, Santa Monica, CA, System Development Corporation.

JENCKS, C., BARTLETT, S., CORCORAN, M., CROUSE, J., EAGLESFIELD, D., JACKSON, G., MCCLELLAND, D., MUESER, P., OLNECK, M., SWARTZ, J., WARD, S. AND WILLIAMS, J. (1979) *Who Gets Ahead? The Determinants of Economic Success in America*, New York, Basic Books.

KAESTLE, C. F. AND SMITH, M. S. (1982) 'The Federal role in elementary and secondary education, 1940–1980', *Harvard Educational Review*, **52**, pp. 384–409.

KENNEDY, M. M., JUNG, R. K. AND ORLAND, M. E. (1986) *Poverty, Achievement and the Distribution of Compensatory Education Services*, Washington, DC, US Department of Education.

KENOYER, C. E., COOPER, D. M., SAXTON, D. E. AND HOEPFNER, R. (1981) *The Effects of Discontinuing Compensatory Education Services*, Santa Monica, CA, System Development Corporation.

KIMBROUGH, J. AND HILL, P. (1981). *Problems of Implementing Multiple Categorical Education Programs*, Santa Monica, CA, Rand Corporation.

KORETZ, D. (1986) *Trends in Educational Achievement*, (Report 59–115 0-86-1). Washington, DC, Congressional Budget Office.

LEVIN, H. J. (1985) *The Educationally Disadvantaged: A National Crisis*, Philadelphia, PA, Public/Private Ventures.

LEVIN, H. J. (1986) *Educational Reform for Disadvantaged Students: An Emerging Crisis*, West Haven, CT, NEA Professional Library.

MOORE, D. R. (1986) 'The relationship between compensatory education and regular education: Reactions' in WILLIAMS, B. I., RICHMOND, P. A. AND MASON, B. J. (Eds) *Designs for Compensatory Education: Conference Proceedings and Papers*, Washington, DC, Research and Evaluation Associates.

NATRIELLO, G. (Ed) (1986) 'School dropouts: Patterns and policies' [Special issue], *Teachers College Record*, **87**, 3.

PETERSON, P. L. (1986) 'Selecting students and services for compensatory education: Lessons from aptitude-treatment interaction research' in WILLIAMS, B. I., RICHMOND, P. A. AND MASON, B. J. (Eds) *Designs for Compensatory Education: Conference Proceedings and Papers*, Washington, DC, Research and Evaluation Associates.

PURKEY, S. AND SMITH, M. S. (1983) 'Effective schools: A review' *The Elementary School Journal*, **83**, pp. 427–52.

ROGERS, M. S., LANDERS, K. L. AND HOEPFNER, R. (1982) *Achievement Growth as a Result of Grade and Length of Participation in Compensatory Programs*, Santa Monica, CA, System Development Corporation.

ROMBERG, T. A. (1986) 'Mathematics for compensatory school programs' in WILLIAMS, B. I., RICHMOND, P. A. AND MASON, B. J. (Eds) *Designs for Compensatory Education: Conference Proceedings and Papers*, Washington, DC, Research and Evaluation Associates.

SMITH, M. S. (1984) *Consideration for the Study of Student Outcomes of Chapter 1*, Madison, University of Wisconsin, Wisconsin Center for Educational Research.

WANG, M., BEAR, M. B., CONKLIN, J. E. AND HOEPFNER, (1981) *Compensatory Services and Educational Development in the School Year*, Santa Monica, CA, System Development Corporation.

WHITE, K. R. (1982) 'The relationship between socioeconomic status and academic achievement', *Psychological Bulletin*, **91**, pp. 461–81.

7

Funding the Individual? A Chapter on the Future of Chapter 1

Denis P. Doyle and Bruce S. Cooper

The subject of this chapter on the future of Chapter 1, the nation's major Federal aid to education law, is framed as a question, 'Funding the Individual?'. The title is a query because the High Court leaves no choice: it has declared institutional funding unconstitutional. The Justices ruled in 1985 that funding school districts for purposes of aiding children in parochial schools did not pass constitutional scrutiny. The Justices found the use of public schools' employees on the premises of sectarian schools 'entangling'. Then, as Congressman Augustus F. Hawkins, Chair of the House Committee on Education and Labor, observed:

> On July 1, 1985 the Supreme Court in *Aguilar vs. Felton* held that the method most commonly employed by local educational agencies to serve private schoolchildren under the Chapter 1 program — that of public school teachers providing instructional services on the premises of nonpublic sectarian schools — was unconstitutional. (After *Aguilar vs. Felton*, 1986, p. vi)

Would that we could ask the question, 'How should services for poor youngsters who attend religious schools be provided?' but the legal rationale for providing aid to parochial school children through the services of public school teachers is gone. With the *Aguilar* decision in 1985, on-site provision of these federally sponsored services is no longer legal. While new 'off-site' options have been tried, they have met with only very limited success. Mobile Chapter 1 vans, brought to the curbside of the private school, portable classrooms parked nearby, and other bizarre remedies have been attempted but they are at best awkward administrative contrivances born of desperation.

No rational person or rational process would produce such practices. They are clumsy, expensive, inconvenient, even dangerous; they are clearly educationally unsound. On what educational basis would private school students be required to travel miles to a nearby neutral site at a public school and back, removing them from their schools and denying them valuable class time, just for a few minutes of remedial reading or mathematics? It is no wonder, then, that services to parochial school youngsters have dropped by 35 to 40 per cent between the 1985 and 1987 school years, with the loss of nearly $75 million in Federal funds.

Ironically, few wanted this decision. The Supreme Court Justices heard not a single complaint that public schools' teachers were using Chapter 1 money and time to teach catechism, Talmud, or liturgy. Local school superintendents seemed to appreciate the responsibility of sharing Chapter 1 services with parochial schools; after all, it meant additional employment for their teachers. Even teacher unions, which have opposed services to private schools, welcomed the additional pay and membership that Chapter 1 provided. And parochial schools had overcome their fear of becoming involved with the government and had actually come to depend on the Chapter 1 teachers to help the least able and poorest students in the religious schools.

The Court itself seemed trapped in its own interpretation of the first amendment, prohibiting the 'establishment' of religion while ignoring the equally important 'free exercise' clause. If the modest practice of despatching public employees to parochial schools 'forges a symbolic link' between church and state, 'entangling' the two, two alternatives remain: abandon Chapter 1 for parochial school children altogether or bypass public schools. The Court leaves supporters of aid no choice but to seek direct student aid, 'funding the individual'.

The issue, however, is more complex and interesting than simply designing a programmatic response to a Court ruling; it raises fundamental questions about the role of government and the education of the public.

We shall suggest in this chapter that the child is the best unit of funding. We shall argue that we should fund the individual for several important reasons:

- Funding the individual allows bypassing the public school system (and state system as well), providing direct support for the family and children, permitting them to attend parochial schools.
- Funding the individual places the locus of decision-making as to what kind of schooling a child should receive with the family, where it rightfully belongs.
- Funding the individual creates an education market, allowing families to 'shop' for schools, and schools to compete for clients.

The reasons for prohibiting direct public services to private schools, while enigmatic to the uninitiated (and some veterans as well), have been developing for the last fifty years. As we noted, in school cases, the Court has systematically emphasized half the first amendment. Establishment of religion is abjured by the courts; and to make matters worse for religious schools, a special twist is added to 'test' whether religion has been 'established'. In theory, public funds can go to religious institutions if the monies serve a purely secular purpose. But the tripartite test developed in *Lemon vs. Kurtzman* (1971) makes it virtually impossible for parochial schools to receive funds:

> First, the statute must have a secular legislative purpose; second its principal or primary effect must be one that neither advances nor inhibits religion ...; finally, the statute must not foster an excessive government entanglement with religion. (cited in After *Aguilar vs. Felton*, 1986, p. 7)

The court in *Lemon* created a Catch 22 situation. To meet criteria 1 and 2, public officials must monitor and supervise public employees on the premises of parochial schools, violating the third test. Hence, to fulfill its responsibilities to see that remedial reading teachers are not preaching the Gospel, leading their pupils in prayer, or performing other forbidden religious acts, the public system must walk the halls and inspect the Chapter 1 classrooms. They must become, in a word, 'entangled'.

In New York City, for example, the Court in *Aguilar* was aware of the school district's attempt to prevent the teaching of religion, in that supervisory staff:

> took specific steps to be sure that its Chapter 1 classes were free
> of religious content. It instructed its personnel to avoid all
> involvement with religious activities in the schools to which
> they were assigned; it directed them to keep contact with
> private school personnel to a minimum; and, most important, it
> set up a supervisory system involving unannounced classroom
> visits. (After *Aguilar vs. Felton*, 1986, p. 10)

To be absolutely sure that government funds were not being used
to 'establish religion' in sectarian schools in New York City, public
officials had to become excessively entangled, violating the third 'test'.
It was a lose–lose situation, for if supervisors ignore the actions of
remedial Chapter 1 teachers, then they ran the risk of overlooking
serious examples of religious practices performed at government
expense. But by inspecting, the Court said, agents of the state:

> had to visit and inspect the religious school regularly, alert for
> the subtle or overt presence of religious matter in Title I classes
> ... [Such] detailed monitoring and close administrative contact
> ... violated an underlying objective of the establishment clause
> to prevent as far as possible, the intrusion of either (church or
> state) into the precincts of the other. (cited in After *Aguilar vs.
> Felton*, 1986, p. 10)

The theory, then, of purely 'secular' purpose without corresponding 'entanglement' seems to be a practical impossibility in elementary
and secondary education; the court has created a legal Gordian knot
which cannot be easily cut, so long as the public schools are the agents
to deliver services to sectarian school students.

Alternatives in Theory

There are alternatives to using the public school system to deliver
Chapter 1 services. We shall spell them out in the next section. Now,
however, we must consider in theory some other basis for funding
religious schools, one that avoids the problem that the off-site provision
presents. Direct aid to parochial schools has been attempted since the
beginning of parochial school education. In the nineteenth century,

when state governments had no places for burgeoning school enrollments, legislatures willingly funded private sectarian schools directly. As McCluskey (1969) notes, 'the State of New York had given financial aid to every institution in the City, practically all of which were operated by churches' (p. 60).

While this form of direct aid gradually disappeared, a theory of government aid began to emerge. Designed to overcome the argument that public aid was supporting private schools, the argument was advanced on behalf of the child.

'Child benefit' theory is based on the idea that public support is not for the religious institution, but the child, in the same way that medical assistance is for the patient, not the doctor or hospital. The institution is simply the instrument through which the benefit is derived. In attenuated form, this theory has been used in the United States for the past thirty years to allow public funds to reach disadvantaged children in parochial schools. The aid was channeled through the offices of the local public schools, and worked reasonably well in the period 1965 to 1985, the first two decades of Title I/Chapter 1. Because this pragmatic and practical accommodation has been found unconstitutional, a new, more direct form of 'child benefit' must be devised, one that funds the individual, not the system on behalf of the child.

Direct benefits to children under Chapter 1 may require a policy as radical as a Chapter 1 voucher. One less radical alternative, however, deserves serious attention. Permit quasi-public secular agencies to act on behalf of parents, preventing 'entanglement' while permitting 'free exercise'. In other developed democracies, public funds have been made available for students to attend religiously affiliated schools since the nineteenth century. Their purpose is to preserve religious freedom. It is an irony that nations with 'state churches', like Denmark, Holland and Great Britain, are now more sensitive to the needs of other religious groups than purely secular states.

The Danes, for example, provide money for private schooling to parents who find government schools objectionable for any reason. The government is explicit about its reasons for providing the opportunity for parents to have virtually complete freedom of choice in education: 'It should be possible for people to choose an alternative kind of education for their children, should they wish, whether their reasons for this be ideological, political, educational, or religious' (Doyle, 1984a, p. 11).

Even more striking, perhaps, is the example of Australia, which, upon independence, adopted — nearly verbatim — the language of the US Constitution's first amendment. Not surprisingly, when the practice of funding religious schools became widespread in Australia, a lawsuit ensued. Infelicitously named the DOGS suit (Defenders of Government Schools), the plaintiffs lost six to one; the Australian High Court ruled that so long as the state treats all religions equally, including irreligion, no 'establishment' of religion has occurred and the individual's 'free exercise' of religion is duly protected (*ibid*). [1]

By way of contrast, the US Supreme Court has by now got itself into an impasse as regards public funding for education in religious schools. Having struck down almost every scheme designed to fund institutions, only funding 'individuals' (families and their children) remains. Although 'individual' funding schemes may not pass judicial scrutiny either, a few recent developments in the courts suggest that the High Court may look more favorably on an approach that gives public resources directly to families.

In Minnesota, in the case of *Mueller vs. Allen* (1983), the US Supreme Court decided that a 'tuition tax deduction' law was constitutional because the benefits went equally to all families which incurred expenses for the education of their children (whether paying fees to a private or public school) and because there was no evident entanglement of church and state. The family simply 'claimed' the costs of education against their state income tax, a scheme requiring no direct public intrusion into private religious life.

And in the *Aguilar* decision, Justice Powell appears to invite a Chapter 1 voucher plan, one which could be operated without government supervision in parochial schools:

> Our cases have upheld evenhanded secular assistance to both parochial and public school children in some areas [see *Mueller vs. Allen*] ... I do not read the Court's opinion as precluding these types of indirect aid to parochial schools ... In the cases cited, the assistance programs made funds available equally to public and nonpublic schools without entanglement ... The constitutional defect in the Title I program ... is that it provides direct financial subsidy to be administered in significant part by public school teachers [and supervisors] within parochial schools — resulting in both the advancement of religion and

forbidden entanglement. If, for example, Congress could fashion a program of evenhanded financial assistance to both public
and private schools [see *Mueller* again] that could be administered, without governmental supervision in the private
schools, so as to prevent the diversion of the aid from secular
purposes, we could be presented with a different question.
(*Aguilar vs. Felton*, 1985)

One purpose of this chapter is to see if such a program, one that
serves all needy children equitably yet removes the public school
system from the business of serving parochial schools, can be fashioned.
The idea is not as farfetched, as it once might have seemed. It is likely,
given Justice Powell's opinion, that the High Court would welcome
some way out of the dilemma its opinions have created. Denying poor
children access to special education services, solely because their parents
exercise religious choice, must offer little comfort to the Court. The
justices have created a 'Scylla and Charybdis' situation for both
religious schools and for the Federal judiciary.

As David Ackerman of the Congressional Research Service notes:

> If a governmental agency channels public aid directly to a
> sectarian school and the aid is not by its nature or as a result of
> controls imposed by the agency limited to secular use, the aid
> program ... is likely to be found by the courts to have a primary
> effect of advancing religion and thus be unconstitutional. If, on
> the other hand, the agency imposes a strict monitoring system
> to be sure that the aid provided is not used for religious
> purposes, the aid program ... is likely to be found to involve
> excessive entanglement between church and state and also be
> unconstitutional. (After *Aguilar vs. Felton*, 1986, p. 10)

By way of contrast and illustration, in the case of *Bowen vs. Roy*, the
Court has offered a strikingly different ruling. Mr. Stephen J. Roy and
Karen Miller, Native American parents of Little Bird of the Snow, were
informed by the Pennsylvania Welfare Department that their Aid to
Families with Dependent Children (AFDC) benefits would be reduced
unless they complied with the statutory requirement that all household
members receive a social security number. Mr. Roy sued, and in court
testified that the use of a social security number would 'rob' Little

Bird's 'spirit'. To require Little Bird to get a number violated fundamental religious tenets, or would force the family to give up their AFDC funds.

> The Court found that while an individual may not compel the government to act in accordance with his religious beliefs, neither as a general rule may the government require that an individual breach a religious precept in order to avoid losing governmental benefits to which he would otherwise be entitled. (Foltin, 1986, p. 1)

Political Considerations

But 'funding the individual' is more complex than legal and constitutional history alone would indicate. There is a political legacy as well. We must consider political history in assessing recent and future developments.

That Chapter 1 exists at all was due to delicate political compromises worked out by President Lyndon B. Johnson and Congress in the 1960s, that eliminated longstanding roadblocks to Federal aid to education. Since the middle of the nineteenth century, three stumbling blocks had prevented the creation of significant Federal programs for elementary and secondary schools in the United States: the three Rs of race, religion and 'republicanism' (with a small 'r'). Republican ideology and democratic practice led to a fear of nationalized education systems and a corresponding preference for local control. To oversimplify only slightly: Southerners feared that Federal aid would lead to integration; Northerners feared that it would perpetuate racial segregation. Protestants feared Federal aid would lead to public funding of Catholic schools; and Catholics were afraid it would not. And finally, the nation as a whole feared the loss of local control with Federal aid.

These impediments were partially removed by 1965. First, President Johnson's Civil Rights Act of 1964 put to rest Northern fears about Federal aid perpetuating racial segregation; and Southerners, however reluctantly, recognized the end of separate schools by race. Second, the design of the Title I legislation (which started as demonstration projects, left up to local needs and decision-makers) put to rest fears about the loss of local control. Only the religious aid issue remained, and President Johnson brilliantly finessed it. By allowing the public schools to hire public school teachers for Title I programs in parochial schools, and to operate and control the program of 'ancillary services', Johnson convinced the public school lobby that they had much to gain and little to lose. After all, why not share education services with all needy children, even those in parochial schools? Either count the Catholics in or lose the entire program, Johnson argued, for the Democratic coalition depended on the Northern, urban (and Catholic) vote as much as the Southern, Protestant supporters.

It appeared in 1965 that literal 'funding the individual' was not necessary at the elementary and secondary level. (It is noteworthy that in higher education Federal policy was — and is — to fund the individual.) Title I, then, was designed to have public schools serve parochial school youngsters, in their own schools. While a number of eligible denominational school pupils were not reached by Title I, the approach was a realistic way to solve a thorny political problem.

Enter *Aguilar*. With this ruling, the Court struck down twenty years of political accommodation and cooperation between private and public schools by destroying the basis for the historic compromises and political coalitions which had brought the very program into being in 1965, and had sustained it through subsequent reauthorizations between 1965 and 1985.

Congress must now act to renew Chapter 1, and it faces the same problem it did two decades ago: how to serve all eligible children, including those who select religious schools.

Legal Scholasticism

In the abstract, the distinction between funding 'individuals' and 'institutions' would not seem very important. After all, the ultimate target of a human service program — however it is funded — is the individual in that program, not the program itself. An institution is simply a 'delivery system'. Institutions exist not for themselves, but to carry out large-scale goals. Picture the formal education of some 43,000,000 children without 'schools'. Chapter 1 programs would be inconceivable without some institutional setting in which to operate them. If the distinction between funding individuals and institutions has meaning, it is that, to oversimplify only slightly, funding individuals reflects a view of society in which the individual is paramount. A decision to fund institutions reflects a view of society in which institutions are more important.

The practical implications of whichever funding mechanism is selected are far-reaching. Letting the individual select the institution introduces choice into the equation. It is not that families will elect a non-institutional alternative for their children's education; rather, by funding individuals, families can select the institution they desire. Choice among institutions places the client in the driver's seat, not the institution. Such schemes as Pell Grants, food stamps, housing allowances, and the GI Bill are all examples of institutions serving the recipient, rather than the clients having to use the funded institution.

Even if *Aguilar* had not been decided as it was the debate about funding individuals or institutions would be germane. Think of the program latitude available if there is no institutional barrier to funding individuals or institutions. For example, the decision to construct great blocks of public housing, rather than using housing vouchers or negative income taxation, is a programmatic decision. Housing officials are not forced by the US Constitution to fund the housing authority instead of the families who need the housing. Similarly, the decision to permit the indigent ill to be treated at a religiously affiliated hospital, at public expense, is made without pressure of constitutional prohibitions; so too, food stamps may be issued rather than having people queue at government commissaries. In these examples, government has determined that the programs are better if choice is allowed and institutions serve that choice, rather than the other way round — not because the Court has ruled one way or the other.

In fact, in virtually all areas of social service, some plan for funding the individual can be found, even if that person, family, or group elects to use that right in a religious institution. Mothers on public assistance can bear their children in a Catholic, Jewish, Methodist, or Lutheran hospital, at public expense; the elderly poor can live in housing owned by a church; crossing guards for a busy street in front of a church or synagogue are frequently provided by the local government. Students can opt to attend a religious university and the government will offer the same grants and loans. And the indigent can be buried in hallowed ground at government expense.

Our point is not that 'institutions' are bad; to the contrary, they are good. But without choice, the tyranny of institutions appears; they become unbridled monopolies.

A case reported in *The New York Times* is informative. In 1985, a newly appointed Director of County Welfare in Sacramento, California, decided to end the practice of cash payments to individuals on general relief. Concerned, perhaps, that they might spend their meager allowances on drink — or God, forbid, something worse — he withheld cash payments altogether. In their stead, he substituted a clean, well-lighted place, a dormitory, with bathing and eating facilities, and a set of rules about behavior and schedules. Participants in the program were required to arrive before a certain time, bathe as necessary, help with kitchen chores, sweep up, police the grounds, and leave early the next morning. Beneficiaries could repeat the process each day but they could not take up permanent residence in the center.

For his pains, the administrator was sued. The charge was that his new scheme was undignified, it stripped the beneficiaries of their independence and choice; indeed, his scheme looked much like the poor houses of the nineteenth century, as his detractors asserted. Perhaps he could have rejoined that his program looked much like Jane Addams' Hull House, but on this matter the newspapers were silent. Was this plan the best or worst aspect of liberal or conservative policy-making? In such opera bouffe tales, one cannot always tell (for a more complete discussion see Doyle, 1984b).

In matters of education, however, the Court takes a different tack: it disallows funding of religious schools, though the same church receives public aid for its health, recreation, housing, and social functions. At a more exalted level, Congress may open with a prayer, recited by a chaplain whose salary comes from public funds, before debating a bill to aid churches in their roles as providers of care; more humbly, servicemen and prisoners in jail may have access to chaplains on the public payroll.

Public support is provided for a wide variety of individual transfer payments which may be used in religious settings to people across the spectra from infirmity to vigor, from youth to age, from poverty to wealth. These payments in cash or in kind, are designed to permit the individual to forge his or her own relationship with institutions, including religious or secular ones. This is true with nearly everything, it appears, except elementary and secondary education (*ibid*).[2]

Private School History

The role of private, religious institutions in American life is not new. As we have already noted, in the mid-nineteenth century, states supported a wide variety of schools which were run by churches. Public schools were, at first, schools for children who could not get into an existing church school, i.e., the poor. The well-to-do, and those who lived in vigorous religious communities, had access to private education.

A close look at the schools of the 1820s reveals two kinds of 'religious' schools. In New York, for example, the 'common' or 'public' schools were Protestant, controlled by the leading citizens of the town, village, or borough. The curriculum included the King James' Bible and Protestant prayer. They represented an effort to Americanize, sanitize, and civilize the hoards of new arrivals who flocked to the nation from dozens of different nations, language groups, and religions. The mission of the 'one best system' was to uplift and reform, to inculcate a common culture.

The other schools were Roman Catholic, schools designed to counter the Protestant pressure to conform and even convert. Bishop John Hughes, for example, proclaimed that every Catholic child should have a Catholic education; and state governments at first were willing to fund these institutions.

In New England, these Catholic schools were known as 'Irish' schools, as apt a euphemism as one can imagine. Here too the government provides support. But by the early 1850s, as Horace Mann's dream came true and the 'free schools' became numerous and powerful, the Catholic schools were systematically disestablished, not by Court edict as was the pattern in the twentieth century, but by legislative action. For the purpose of this chapter, we need not dwell on anti-Catholic sentiment; the process of denying funding is more important than the reasons why: state legislatures simply cut them off.

As Catholics grew in number and local political strength, anti-Catholic sentiment increased, and a major effort to amend the US Constitution to forbid aid to Catholic schools was launched. Named after its chief sponsor, James G Blaine, it failed nationally, but was enacted by a number of states where it survives in their constitutions to this day.

In the 1940s, however, as Catholics came to real power in the industrialized states (New York, New Jersey, Michigan, Massachusetts, Illinois and Rhode Island, for example) and were able to get state legislatures to pass direct aid laws, opponents sought redress in the courts. The principle of the 'separation of church and state' became constitutional doctrine, disallowing numerous plans to aid private schools. Building loans, teacher salary schemes and other forms of special aid were struck down. A decade and a half after *Everson vs. Board of Education* (1947), the public schools themselves were denied explicit devotional activity. The separation doctrine has had two ironic outcomes, then: children in religious schools were denied public support, those in the public system could no longer engage in group prayer. It is a far cry from the nineteenth century effort to make religion an integral part of school in both the private and public sectors.

Not only does the present antipathy to religious schools have historical roots, it also rises in a pedagogical sense as well. After all, Chapter 1 is designed to improve the educational performance of individuals; school-based programs, from a pedagogical standpoint, are simply an instructional strategy. Do individuals learn better, which is to say more and faster (as well as more amiably), in group settings? Is there an academic or intellectual critical mass, in which a certain minimum number of youngsters is necessary to succeed? These questions, though intrinsically and practically interesting, are not germane to this chapter except as they illuminate the ways in which Chapter 1 might be thought about, unencumbered by the weight of Court decisions.

If there is a 'critical mass' of youngsters which improves learning, that fact would have only limited bearing on whether we should fund individuals or institutions. If groups of students provide a more effective 'instructional' target, then it would make sense to 'target' funds to groups of students. But that objective too could be achieved by funding students rather than institutions; individual student eligibility could be predicated on concentration requirements. In any case, the debate about funding individuals or institutions does not hinge on pedagogical considerations. Rather, it should hinge on fundamental questions of individual liberty and dignity; today it hinges on narrow court interpretations.

There is a methodological dimension to the question of funding the individual that deserves brief note. It arose when the original Elementary and Secondary Education Act of 1965 was passed. As noted in the congressionally mandated study of the mid-1970s:

> Since 1965 Congress has considered reformulating its funding objectives to allocate funds on the basis of low achievement instead of poverty. In 1974 Congress decided to continue to allocate Title I funds on the basis of numbers of low-income children, while instructing the National Institute of Education (NIE), as part of the Compensatory Education Study, to explore alternate methods of funding (National Institute of Education, 1977, p. v).

This issue is more than methodological, however. The practice of funding programs, including targeting and concentration requirements, has meant that Title I funds are heavily concentrated in cities; suburban children who are poor — and poor students as well — have limited access to Title I services. And city kids who are poor but who attend schools in wealthier areas are denied aid by virtue of geography, not need. If individuals rather than programs were funded, funds would be more evenly distributed among students even if they would be less concentrated in specific schools.

Not surprisingly, the issue of funding allocations on the basis of test scores was not supported by the National Institute of Education study of Title I. The study concluded that it was not administratively feasible to pursue a strategy of using achievement test scores rather than poverty and achievement criteria for Title I funds allocation. No doubt the study was fully and fairly conducted, and given the realities of the day it would have been administratively difficult to pursue such a strategy. But that hardly puts the issue to rest. Individuals could receive Chapter 1 funds — or, dread word, *vouchers*, — on the basis of poverty criteria. Indeed, there is one important example of just such a program being tried. The Alum Rock Voucher experiment in San Jose, California, employed 'compensatory vouchers' for all children who met specified poverty criteria. 'Comp vouchers', as they were called, were in addition to the basic voucher, an amount equal to current per pupil expenditure in the district.

The demonstration — which lasted five years — had a number of interesting outcomes, but none more interesting than this: youngsters with 'comp vouchers' became attractive to schools, because they brought with them substantial funds to be used for education programs on their behalf. For once in their lives, they were sought after, not rejected.

We have many other examples of programs in which the individual is funded on the basis of income, from food stamps, to social security, to medicaid, to Pell Grants, to the GI Bill. In each case, whatever difficulty attached to the decision to fund the individual was overcome by the importance of the policy. Individual funding was chosen for policy reasons, and administrative problems were solved in the larger context of the policy decision.

Title I vouchers have been so widely discussed they need not be described here. Suffice it to say, no serious analyst expects their immediate enactment. A related scheme, however, may have brighter prospects.

Local Option Vouchers (LOVs)

Another approach, which may gain wider support, would be to allow local education authorities to issue their own vouchers to local parochial school students, permitting them to buy the Chapter 1 services in a variety of places.

The advantages of LOVs over national vouchers is that control would be local: public schools that attempted direct aid to private schools might continue using local public schools or vans. But, if, after trying such approaches, the public and parochial school leadership decide that 'it's not working', a simple voucher for children in the private sector could be used. In the event of significant disagreement as to whether services are equitable and effective, an appeals process could be used, much like the bypass procedure now available for districts which cannot or will not provide Chapter 1 to private school children. If the appeals panel found that local public schools were not helping parochial school students equally, then a LOV could be invoked and the public system bypassed.

The political advantages of LOVs are several. Local school districts control their own funds which they can 'privatize' when they need to. It also allows the coalition that has supported Chapter 1 for over twenty years to remain intact. Rather than pitting Catholics against teachers' unions, industrial states against the rest, the LOV proposal, like the President Johnson compromise of 1965, has the elements of 'something for everyone'. Public schools continue to get the lions' share of Federal Chapter 1 funds; parochial schools have an out; and politicians serve all their neediest students and families. From a cost/benefit viewpoint, LOVs mean more service for more children for less money. With LOVs, the entire costly apparatus of buying and maintaining mobile classrooms, of transporting parochial schoolers long distances, or renovating neutral sites, is eliminated.

The final possibility merits brief discussion.

Family Bypass

One measure, which might be done immediately, even before Congress reauthorizes Chapter 1, would be to declare a national 'bypass' to allow parents or groups of parents to become the bypass 'agent'. In four states the Secretary has already declared the local/state program ineffective or non-existent and has allowed 'third parties' to be the funding agent for parochial school pupils. In states like Missouri, where the state constitution forbids aid to religious schools, the Secretary has invoked the Federal bypass provision and has allowed local contract agents to be the conduit for funds to local Chapter 1 programs. Other states, such as Oklahoma, Wisconsin, and Virginia, have used bypass provisions as well.

The virtue of 'family bypass' is also its vice. The Secretary could move without consulting Congress which would infuriate both houses. The political fallout would be high. The Secretary could buy a year of services for parochial school children, but such an action would produce a furious reaction by the opposition. But like the Local Option Vouchers, 'family bypass' might be a blessing in disguise for public schools, which are saddled with the nearly impossible task of serving children in parochial schools.

Conclusion

One final issue warrants brief discussion before closing. The history of American aid to elementary and secondary education of any kind is replete with stories of religious tension and even bigotry. Chapter 1 is only one part of a long story. But in some important respects it is the most important part and as a consequence its demise is more poignant. Remember, Chapter 1 (then Title I) was the fulcrum by which President Johnson levered a reluctant Congress into a break with more than a century of tradition — his Title I compromise made Federal aid to elementary and secondary education a reality. No other President had been able to do so. With the exception of P.L. 94-142 (a civil rights act for the handicapped) no other President has enlarged it.

Even though the legislation was enacted, however, suspicion remained. Between the idea and the act 'falls the shadow' as T. S. Eliot reminds us. In the world of politics, the shadow is implementation. It took nearly two decades to overcome the suspicion and even hostility that characterized public-private school relationships; no sooner were they overcome than the Court stripped private schools of their right to participate. It is a consummate irony.

Equally ironic, but not surprising, public schools are not springing to the defense of denominational schools. The largesse the public schools enjoy is a product of that compromise too; had private schools been excluded in the beginning, public schools would have no program. Now they have a program, with no private school participation likely, because there is only one instrumentality that is likely to survive judicial scrutiny, and that is 'vouchers', a word which fills most public school educators with fear and loathing. The final irony, if Justice Powell's wording is taken to heart, is that 'vouchers' just for parochial school children would not do. Justice Powell — and by extension, the Court — could only be satisfied by 'Chapter 1 vouchers' for everyone, public and private school student alike. Then, all would be treated equally. Earlier, we noted that 'one purpose of this chapter' is to see if a program could be fashioned. As we have tried to suggest, the intellectual task presents no overwhelming obstacles. The political task, however, is daunting. It is one thing to draft legislation, another to enact it.

The obvious solution, 'Chapter 1 vouchers' is almost certainly destined to fail. The Administration is not prepared to order them by fiat or edict. The Congress, for a variety of reasons — not least opposition by powerful public school interest groups — will not enact such legislation in the near future. Instead, Congress appears to be moving toward a continuation of Chapter 1 as is with a small ($30 million) 'sweetener' to help public schools buy more (perhaps 300 at $100,000 each) vans. More money hardly overcomes the inherent weakness of funding public institutions which can't effectively reach children in private schools. Our reading of the current situation is both straightforward and grim: Chapter 1 funding for children in religious schools will soon be over. An extraordinary period of American education history is coming to a close, not for lack of ideas, but for lack of vision.

Notes

1   See High Court of Australia, Her Majesty's Attorney General for the State of Victoria (at the Relation of Black and Others) and Others, (Appellant), and Commonwealth of Australia and Others (Respondents), 10 February 1981.
2   The difficulty, even absurdity, of the present situation is revealed in the following hypothetical example. The government could, if it so chooses, give every child in the nation a cash payment in any amount the Congress could be convinced to appropriate. It might be $5, $500, or $5000. Indeed, cash benefits for children — family allowances — are the rule in every developed country, totalitarian or free. Such an allowance would withstand scrutiny in the United States *so long as it were not earmarked for education.* As a cash grant to be used for any purpose, from drink to transportation, it would pass court muster; similarly, if it were dedicated for food, housing, or health care, it would pass court muster, but *not if it were for education.*

References

After Aguilar vs. Felton: Chapter 1 Services to Nonpublic School Children (1986) (A report prepared for the Sub-committee on Elementary, Secondary, and Vocational Education of the Committee on Education and Labor, U.S. House of Representatives) Washington, DC, US Government Printing Office.
Aguilar vs. Felton. 105 S.Ct. 3232 (1985).
DOYLE, D. P. (1984a) *Family Choice in Education: The Case of Australia, Holland and Denmark* (Occasional paper), Washington, DC, American Enterprise Institute.
DOYLE, D. P. (1984b) *From Theory to Practice: Considerations for Implementing a Statewide Voucher System* (Occasional paper), Washington, DC, American Enterprise Institute.
Everson vs. Board of Education, 330 U.S. 1 (1947).
FOLTIN, R. T. (1986) *Bowen vs. Roy: Accommodation of Religious Practice Under the*

First Amendment. A Summary and Analysis, New York, The American Jewish Committee, Institute of Human Relations.

Lemon vs. Kurtzman, 403 U.S. 602 (1971).

MCCLUSKEY, N. S. (1969) *Catholic Education Faces Its Future*. Garden City, NJ, Doubleday.

Mueller vs. Allen, 463 U.S. 388, 399 (1983).

NATIONAL INSTITUTE OF EDUCATION. (1977) *Using Achievement Test Scores to Allocate Title I Funds*, Washington, DC, National Institute of Education.

8
The Problem of Quality in Chapter 1

Richard F. Elmore

The Problem

How can Federal policy enhance the quality of local programs in Chapter 1? This is a plausible question, given the amount of Federal money spent on Chapter 1; the considerable Federal, state, and local program experience accumulated over the past twenty years; and the needs that the program will be expected to meet over the next twenty years. Yet relatively little attention has been focused explicitly on the issue of quality in Title I/Chapter 1, and there is relatively little systematic understanding or analysis of the issue in the evaluation literature growing out of the program.

Everyone — members of Congress, Federal, state, and local administrators, teachers, parents, evaluators, and analysts — is concerned about quality. The rationale for a federally funded compensatory education program rests heavily on assumptions about quality: additional money buys compensatory services for a small portion of the population for a relatively small portion of the school day, and this money is assumed to provide the difference needed to pull a significant proportion of the educationally disadvantaged into the educational mainstream. If the additional money introduced by Chapter 1 buys no more than the service a student would otherwise receive in the regular school program, then the key assumption underlying compensatory education is faulty.

For all its importance, though, we know very little about what quality is in educational programs and even less about how to produce it reliably with policy. Seemingly straightforward definitions of quality, for example, concentrations of resources, staff characteristics, program design, and student performance, raise serious operating problems when they are translated into policy. These problems, we shall see, are intrinsic to a large-scale Federal grant program. So while quality is central to a program like Chapter 1, it is also difficult to define and even more difficult to realize in practice.

Consequently, the fiscal and administrative machinery of Chapter 1 does not deal explicitly with quality. In some cases, the program has mandated or encouraged practices that are assumed to be associated with quality, such as concentrations of funds, but it is not clear that these practices actually result in higher quality local programs. In other cases, the program has encouraged local practices that are questionable under certain definitions of quality, for example, pullout programs. In still other cases, the program takes a deliberately agnostic posture toward quality. For example, with fiscal accountability the program says, in effect, that protections against displacement of local funds by Federal funds are essential even if they make it more difficult to mount high quality local programs.

The single most important characteristic of Chapter 1 is that it is a marginal program (for a more detailed discussion of the marginal role of Federal policy, see Elmore and McLaughlin, 1982). That is, Chapter 1 'works', if at all, by augmenting existing instruction in existing schools. The typical recipient of Chapter 1 services is exposed to about three-quarters of an hour of reading and math four times a week with about ten students and two adults in a separate classroom (Advance Technology, 1983). Depending on how it is used this can be a significant increment to a student's education, but it is still marginal, in several senses. It constitutes about 12 to 15 per cent of a student's time in school; it draws on available staff within the school or district, who reflect the general ability level in those settings; it augments an existing instructional program which is determined by local preferences, state requirements, and local fiscal capacity; and it works on young people who come from home environments that influence their orientation to learning in various ways. My point is simply that the 'quality' of Chapter 1 services, however defined, is heavily dependent on the setting in which those services are delivered.

Quality is important to Chapter 1. But it is difficult to define and even more difficult to realize once defined. It is also, once defined and translated into administrative machinery, heavily dependent on the setting in which services are delivered.

Definitions of Quality

Acknowledging these problems is not to say that quality is unimportant, that it is unachievable on a large scale, or that concern for quality cannot play a major role in shaping the future of Chapter 1. In this section, I will develop working definitions of three types of quality that might be used to shape Federal policy toward Chapter 1 — the resources applied to a local program (inputs), the operating characteristics of local programs (process), and the consequences of local programs for students (outputs). And I will speculate about the strengths and limitations of using each of these approaches as a basis for policy.

Input Standards

In its simplest terms, Chapter 1 supplies money to states and localities to purchase compensatory education. This money is spent on certain things — teachers, aides, administrators, instructional materials, tests, etc. — and these expenditures are related in some way to the services students receive. Some of the things on which money is spent — teachers, for example — have attributes — such as experience, training, and knowledge — that may also affect the services students receive. Finally, these expenditures funded by Chapter 1 supplement existing expenditures for the same things — teachers, materials, administrators, etc. — in the broader academic program. This package of things purchased by Chapter 1, their important attributes, and the base level of resources constitutes the package of 'inputs' that students receive.

One could, in theory, design a set of indicators based on inputs and use those indicators to define an acceptable range of quality. For example, these indicators might stipulate that a per student Chapter 1 expenditure of $400–700, on a local instructional base of $1500–$2000 per student, would have a reasonable likelihood of purchasing the package of resources (teacher skill, experience, materials, evaluation, etc.) necessary for a program of acceptable quality for a particular number of students. One could also look in a more fine-grained way at packages of inputs and attempt to determine which packages seem to have the closest fit with student needs or outputs.

An input-driven system could have several possible consequences. First, by defining an acceptable or exemplary range of inputs, it would tend to focus the attention of Federal, state, and local administrators on the delivery of resources to students. Second, by calling attention to the mix of inputs and their characteristics in local programs, it would make explicit certain trade-offs involved in local administration. If additional years of teacher experience are costly, for example, some local administrators might trade less instructional time by more experienced staff for more instructional time with less experienced staff. While these trade-offs are inherent in the administration of any service delivery program, they are seldom made explicit, and are consequently seldom understood by policymakers or administrators. Third, by making explicit the relationship between Chapter 1 expenditures and the state and locally funded instructional base, it would call attention to distributional variations in the actual resources reaching students served by Chapter 1, rather than the distribution of Chapter 1 funds alone.

Input-driven systems raise certain problems, though. While it may be reasonable to stipulate acceptable or exemplary ranges on inputs, there is no reason to believe that inputs at the gross level measurable by per pupil funding, student-staff ratios, and Chapter 1/base program ratios will be meaningfully related to other measures of program quality. In simple terms, the same level of inputs 'buys' very different program characteristics and very different student performance from one setting to another. There may be discernible correlations between inputs, programs, and performance in the aggregate, but those correlations conceal enormous variations in local practice.

Specifying acceptable or exemplary ranges of inputs also sends certain signals to state and local administrators about what Federal policymakers and administrators value. Used by itself, an input-driven system says, 'if you keep certain indicators within a certain range, we don't care what else you do with the money'. This philosophy has certain advantages. It does not prejudge whether certain types of instructional programs are effective. (I will use the term 'effectiveness' throughout to refer only to effects on students.) But neither does it provide incentives for local administrators to look for more creative, innovative, or effective ways of using Federal funds. In this respect, input-driven quality indicators are much like the current regulatory regime of Chapter 1, which values compliance with administrative guidelines more than the search for new or more effective programs.

Perhaps the most serious problem with input-driven measures of quality is their insensitivity to local context and student background. Two of the most robust findings of research on the effects of schooling in general and Chapter 1 in particular are (i) that student performance is strongly related to the race, family income, and family resources of students; and (ii) that the higher the concentration of minority, low-income students, the lower the achievement level of the school (see Kennedy, Jung and Orland, 1986). To be sure, these findings describe overall patterns; there are many important and interesting exceptions that merit study in their own right. But the fact is that student background exerts strong influences on educational programs, both in terms of what must be taught and what it is possible to expect by way of student achievement. Input measures focus attention on the allocation of resources to schools and classrooms, rather than on the characteristics of the student population served. They carry the assumption that a certain standard of input should provide an adequate level of service to students. In fact, though, the educational problems of so-called disadvantaged students vary widely and have very different resource implications. Standardized input measures discourage attempts to treat different types of students differently.

Process Standards

Another way to think about quality is in terms of the design of local programs and the processes that surround them. Chapter 1 can be thought of as buying certain packages of instruction, for certain types of students, within certain stipulated structures and procedures. In their pure form, process standards would take as given the existing allocation of resources to districts and schools and focus on the package, or alternative packages of instruction, students, and procedures that a given level of resources would purchase.

The level of detail at which process standards can be specified is a major political and administrative issue. The Federal government has long adhered to the principle that it does not dictate curriculum content to states and localities, so requiring the selection of model curricula for local Chapter 1 programs is not a feasible option, even if it were

171

desirable. But the Federal government does have a long tradition of sponsoring research, development, and evaluation designed to identify exemplary educational practices. These date back to the 1950s (with the Cooperative Research Act), through the Sputnik Era (with the development of model science and math curricula), into the 1960s and 1970s (with the *What Works* series and the National Diffusion Network), up to the most recent publication of compendia of successful educational practices. While it does not seem feasible that the Federal government could require specific types of instructional programs, even if it were desirable, it is feasible for the Federal government to reward states and localities differentially for engaging in certain types of practices. I will return to this issue in the final section on strategy.

Process-driven standards of quality could have certain consequences for local programming. First, if they were constructed on the assumption that a 'program' is a package of students, content, and structure, they would call attention to the fit between student characteristics and program content. The student population served by Chapter 1 presents relatively diverse problems — content-specific achievement (reading, math, etc.), language acquisition, behavior, motivation, etc. Different combinations and levels of problems presumably require different levels of resources, different types of content, and different structures (grouping practices, teacher–aide combinations, etc.).

Second, unlike input and output standards, process standards focus local administrators' and teachers' attention on educational practice, rather than on the allocation of dollars or on the measurement of achievement. Implementation of Chapter 1, under process standards, would increasingly consist of finding the appropriate match of students, content, and structure, rather than meeting some predetermined mix of resources or student achievement level.

Process standards have their own characteristic problems. The state of knowledge about the appropriate fit between student characteristics, content, and structure is far from amenable to straightforward, easily implemented prescriptions. There is such a base of knowledge, it does have useful implications for educational practice in local compensatory programs, and its systematic application to those programs could improve content and performance. But saying that such knowledge could be useful is something very different from saying that it should be turned into authoritative standards for local practice.

All conclusions about effective practice are statements of average relationships with large intervals of uncertainty around them. Among the most significant sources of uncertainty are the existing skill and orientation of teachers and the characteristics of the process by which new practices are introduced to schools and classroom. Certain packages of students, content, and structure will perform according to expectation in certain settings, but will not in other settings. So process standards send incomplete signals to state and local administrators. They say, 'this kind of program generally works well', but they do not allow for the fact that it will fail to produce the same effect across diverse settings. One of the most robust findings of research on policy implementation is that for a given array of program models, variation across sites in degree of implementation and effectiveness for a particular model is considerably greater than variation in average performance among models. In other words, the setting in which the model is implemented exercises more influence than the model itself.

Another significant problem with process standards is that they tend to set artificial constraints on the development of new practices. For example, in environmental policy, standards for the discharge of pollutants were once determined by industry-wide agreements on 'best practicable technology'. After pollution abatement technology was installed the technology continued to change, but the standards reflected earlier technology. This introduced a complex set of problems about whether to update standards, whether to apply them retroactively to firms that were earlier in compliance, and whether less stringent technologies could be used in areas where pollution was not as serious a problem. In education, one could imagine the same kind dynamic. Exemplary practice at one time could become obsolete or retrograde at another time. Exemplary practices at one time could become institutionalized and rigidified, making it more difficult to introduce new practices at some future time.

Finally, process standards send an important signal to local administrators and teachers about who is responsible for generating knowledge about successful practices. In effect, they say that knowledge about what works is generated outside local settings by people with expert knowledge and that these ideas are then supplied to school practitioners who often screw up their execution because they don't have the skill or understanding to do them correctly. Expert knowledge is important to the development of educational practice, but this version of the

173

relationship between the two is destructive to the development of professional responsibility within schools.

Output Standards

A final way to think about quality is in terms of effects on students. In this view, high quality local programs are programs that produce results, measured by such indices as students' achievements, attendance, attainment, reductions in dropout rates, and the like. In this view, Chapter 1 is a way of purchasing capacity in local districts for the purpose of remedying performance problems for certain parts of the student population. In their pure form, output standards make no assumptions about the correct allocation of inputs or the best fit between students, content, and structure. They stipulate either that a given level of performance is expected from a given level of funding, or that performance above some level will be rewarded.

Output standards send a signal to local teachers and administrators that says, 'do whatever is necessary to produce these effects with this amount of money'. They also say implicitly that the necessary knowledge for solving detailed problems of student selection, content, and structure ultimately lies within the organizations that deliver educational services. No amount of external prescription of inputs or processes will supply the knowledge needed to mount an effective program in the absence of a strong incentive to mobilize that knowledge. Output standards supply that incentive.

The technical problems associated with output standards are similar to those associated with process standards. That is, the ability to set output standards assumes a technical knowledge of how much of a given output can be attributable to a given infusion of money. Otherwise, there would be no feasible relationship between rewards and expected effects. Empirical estimates of these relationships are statements of average relationships that conceal large variations.

Given this diversity, where should output standards be set? If they are set at the median level of performance, then half the distribution will be below standard, by definition. If they are set at a level significantly below the median, then policymakers appear to be endorsing below average performance. Another option is to set output standards by criterion levels, rather than by reference to a distribution. That is, policymakers could say that a compensatory program should, at a minimum, produce people who know how to read and write a complete sentence, do complex multiplication and division, etc. There is considerable expertise at the national and state levels in constructing such tests, so the issue is not whether it is possible to measure outputs, but rather how feasible it is to use them as indices for enhancing quality in Chapter 1.

When output standards are applied to programs like Chapter 1, which serve only a fraction of their eligibility clientele, they introduce strong selection incentives. Local programs can improve their performance by changing their student composition, rather than by improving the quality of the programs. Sometimes these selection incentives operate to focus administrators' and teachers' attention on what kind of students can best be served by a given array of services. In this case, they tend to improve the fit between program characteristics and student characteristics. On the other hand, Chapter 1 is explicitly designed to focus attention on students who are the most difficult to reach. To the extent that output standards reward selection of eligible students who present the least difficult problems, they undermine Chapter 1's central purpose.

Specifying which outputs will serve as performance measures is a complex and slippery task. Student achievement, measured by norm-referenced or criterion-referenced tests, is an obvious choice. But no responsible analyst or policymaker would advocate the exclusive use of achievement measures, since they typically tap only a narrow range of skills and they fail to capture important dimensions of what compensatory programs are trying to do. So a responsible array of output measures would include other measures — attendance, attainment, attitudes, dropout rates and the like. But specifying multiple output measures creates the problem of how much value to attach to which measures. Will we accept a lower average achievement level in return for higher attainment and lower dropout rates? That is, is it more important for low-achieving students to stay in school or for those who stay to learn more? Relationships among output measures are very poorly understood.

An output-driven system is predicated on the assumption that the increment of funding introduced by Chapter 1 is significant enough to produce certain effects with some consistency across very diverse settings. This assumption is unlikely to be true, since variations in funding for the basic instructional program in Chapter 1 schools are likely to be considerably more than the value of the additional money introduced by the program. Other variations are also likely to overwhelm the effect of the Chapter 1 increment — teacher skill, instructional content, and the characteristics of the populations served. In theory, it is possible to produce estimates of student outputs that control statistically for these background variations. In operation, these systems introduce unresolvable methodological wrangles into debates on program effects. One can imagine the spectacle of localities suing states or states and localities suing the Federal government over the legal and statistical validity of funding decisions based on student outputs.

Several feasibility questions cut across input, process, and output standards of quality in Chapter 1. Most of these questions stem from the fact that Chapter 1 is a complex intergovernmental grant program. At least in my formulation, standards of quality apply to local program decisions, which seems logical because Chapter 1 services are mounted and delivered in local schools and school systems. But Chapter 1 as a political and administrative system is considerably more complex than this formulation suggests. States play a significant role in the routine evaluation of Chapter 1, and would have to play a significant role in any attempt to introduce quality standards to the program. States have dramatically different policies toward these quality issues and dramatically different capacities to influence local decisions about the administration of Chapter 1. Hence, federally initiated quality standards, by any definition, would be differently implemented by different states and state actions would be differently implemented in local settings.

Another closely related question is the effect of existing policy and regulations in Chapter 1 on attempts to influence quality. The existing policy and regulatory structure of Chapter 1 represents a carefully constructed resolution of a myriad of issues that have arisen over the history of the program: targeting, non-public recipients, displacement of local revenues by Federal revenues, etc. For the most part, these issues have been resolved by stimulating increasingly specific Federal requirements that apply to an increasingly narrower range of activities. Since the mid-1970s, the Federal government has not tried in any serious way to influence the actual instructional content of local Chapter 1 programs or the standards by which those programs are judged.

Hence, a new concern for quality, manifested in standards, would be perceived by the Chapter 1 subgovernment — interest groups, state and local administrators, and clients — as a significant shift in Federal policy. Regardless of how those standards were applied, the move would be perceived as signaling a new period of Federal activism in Chapter 1, following a long period of relative passivity. The Federal role — in Chapter 1 and in education generally — has long been characterized by these cycles of activity and passivity. But there is some question whether the Federal government is prepared to develop the kind of administrative capacity necessary to oversee an initiative aimed at increasing quality in Chapter 1, given the foreseeable fiscal situation.

Federal Strategies for Enhancing Quality

Here is the situation confronting Federal policymakers: education policymakers at all levels have a great concern for the quality of the educational program provided to public school students. Many states and localities are already engaged in quite ambitious and detailed programs to enhance quality. Chapter 1 is unlikely to be exempt from this broader concern. By any of the definitions discussed here — inputs, processes, or outputs — serious conceptual and practical problems impede the introduction of quality standards to Chapter 1. The issue boils down to how Federal policymakers might seriously broach the issue of quality in Chapter 1, while simultaneously acknowledging the problems raised by alternative definitions of quality.

One overall conclusion seems clear. The Federal government will not muster the legislative authority or the administrative capacity to impose standards of program quality directly on local districts. In the present political and fiscal context, it is highly unlikely that the issue of quality will be addressed by writing Federal regulations that specify input, process, or output standards. For all the reasons sketched out above, writing such regulations and enforcing them would be a difficult and dubious enterprise under the best circumstances.

Ruling out direct Federal regulation of program quality does not mean that the Federal government has no resources for influencing the quality of local Chapter 1 services. A Federal concern for program quality can be manifested in ways that are consistent with a limited

177

Federal role and with the serious practical and conceptual issues that underlie alternative definitions of quality.

By way of example, let me sketch three alternative Federal strategies for focusing increased attention on program quality in Chapter 1. I will call these strategies jawboning, piggybacking, and bootstrapping. They correspond to relatively well-established strategies already in the Federal repertoire, so they do not require extensive strategy departures from existing practice. They all take account of the limits on Federal influence imposed by the marginal nature of Chapter 1 and the wide variation in capacity at the state and local level. And they are all consistent with relatively modest changes in Federal Chapter 1 expenditures.

Jawboning is essentially the systematic use of information to draw attention to either good or bad behavior. When school systems or state agencies use student test scores to call attention to high or low-performing schools, or when the Secretary of the US Department of Education publishes a pamphlet describing exemplary practices in schools, the expectation is that people in schools will pay serious attention and change their practices over time. The key characteristic of jawboning is that it involves no material rewards or penalties, and only occasionally praise or humiliation.

Jawboning is a weak treatment, in the sense that it does not use direct intervention to influence behavior. It is relatively powerful in shaping people's perceptions of ideas in good currency. It legitimates certain practices by giving them the imprimatur of authority.

Chapter 1 carries the dominant image of a social pork barrel program, whose primary purpose is to distribute large amounts of money as broadly as possible among states and localities with a socially and politically defensible rationale. This image has been reinforced by the politics of Chapter 1, which consist mainly of education interest groups and congressional allies defending the program against its critics by invoking the kids, but never taking the lead in giving it a positive, ambitious new agenda. Federal leadership could play a major role in changing this image by engaging in systematic attempts to surface and publicize information about exemplary local programs and practices. Leadership might also call attention to programs and practices that undermine Chapter 1's effectiveness. The *What Works* series of the 1970s was a pallid version of jawboning, but it reached a fairly narrow audience and it never established real authority with the educational community.

Piggybacking is the use of discretionary funding to reward and claim credit for local successes. Like jawboning, piggybacking involves some kind of systematic surfacing of exemplary local programs, but unlike jawboning, it involves the deliberate use of financial rewards. For example, states might be asked to identify some number of exemplary local programs according to federally mandated criteria as part of their evaluation responsibility under Chapter 1. The criteria could include the nature of the student population served and the creative use of federally funded activities to complement the basic instructional program. These programs could be asked to propose a plan for how they might use some significant increment of funds over a two- or three-year period, and the progress of their efforts before and after the awards could be described in a literature designed to reach a broad audience of practitioners and policymakers.

The principle underlying piggybacking is to bankroll creative local people, call attention to their efforts, and claim credit for some portion of their success through the use of financial rewards. Publicizing their efforts lends authority to a view of Chapter 1 as aggressively searching out and rewarding creativity.

Bootstrapping is the use of discretionary funding to underwrite program development in the most difficult circumstances, with the least likelihood of success, and to claim credit for success against the odds. For example, states might be asked to nominate elementary and middle schools feeding into high schools with high dropout rates and low academic achievement records. Those feeder schools could be the recipients of discretionary funding to develop Chapter 1 programs around the explicit objective of guaranteeing high school completion and meeting achievement standards. The discretionary funding could follow a cohort through the system, or, more likely, it could support the development of activities designed to complement the regular school program for all students. These efforts could be described in a literature designed to reach a broad audience of practitioners and policymakers.

The principle behind bootstrapping is to use discretionary funding to score successes on the most difficult problems confronting compensatory education, and to use those successes as a goad to the rest of the program. Publicizing these types of success lends authority to the view that Chapter 1 searches out the most difficult problems and finds solutions.

None of these approaches to quality is likely to be politically popular with Chapter 1's traditional political constituency. Any effort to distinguish among more or less successful programs will not be greeted with enthusiasm by a coalition whose main collective interest is in preserving its funding base. There may be a political constituency supportive of these ideas among local teachers and administrators and among friendly critics of the program who see it as having lost sight of its original compensatory purposes.

A major advantage of these approaches is that they do not require the Federal government to endorse any single operating definition of quality, but only to specify broad criteria (which may be based on inputs, processes, and outputs) and allow states and localities to grapple with the problems of defining quality operationally. This approach is, I think, consistent with a view which says quality is essential to the success of Chapter 1 even if we don't know exactly what it means and even if any single definition of it leads to consequences we may not like.

References

ADVANCE TECHNOLOGY, INC. (1983) *Local Operation of Title I, ESEA 1976–82*, McLean, VA, Advance Technology, Inc.

ELMORE, R. AND MCLAUGHLIN, M. (1982) 'Strategic choice in Federal education policy: The compliance-assistance trade-off' in LIEBERMAN, A. AND MCLAUGHLIN M. (Eds) *Policymaking in Education* (Eighty-first Yearbook of the National Society for the Study of Education) Chicago, IL, University of Chicago Press.

KENNEDY, M. M., JUNG, R. K. AND ORLAND, M. E. (1986) *Poverty, Achievement and the Distribution of Compensatory Education Services* (First interim report of the National Assessment of Chapter 1) Washington, DC, U.S. Department of Education.

9
How Fiscal Accountability and Program Quality Can Be Insured for Chapter 1

Allan Odden

For fifteen years after the enactment of Title 1 of the Elementary and Secondary Education Act of 1965 (now Chapter 1 of the Educational Consolidation and Improvement Act of 1981), regulations were developed to insure that Federal dollars were spent on supplemental educational services for low-achieving students in schools with concentrations of pupils from economically disadvantaged homes. It was not an easy task. There are tens of thousands of Chapter 1 eligible schools across the nation's more than 16,000 school districts in the fifty different state educational systems. Developing a regulatory structure that worked across the widely diverse schools in which Chapter 1 students were taught proved to be time consuming and challenging.

By the late 1970s, however, that task basically was accomplished. Yet, almost immediately, people began to raise issues about the quality of Chapter 1 educational services. Many felt that fiscal accountability had been realized 'on the back of program quality'. As evidence in support of concern, some state and local Chapter 1 coordinators were even quoted as saying that: 'program quality was fiscal compliance'. But most scholars, local educators involved in Chapter 1 programs, and even policymakers admitted that the fifteen-year focus on developing a regulatory system to insure fiscal integrity had drawn attention away from the substance of programs provided with Chapter 1 funding and that insuring program quality was a key, unresolved issue that needed to be addressed.

The purpose of this chapter is to identify policy options that retain adequate fiscal accountability as well as insure program quality. The first section briefly summarizes the economic and political science literatures related to these issues. The economic literature covers intergovernmental grant structures and empirical research on the effects of various grant designs on education spending in local districts and schools. The political science literature covers the politics surrounding redistributive programs, of which Chapter 1 is a major example. The second section reviews more specifically the literature on Chapter 1/Title I, and within that, current knowledge about how the current fiscal accountability structure works. The third section addresses the issue of program integrity, and reviews various approaches to insuring the quality of Chapter 1 educational programs and services. The chapter concludes with alternative policy recommendations.

Economic and Political Science Knowledge Concerning Chapter 1 Fiscal Accountability

Economic literature that informs thinking about how to insure Chapter 1 fiscal accountability includes that on intergovernmental grant design and empirical research on how various grant structures have worked in education, including the grant structure for Chapter 1/Title I. The political science literature includes that on Federal program implementation, the bulk of which concerns Title I/Chapter 1 implementation, and the current theory of program implementation.

Economic Literature

The public finance literature suggests that intergovernmental grants can be divided into a number of categories. First, education grants can be unrestricted or restricted, i.e., either block grants with few, if any, restrictions on how the dollars can be spent (other than on education generally) or targeted, categorical grants which specify the type of program and/or student on which the funds must be spent. Second, education grants can be non-matching or can require districts to match, under some formula, Federal (or state) dollars with local dollars. The matching rate can be a constant percentage across all districts or variable according to specified characteristics. If variable, the characteristic generally used to determine the matching rate is a fiscal capacity measure so more Federal (or state) revenues would be provided to districts lower in fiscal capacity and less to districts higher in fiscal capacity. Chapter 1 is an example of a restricted grant without a required local match; funds are restricted to expenditures on services provided to Chapter 1 eligible students.

Economic grant theory predicts how local governments — school districts in the case of Chapter 1 — would respond in terms of changes in expenditures to funds received under different grant designs. General, unrestricted or block grants (now provided through state school finance equalization formulas) are predicted to change expenditures the least. So, some of an education block grant (from the Federal or state government) would be used to increase local educational expenditures but some also would be used to substitute for local revenues, thus lowering local tax rates or increasing local expenditures on some other function. Restricted, categorical grants for special student needs are predicted to increase local expenditures about the same amount as the grant. Restricted grants with matching requirements are predicted to increase local expenditures the most, at least the sum of the amount of the Federal grant and the required local match.

Empirical research pretty much supports these predictions. A recent synthesis of the local impact of intergovernmental education aid programs (Tsang and Levin, 1983) found that state equalization (unrestricted) aid produced a local expenditure response elasticity that ranged from 0.16 to 1.06, with most elasticities in the 0.3 to 0.7 range. In other words, the average response was to use about half of unrestricted aid on higher education expenditures and to use the other half to substitute for local revenues. State categorical (restricted) aid produced a local expenditure elasticity that ranged from 0.17 to 1.8, with the average elasticity being around 1.0. So restricted aid tended to produce a larger local response with spending, on average, increasing dollar-for-dollar of categorical aid.

The local expenditure response for Federal restricted aid was even larger than for state restricted aid. The elasticities ranged from 0.7 to 1.0, with one study finding an elasticity of 4.4 for Federal Title I aid. Moreover, the lower elasticities for Federal aid tended to occur in studies prior to 1975, i.e., before the development and firm implementation of the Federal, Title I (now Chapter 1) regulatory structure. Nearly all elasticities in post-1975 studies were at least 1.0. Thus it is safe to conclude that Federal Chapter 1 aid produces at least a dollar-for-dollar local increase in educational spending, which is precisely its minimum goal.

In other words, the current functioning of Chapter 1 produces the desired local allocative effects, as compared to less than desired effects produced in the early 1970s (Barro, 1978). As a result, it can be argued that the current structure of the Chapter 1 formula is adequate — it stimulates an increase in local spending at least equal to the size of the Federal grant. While the formula could be redesigned to strengthen its local fiscal impact, that would entail a change in the fiscal goal of Chapter 1. As currently designed, it produces the desired local fiscal effect.

Political Science Literature

Political science literature that pertains to Chapter 1 fiscal accountability includes that on Federal policy implementation, of which the bulk of studies analyze Title I/Chapter 1 implementation, and emerging theory concerning program implementation. In research syntheses in the mid-1970s and again in 1986, Kirst and Jung argue that initial problems in local Title I/Chapter 1 implementation essentially were overcome over time, that initially the task of implementing a large Federal program was a new and unknown task to local educators who made many mistakes in responding to the initial law and fledgling initial regulations (Kirst and Jung, 1980; Jung and Kirst, 1986). But over time, both local educators and Federal and state regulation writers and compliance monitors were able to develop a structure that was understandable and implementable at the local level. Basically, Kirst and Jung argue that the well-known early problems surrounding Title I implementation should not prejudice conclusions about current local capacity to implement a Federal program of targeted educational services; that capacity essentially has been developed and local practices, on balance, reflect the intent of extant law and regulation. Peterson, Rabe and Wong (1986) make essentially the same argument for Federal redistributive programs across several functional areas, including education.

From a different theoretical perspective, Hargrove (1983) provides reasons for why a strong regulatory structure is needed for Chapter 1, reasons that reflect the realities of political pressures in the USA. For redistributive governmental programs that allocate dollars disproportionately (such as Chapter 1 which allocates more funds to areas with more poor children), Hargrove postulates that political pressures function to blunt the strength of a redistributive program and transform it over time into a more proportionally distributive program. Thus, Hargrove argues that redistributive policies must be accompanied by tough regulatory structures that maintain the redistributive characteristics.

Indeed, analyses of the long-term impact of state school finance reforms, which were designed to distribute more state aid to property poor school districts, support Hargrove's assertions. In nearly all states, political pressures produced legislative changes over time that diluted the redistributive elements of new school finance formulas enacted in the 1970s (see the series of articles in the *Journal of Education Finance*, edited by Goertz and Hickrod, 1983a and 1983b).

Moreover, Hargrove's example of his theoretical point is Chapter 1. He reviewed the early history of Title I which shows that most districts and schools initially spread Title I dollars across all students in a school. That practice led to the development of a regulatory structure to target funds to low-achieving students in schools with concentrations of poor children. He also notes that the energy expended in developing and implementing these regulations resulted in a shifting of attention from program quality to fiscal compliance and accountability. While he leaves the reader with this unresolved dilemma, his basic point is that political theory holds that redistributive policies must be accompanied by a set of regulations 'with teeth' in order for the policy to maintain its redistributive thrust over time.

In short, both the economic and political science literatures suggest that the main elements currently embodied in Chapter 1 — a restricted, categorical funding formula together with a stringent regulatory structure — are needed in order to maintain the integrity of Chapter 1 as a program of targeted assistance. While the empirical literature on the spending effects of Chapter 1 seems to lend overall support to these claims, in order to determine whether Hargrove's dilemma can be resolved, it is still necessary to have a more detailed analysis of the functioning of the regulations, an outlining of strategies that can improve program quality, and an analysis of whether the two are inherently in conflict.

Current Functioning of Chapter 1 Rules and Regulations

There are dozens of rules and regulations covering both fiscal accountability and program integrity for Chapter 1. The following represent the key areas related to fiscal distribution and accountability:

- allocation to local districts,
- comparability of resources across schools before the allocation of Chapter 1,
- allocation to (targeting) schools and students within districts,
- maintenance of effort, and
- supplement, and not supplant requirements.

In the main, recent research concludes that these provisions are working pretty much as intended. The congressionally mandated study conducted in the mid-1970s found that Title I funds were allocated to districts according to the poverty criteria in the law. Districts with greater numbers and per cent of students from low-income families received more Chapter 1 (then Title I) funding than districts with fewer such students. In short, the Federal goal for Chapter 1 of providing additional resources to districts enrolling students from economically disadvantaged backgrounds is attained by Chapter 1. While there always can be technical arguments about which poverty criteria to use in allocating funds, the criteria that have been used for nearly two decades work and determine how Federal funds are distributed to local districts.

The remaining regulation categories pertain to within district allocations. Comparability regulations were created to insure that, within a district, schools had equivalent resources before Chapter 1 funds were distributed. The regulations were developed in earlier times when research showed significant intra-district inequities in the allocation of state and local resources, and that the impact of Title I funds often was simply to raise the level of Title I school resources closer to the district average. Comparability also was a critical issue when many districts paid elementary teachers less than secondary teachers before the advent of widespread collective bargaining. Today, most collective bargaining agreements require equal teacher salaries for all teachers in a district and equitable mechanisms for distributing resources across schools.

Thus even though Chapter 1 regulations have 'loosened' the

comparability regulations, recent studies of Chapter 1 administrative practices and policies in several states conclude that the changes appear not to have eroded within district, across school comparability. Again, while several technical issues surround the comparability issue, current practice in most states is guided by policies that insure uniform teacher salary policies within districts, and equitable distributions of teachers and instructional materials across schools before the allocation of Chapter 1 funds. In other words, comparability regulations seem to be having their intended effect.

District allocations of Chapter 1 funds to schools and students are constrained by targeting regulations that are designed to funnel Chapter 1 dollars into schools with the highest concentrations of poor students and, within those schools, to students with the greatest academic needs. Recent studies also confirm that these regulations are generally working as intended. Most districts identify poor students as either those students from families receiving Aid to Families with Dependent Children (AFDC) assistance or those students eligible for free or reduced lunch. Further, districts tend to allocate Chapter 1 funds to schools with a concentration of these students, that is, at or above the district average, or distribute funds on a school-by-school basis beginning with the school with the highest concentration. Sometimes, districts identify particular grade ranges for computing poverty concentration, such as just K through 3 or just 7 through 12, but then distribute funds on the basis of poverty concentration within those grades.

Within schools, general practice is to identify eligible students as those scoring below a certain level on a standardized achievement test. In most cases, services are provided to students scoring below the fiftieth percentile; the plurality of districts target the lowest scoring students as those to serve first.

Again, there are numerous technical intricacies surrounding these school and student targeting provisions, but recent research confirms that general practices reflect the letter and spirit of Chapter 1 — that, within districts, funds are distributed to the schools with the highest concentrations of poor students, and within those schools, to students with the greatest academic needs (Farrar and Milsap, 1986).

The 'maintenance of effort' requirement today has little practical effect. When first implemented, it required states, districts and schools to maintain the level of fiscal support for schools that was present before the onset of Title I (now Chapter 1) funds. Since education revenues rise every year, maintenance of effort has rarely been a problem. Even in the depths of the early 1980s recession, all but a handful of states and districts were able to meet the exact letter of maintenance of effort. This regulation could be given more teeth by indexing the requirement by an inflation factor, to require an inflation-adjusted maintenance of effort. It also could be strengthened, now that enrollments are rising in many places, by requiring maintenance of effort in per pupil terms. However, there is no groundswell of support for strengthening maintenance of effort requirements. Its general intent — to prevent the retraction of resources upon the arrival of Chapter 1 funds — seems pretty much to have been accomplished.

'Supplement, not supplant' regulations are designed to insure that services provided with Chapter 1 funds are actually additional services for students served and do not just supplant other services they otherwise would have received. Initially, supplement, not supplant regulations remedied a major flaw in the delivery of Chapter 1 (then Title I) services in numerous schools. Students often were 'pulled out' of regular reading classes and provided remedial reading by a Chapter 1 funded teacher. Even though the class size in the pullout arrangement might have been lower and even though, in some cases, the services were provided by a reading expert, the fact remained that students missed their regular reading instruction. The initial supplement, not supplant regulations addressed this obvious problem.

But subsequent attempts to comply with this regulation have raised equally important, though more subtle questions about what constitutes compliance. Common practice today is to continue the pullout structure. While students are not pulled out of reading and mathematics classes, they tend to be pulled out of science or social studies classes, physical education classes or even elective classes. Even though the Chapter 1 instruction in reading/language arts and mathematics clearly supplements their regular reading/language arts and mathematics instruction, it nevertheless supplants other instructional and educational services to which the students normally are entitled.

A problem is that auditors like a pullout arrangement since it leaves a cleaner audit trail. With respect to reading/language arts and mathematics, such a practice for delivering Chapter 1 services clearly supplements and does not supplant services for those academic subjects.

But it is a tricky task to provide Chapter 1 services that clearly supplement services regularly provided in specific subjects but do not supplant any other regularly provided educational services. Accomplishing the task and leaving a 'clean' audit trail entails additional challenges. 'Clean' examples would include before or after school programs and summer school programs, strategies that are being tried in some places across the country. Not so obviously clean examples (at least to most auditors) include the use of resource teachers for individual and small group attention for Chapter 1 students during regular seatwork, pullout programs for more intensive work during regular seatwork, small classes for Chapter 1 students (instead of the regular large class), and additional classes with different teaching strategies for Chapter 1 students who do not learn an instructional objective in the regular class.

The point here is that compliance with supplement, not supplant regulations merges fiscal accountability and program quality issues, and begins to highlight differences between auditors and education program specialists. The point also is that the standard pullout practice, which auditors have accepted as compliance with supplement, not supplant regulations, is more clearly becoming the potential juncture at which fiscal accountability and program quality may be at odds.

Nevertheless, the overall conclusion on Chapter 1 fiscal accountability regulations and requirements is that they seem to be in place and working as intended. In the main, if not enhancing program quality, they do not seem to be interfering with program quality (*ibid*).

Chapter 1 program quality regulations cover three basic arenas:

- needs assessment
- size, scope and quality, and
- evaluation and sustained effects analysis.

Most districts and schools already had and continue to have ongoing needs assessment activities associated with Chapter 1. The idea is to have a mechanism in place, different from any testing program that might be used to identify Chapter 1 eligible pupils, to assess generally and specifically the academic areas/subjects in which Chapter 1 eligible students need additional help. The needs assessment then identifies the substantive focus of Chapter 1 services.

The evaluation and sustained effects requirements were substantially modified when the Congress changed Title I to Chapter 1. But most states and school districts still require some type of annual pre- and post-testing for evaluating the effectiveness of local Chapter 1 programs, so evaluation practice has changed relatively little. The sustained effects requirement under Title I was designed to assess the longer term impact of services, but it had difficulty being implemented across the country, was eliminated in Chapter 1 and is part of state and local practice in some but far from all places.

While both the needs assessment and evaluation requirements have a clear rationale, and generally are part of local Chapter 1 practice, they tend to affect only minimally the substance of Chapter 1 services. Their clearest impact has been to target reading/language arts and mathematics as subjects in which to concentrate the provision of additional services and as subjects to test to identify annual student performance change. In some places, needs assessments have identified weaknesses in higher level thinking skills, but this is an emerging trend and does not reflect average practice.

The size, scope and quality regulations are those which could be expected to have the most impact on the substance of local services, but here too the impact has been minimal. General practice under these regulations has been to identify the minimum number of dollars per pupil that must be provided in order for a school to have enough funds to create a program of sufficient size, scope and quality. Rarely has this potentially substantive regulation gone beyond the minimum dollar requirement.

Finally, Chapter 1 has required a fiscal and program audit for many years. Conducted by people external to the district and school, the audit has served as a check on both funds allocation and funds use. Typically, however, audits focus on tracking funds down through the system to the student receiving services in a Chapter 1 program. Thus, the audit side of the Federal and sometimes state governments has functioned to create a 'press' for districts and schools to have 'clean' audit trails. Put differently, there is little if any push from auditors on program quality issues, and as the discussion on the supplement, not supplant regulation suggests, at times the auditor press can negatively influence program quality.

In summing up all of the above, it is fair to conclude that the current regulatory structure is working at least as far as fiscal accountability is concerned. Yes, technical adjustments probably could improve practice in some places, and technical changes in other places could probably alter the distribution of funds and perhaps even improve the efficiency of the uses of Chapter 1 funds. But as currently structured, Chapter 1 law, regulations and rules pretty much channel funds to districts with poor children, within those districts to schools with the highest concentration of poor children, and within those schools to students with the greatest academic needs. State and local resources are distributed comparably across schools before the allocation of Chapter 1 funds, and Chapter 1 services supplement and do not supplant other regularly provided educational services.

Further, the regulatory and program structure of Chapter 1/Title I is understood and can be implemented without administrative, paper work or procedural overburden at the state, district and school level. Indeed, several research studies conducted for the Congress at the beginning of the 1980s reached these conclusions. Further, syntheses of research studies (Moore *et al*, 1983; Knapp, Stearns, Turnbull, David and Peterson, 1983) on Federal program implementation over the last twenty years also reach such conclusions (Kirst and Jung, 1980; Jung and Kirst, 1986).

In addition, when the initial Chapter 1 legislation essentially eliminated the Title I regulatory structure, Federal pressure from the audit side combined with pressure from both state and local program levels essentially reinstated the old Title I regulations as non-regulatory Federal guidance. When regulations for Chapter 1 were finally adopted, most of the non-regulatory guidelines were adopted, save for the identified substantive changes in comparability, and essentially minor changes in the other areas discussed above. Finally, a recent study of the impact of these regulatory changes on administrative policy and practice and actual behavior at the state and local level concluded that Chapter 1 modifications had changed actual resource allocation practices very little, that practices characteristic of Chapter 1 in 1985 pretty much reflected practices characteristic of Title I in 1980 (Farrar and Milsap, 1986).

These findings are not altogether surprising. Chapter 1 is a mature program, now more than twenty years old. It is administered by a fairly tightly coupled, vertically aligned structure of Title I/Chapter 1 professionals (loyalists) from the Federal government, to the fifty states and to the local Chapter 1 coordinators. These people have learned over the years how to implement Chapter 1/Title I, they have intimate familiarity with its rules and regulations, and, in the main, believe in both the program and in the regulations. They generally feel the regulations 'protect' Chapter 1 as a program of services to educationally needy students in schools with high concentrations of children from poverty backgrounds.

Further, over the years, these people have painstakingly helped develop a set of standard operating procedures that implement the law, rules and regulations. Thus, when given freedom to stray from that structure by the lack of regulations in the early days of Chapter 1, most did not. Many used the old Title I regulations to establish state policy on Chapter 1 for both fiscal distribution and accountability. These same people tended to be relieved, then, when the non-regulatory guidelines became Chapter 1 regulations, save for the above mentioned changes.

But concluding that Chapter 1 probably has a regulatory structure that insures fiscal accountability and seems not to be in need of drastic overhaul is not the same as concluding that this structure also addresses adequately the issue of program quality. Those issues are discussed in the next section.

Insuring Chapter 1 Program Integrity and Quality

'Compliance is quality', is a comment made by many state and local Chapter 1 coordinators. That comment underscores an apparent dilemma between fiscal accountability and program quality: does accomplishment of the former negate accomplishment of the latter? The answer is no, but the reality is that the intensive focus on developing a fiscal accountability structure that works has, for whatever reasons, substantively overlooked issues of program quality. So the regulatory structure insures the correct distribution of dollars and the provision of services to Chapter 1 eligible services, but is essentially silent on the substance of those services. Whether the fiscal accountability structure is in conflict with what can be done about program quality can be answered only after identification of how the Federal government can address the issue of program quality.

In addressing this issue, the Federal government must face the reality that it is at least two major levels away from the actual delivery of education services. Constitutionally states control education; in most states, local districts administer and deliver education services. Thus,

Federal programs are developed and delivered within the context of state as well as local curriculum and teaching policy.

Put differently, the Federal government does not 'run' Chapter 1 programs. They are 'run' by states and local districts and schools. Services funded by Chapter 1 dollars are delivered by individual teachers in local school settings, which are under the control of local policy and state law. In short, the Federal government is dependent on state and local educators to deliver the Chapter 1 program. Whatever the regulations, the Chapter 1 program becomes what local educators deliver. Thus, what the Chapter 1 program 'is' depends on the nature and substance of services teachers provide to Chapter 1 students in thousands of classrooms across the country.

While the Federal government can channel resources that support the provision of extra services to Chapter 1 eligible students, a key issue for the Federal government in addressing the program quality issue is how it can energize state and local talent towards the substantive goals of Chapter 1 knowing that it cannot dictate the substance of curriculum and teaching policy. Put differently, the challenge is to determine how the Federal government can influence local educators to apply the best educational practices in the delivery of Chapter 1 programs without being able to regulate the key arenas — curriculum and teaching policy — associated with those effective practices.

This, however, may not be as large a problem as thought. With fiscal accountability 'in place', Chapter 1 programs in several states are gradually beginning to refocus on program quality issues. The substance of Chapter 1 programs in many places is beginning to include some of the best educational practices deriving from the effective teaching and schools research.[1] These program transformations are quite exciting, have occurred essentially outside of any Federal prodding, and can be seen in Chapter 1 programs in numerous states. In Vermont, for example, Chapter 1 resources are being used to develop and implement effective teaching and schools practices across the entire state, and in many schools across the entire curriculum. But in most states, these developments are still contained within state and local Chapter 1 offices, and often do not affect the core education program.

Thus, even in the many states in which long overdue attention is shifting to Chapter 1 program quality issues, it still seems to be insulated from penetrating overall curriculum and teaching policy which really defines the substance of the state/local education program.

In short, even though the emergence of research-based effective teaching and schooling practices in Chapter 1 programs is a good sign, it is still a vulnerable trend because its influence on the core education program is constrained by the policies, outside of its control, that surround that core.

Not only is curriculum and teaching policy for the core program formally under the direct control of the state, but also states see those arenas as under their control and that which ought to be the substance of their primary policy attention. A recent, federally supported study (Milne, Moskowitz and Ellman, 1983) looked at state approaches to programs for special student populations, including those receiving compensatory education. A key conclusion was that the primary state education concern was for the core education program, and that special needs, categorical programs (like Chapter 1 or state compensatory education programs) take a secondary place to this driving interest.

This ranking of priorities, though, makes sense. Education is a state responsibility and thus states must make the core of the education program its primary focus. Whether the divergence in priorities between the Federal and state governments is cause for concern depends in part on the degree to which categorical program quality and the core education program quality are linked. The fact is that they are inextricably linked, although both states and the Federal government not only lost sight of this reality in the 1970s but also let the quality of the core program slip into decline. Attempts to solidify the integrity of Chapter 1, then, drifted unconsciously into a total focus on the categorical program per se.

Thus, primary state concern for the quality of the core program was viewed as problematic at the Federal level because it seemed to demote the issue of Chapter 1 quality to a second level status. Today this state perspective is viewed as a strength for two reasons. First, the dependence of categorical program quality on the quality of the core education program has been rediscovered. Second, nearly all states have taken a series of steps to improve the quality of the regular, core educational program. Put differently, the state education reform movement emerged at the right time for Chapter 1 because if the issue was how to improve Chapter 1 program integrity, the answer primarily hinged on the quality of the core program, how to improve the quality of that program and how to attach the Chapter 1 program to it.

California's recent education reform initiatives and administrative changes in compensatory education provide one example of these reconnections. First, and contrary to popular opinion, the thrust of California's recent education excellence initiatives has been to strengthen the curriculum program provided students in the middle and bottom quartiles, the students for whom program quality had withered the most. A major problem for the middle track was that they faced the 'Shopping Mall' high school and were offered mainly 'soft' courses to take which, even if passed, did not add up to any body of substantive knowledge. The problem for the bottom track, categorical program-eligible students was that most of their curriculum was 'watered' down, so even if they mastered it, they simply learned less than other students. However analyzed, the system benefited the bottom three quartiles of students too little.

The strategy in response was to *define a core, academic curriculum program to which all students would be exposed and which all students would be expected to master.* California's reform was essentially targeted on this issue and included increased high school graduation requirements, development of state model curriculum standards in the core academic areas, modification and expansion of state testing programs, changes in state textbook adoption criteria, and changes in teacher and administrator training and evaluation. California accompanied these attempts to strengthen the core curriculum with several administrative changes for categorical programs, all essentially designed to require local educators to align services provided under categorical funds with the regular curriculum program; the extra, supplementary services were to help students learn the regular curriculum program. Each school receiving categorical funding also was required to develop an overall school improvement plan (reflecting knowledge that education improvement is a schoolwide phenomenon) and to show how the needs of students eligible for categorical program services were integrated into the overall school program.

Not all states have enacted the breadth of changes included in California's strategies, but many have. Of course, for states or local districts that still have weak regular education programs and are not taking initiatives to strengthen them, the Federal government and Chapter 1 programs remain at a fundamental disadvantage. Nevertheless, the fact remains that the primary element related to Chapter 1 program quality is beyond the direct grasp of the Federal education arm, that Chapter 1 is a program on the periphery of that which determines its quality. The challenge is to determine how the Federal government can exert indirect influence on the core so that local core programs are sound and so local Chapter 1 programs are attached, as they should be, to it.

Even if that challenge could be met, the issue remaining is whether state attempts to strengthen the core curriculum program actually result in improved curricula at the local district and school level. Since state efforts to accomplish that task are still in their infancy, firm answers cannot be provided at this point. But several pieces of knowledge suggest that these state strategies are experiencing success. First, student exposure to curriculum content is a primary determinant of student learning of that content; thus, insuring that all students are exposed to a defined, core curriculum ought to improve student knowledge of the substance included in that core. Second, curriculum alignment seems to be a characteristic of instructionally effective schools and districts. State attempts to align academic goals, curriculum objectives, texts and tests reinforce at a higher level of government this school and district policy. Third, nearly all emerging reports on the impact of state education reforms document structural changes in the direction of reform goals and improved student performance on academic tests. In California, specifically, there have been dramatic changes in academic course offering with large increases in mathematics, science, world history, economics and foreign language (Guthrie *et al*, 1986). Fourth, states can combine these content initiatives with process strategies to support implementation on a school-by-school basis; such strategies reflect knowledge not only that the site for education improvement is the school unit, but also that states *can* design effective school site education improvement programs (Odden and Anderson, 1986). Fifth, recent knowledge on local implementation and educational change documents the importance of top level vision, leadership, management and implementation assistance. Further, this research concludes that top-down initiation can be successful if accompanied by long-term commitment and ongoing technical assistance (Fullan, 1985). Finally, there is at least preliminary data suggesting that this combination of state curriculum focus, categorical program alignment and school site improvement can work for Chapter 1 students (Odden, 1986).

In short, the key ingredients for improving Chapter 1 program quality seem to be the following:

- a strong regular curriculum program,
- alignment of Chapter 1 services with the regular program,
- a school-based education improvement plan that specifically stipulates how Chapter 1 services are integrated within it, and
- a school plan that specifically incorporates the programs and strategies based on the education effectiveness literatures.

Strategic Alternatives and Policy Implications for Insuring Chapter 1 Fiscal Accountability and Program Quality

Five basic strategic alternatives could be considered on the basis of the issues discussed in the previous sections. They will be covered from the least to the most effective.

The first would be to *completely deregulate Chapter 1*, a strategy proposed in the early 1980s. This strategy mainly reflects ideological rather than substantive grounds. This strategy will accomplish neither Chapter 1 fiscal accountability nor program quality. Both the theoretical and empirical economic literature concludes that such a policy would dilute Chapter 1 as a program. Further, both the theoretical and empirical political science implementation literature suggests the same result.[2] And finally, if the road to program quality is a strengthened core program and the linking of Chapter 1 to the core, complete deregulation is silent on both matters. In short, deregulation may eliminate governmental interference at the local level but it is unlikely to strengthen either Chapter 1 fiscal accountability or program quality.

A second strategy would be to take seriously the school site as the unit of education improvement and to *require schools to develop a schoolwide education improvement program* and show how Chapter 1 services would be part of that overall plan. A specific requirement would be to *align all Chapter 1 services with the regular curriculum program* to insure that such services were provided to help Chapter 1 students master that program. This strategy retains the current fiscal accountability structure and adds modifications to the size, scope and quality regulations. This strategy does not address directly the quality of the regular school program but does take seriously the school site as the locus of education improvement and the alignment of categorical services with the core education program.

A third strategy would consider both *fiscal accountability and program quality issues primarily on a schoolwide basis*. Schools could be required to develop a school-site education improvement program and to design mechanisms for Chapter 1 students to participate and be successful in this overall program. An additional requirement could be to align all Chapter 1 provided services to the regular curriculum program to insure that such services were designed to help Chapter 1 students master that program. Fiscal accountability could stop at the school level if there were evidence of adequate Chapter 1 student performance. The Chapter 1 grant could even be accompanied by an incentive bonus if Chapter 1 student performance met or exceeded certain performance targets. These modifications would link the schoolwide thrust to individual impacts. The danger in this approach is that schools with concentrations of poor children might 'narrow' the curriculum to basic skills and knowledge, ignoring both the need for a broadly-based curriculum program and a curriculum which develops higher level thinking skills.

This strategy would include such new program structures as intensive extra help during individual seatwork, before and after school services, summer school programs, and other ways to provide services that are really supplemental. Consideration also could be given to providing Chapter 1 services in *very small classes* now that research shows class size can make a major positive impact on student achievement if it is small enough and if more than 100 hours of instruction are provided over the year (Glass, Cahen, Smith and Filby, 1982). Since this strategy includes requirements for showing performance improvements for Chapter 1 students, somewhat 'bolder' program structures could be allowed.

A fourth approach also would focus on the school as a unit but would *condition school level fiscal accountability upon demonstrated schoolwide use of proven effective strategies from the effective teaching and schools research*. Use of this option could be further conditioned by a minimum requirement for poor student concentration, such as 50 per cent. Several pilot projects of this type have been tried across the country with promising success (Stallings and Krasavage, 1986; Robbins, 1986). The idea here is that effective teaching and schools techniques have been developed from research on what works in classrooms and schools with concentrations of Chapter 1 type students. The assumption is that if both these school characteristics and effective teaching practices were put into place, all students, including Chapter 1 students, would likely perform better. The further assumption is that the impact on Chapter 1 students would not be diluted even if non-Chapter 1 eligible students benefited from the new activities.

The fifth strategy would include all of the components of strategy two and any of the other components of strategies three and four and would *add initiatives to strengthen the regular curriculum program*. Set-asides could be provided for states (and possible local districts) to develop a sound and deep regular curriculum program; to develop model curricular guides to help implement that curriculum; to develop a testing and assessment program to identify student performance in that curriculum; to provide specific analyses of how Chapter 1 students perform in order to target school, district and state foci for Chapter 1 services, to identify textbooks and materials that would be appropriate for that curriculum; and to identify supplementary instructional materials and strategies aligned with that curriculum that could be used in Chapter 1 programs. The idea here would be to stimulate states to strengthen the core curriculum program for all grades, on the assumption that it conditions the basic impact of even the highest quality Chapter 1 program. The state assessment program — if it were aligned with state curriculum objectives, and included several subjects and higher level thinking skills as well as basic skills — would help stimulate local response to a state-outlined core, curriculum program.

All of these strategies could be implemented with modest changes in the size, scope and quality regulations.

Summary

This chapter has two basic points. The first is that the current structure of Chapter 1 — the law and its accompanying rules and regulations — is adequate for insuring fiscal accountability, and the means for implementing this structure at the state and local level are firmly developed and function relatively well. The second point is that the quality of Chapter 1 programs depends primarily on the quality of curriculum and teaching in local school districts, two arenas essentially beyond direct influence by the Federal government. Nevertheless, there are several strategies available to the Federal government for improving Chapter 1 program quality including the following:

- requiring all Chapter 1 sites to have a schoolwide education improvement program with Chapter 1 integrated into it;
- requiring Chapter 1 services to be aligned with the regular educational program so Chapter 1 helps low-achieving students to learn the regular curriculum;
- conditioning receipt of Chapter 1 funds on schools implementing research-based effective teaching and schools strategies; and
- providing new funds for states to develop model curriculum guides for a strengthened academic program, a testing program to assess student progress in that program, and supplemental instructional strategies and materials to help students such as Chapter 1 students who do not fully learn curriculum objectives during regular instruction.

Notes

1 See Wittrock (1986) Chapters 12, 13, 14 and 18 for summaries of this research and Kyle (1985) for programs and policies to implement the results of this literature in state and local school systems, schools and classroom.
2 Recent experience with Chapter 2 funds reinforces this point. The major redistributive program that was 'rolled into' Chapter 2 was federal desegregation assistance that had benefited mainly large cities. Without regulations requiring this disproportionate allocation, states redistributed these funds on about an equal per pupil basis to all districts in the state within three years.

References

BARRO, S. M. (1978) 'Federal education goals and policy instruments: An assessment of the "strings" attached to categorical grants in education' in TIMPANE, M. (Ed) *The Federal Interest in Financing Schooling*, Santa Monica, CA, The Rand Corporation.
FARRAR, E. AND MILSAP, M. A. (1986) *State and Local Administration of the Chapter 1 Program*, Cambridge, MA, Abt Associates.

FULLAN, M. (1985) 'Change processes and strategies at the local level' *Elementary School Journal*, **85**, pp. 391–422.

GLASS, G. V., CAHEN, L. S., SMITH, M. L. AND FILBY, N. N. (1982) *School Class Size*, Beverly Hills, CA, Sage.

GOERTZ, M. E. AND HICKROD, G. A. (Eds) (1983a) 'Introduction: Evaluating the school finance reforms of the 1970s and early 1980s' [Special issue], *Journal of Education Finance*, **8**, 4.

GOERTZ, M. E. AND HICKROD, G. A. (Eds) (1983b) 'Evaluating the school finance reforms of the 1970s and 1980s: Part 2' [Special issue], *Journal of Education Finance*, **9**, 1.

GUTHRIE, J., KIRST, M., HAYWARD, G., ODDEN, A., EVANS, J., ADAMS, J., EMMET, T. AND HARTWIG, F. (1986) *Conditions of Education in California, 1986–87.* Berkeley, CA, University of California, School of Education, Policy Analysis for California Education.

HARGROVE, E. (1983) 'The search for implementation theory' in ZECKHAUSER, R. J. AND LEEBAERT, D. (Eds) *What Role for Government?* Durham, NC, Duke University Press.

JUNG, R. AND KIRST, M. (1986) 'Beyond mutual adaptation and into the bully pulpit: Recent research on the Federal role in education', *Educational Administration Quarterly*, **22**, 3, pp. 80–109.

KIRST, M. AND JUNG, R. (1980) 'The utility of a longitudinal approach in assessing implementation: A thirteen-year view of Title I, ESEA', *Education Evaluation and Policy Analysis*, **2**, 5, pp. 17–34.

KNAPP, M. S., STEARNS, M. S., TURNBULL, B. J., DAVID, J. L. AND PETERSON, S. M. (1983) *Cumulative Effects of Federal Education Policies on Schools and Districts*, Menlo Park, CA, SRI International.

KYLE, R. (Ed) (1985). *Reaching for Excellence*, Washington, DC, US Government Printing Office.

MILNE, A., MOSKOWITZ, J. AND ELLMAN, F. M. (1983) *Serving Special Needs Children: The State Approach*, Washington, DC, Decision Resources Corporation.

MOORE, M. T., GOERTZ, M. E., HARTLE, T. W., WINSLOW, H. R., DAVID, J. L., SJOGREN, J., TURNBULL, B., COLEY, R. J. AND HOLLAND, R. P. (1983) *The Interaction of Federal and Related State Education Programs*, Princeton, NJ, Educational Testing Service.

ODDEN, A. (1986) *Education Reform and Services to Poor Students*, Los Angeles, CA, University of Southern California.

ODDEN, A. AND ANDERSON, B. (1986) 'How successful state education improvement programs work', *Phi Delta Kappan*, **67**, pp. 582–5.

PETERSON, P., RABE, B. AND WONG, K. (1986) *When Federalism Works*, Washington, DC, The Brookings Institution.

ROBBINS, P. (1986) 'The Napa-Vacaville Follow-Through project: Qualitative outcomes, related procedures and implications for practice', *Elementary School Journal*, **87**, pp. 139–58.

STALLINGS, J. AND KRASAVAGE, E. (1986) 'Program implementation and student achievement in a four-year Madeline Hunter Follow-Through project', *Elementary School Journal*, **87**, pp. 117–39.

TSANG, M. C. AND LEVIN, H. (1983) 'The impact of intergovernmental grants on education spending', *Review of Educational Research*, **53**, pp. 329–67.

WITTROCK, M. (Ed.) (1986) *Handbook of Research on Teaching* (3rd edn) New York, Macmillan.

Section 3:
Lessons for Implementation

10
The Next Steps in Urban Education

Charles Glenn

Participation in the conference sponsored by the Office of Educational Research and Improvement (OERI) on 'Alternative Strategies in Compensatory Education' brought into focus a number of concerns about the educational equity efforts to which we have devoted so much attention in Massachusetts.

During my sixteen years as state director of equal educational opportunity, our legislature has adopted a succession of path-breaking funding programs designed to support the education of poor and minority children. These 'carrots' have been paralleled by a series of 'sticks', new requirements upon local school systems designed to prevent segregation and discrimination and to assure the right of students to an effective education. State education staff have employed the most varied forms of monitoring, exhortation, training, publications, litigation, and general nagging, and Boston in particular has been the object of state and Federal court orders on every imaginable aspect of education. As each new effort began, we thought that it would enable us to turn a corner in serving at-risk children. Why have the results been so disappointing when compared with our high expectations?

The two-day discussion of compensatory education came together in my mind with our recent discussions in Massachusetts. The comments that follow are expanded from the notes from which I reacted to several of the papers; they give a state perspective on an issue that is often seen in terms of Federal policy and local services.

Charles Glenn

The Problem

A review of the annual racial statistics in Massachusetts shows that we
are reaching the outer limits of the desegregation strategies that have
absorbed so much of our energies over the past decade. In a number of
communities — Boston, Chelsea, Holyoke, Lawrence, Springfield —
minority students are now in the majority and even our best efforts will
leave some schools predominantly minority in enrollment. In others —
Worcester, Lowell, Lynn, New Bedford, Brockton — there is a
continuing need to assure that the right steps are taken and the wrong
ones avoided. In all cases, however, our attention can now turn to
assuring that 'equal opportunity' has specific educational content and
produces results that make a difference in the lives of poor children.

At the same time, the recent school-by-school assessments
required by our school reform legislation have documented in a
systematic way what we have known all along: that those schools in
which there is a high concentration of poor and minority students show
very disappointing achievement levels. This is true even of some
schools about which we are justly proud. Racial integration may be
producing solid respect and friendship across racial differences. Parents
may feel that the school is responsive to their concerns. Teachers may
take pride and satisfaction in their work. Students may enjoy going to
school. All of this may be happening, and is happening to many urban
schools. Yet students exhibit achievement lags in mastering essential
skills and knowledge, not to mention the higher order ability to 'put
things together' without which the basics are of little use. The bill
comes due in the intermediate and high school, when students suddenly
flop, seem lost, become discouraged, lower their expectations, or quit in
frustration although their elementary education has been in many
respects a substantial success.

We have often said that desegregation of the elementary schools in
Holyoke was a great success and was accompanied by solid educational
improvement, but Hispanic students are dropping out of high school at
an epidemic rate. Worcester could tell the same story, so could
Cambridge and Springfield. Even Boston, where everything seems
more complicated, can point with pride to a number of outstanding
elementary schools with 75 per cent minority enrollment, but lagging
achievement of minority students at the secondary level.

What are we failing to do? How can we assure that the education provided in what are now several hundred desegregated schools can be as consistently solid as it is frequently exciting? How can we focus on achievement without turning our backs on what has been accomplished and learned through twenty years of desegregation effort?

In the operational plan for the fiscal year 1987, the Massachusetts Board of Education placed a coordinated approach to improving urban schools first among its objectives. Rather than undertaking a state-wide effort, the department will work with perhaps fifteen target schools. It intends to continue this work at an accelerating pace for at least five years until every school with a high proportion of poor and at-risk students has developed the capacity to educate them effectively. In the words of the plan:

> The Department will provide assistance to at least six school districts to strengthen programs and services in selected elementary schools enrolling low income and minority students. 1986 state-wide assessment results will be used to select elementary schools in particular need of such assistance, as well as effective schools to serve as models and technical assistance centers. Specific educational objectives designed to benefit at least 3,000 students will be negotiated for each school with an emphasis on the following:
>
> - Strengthening overall educational leadership.
> - Identifying student strengths and needs, and providing programs and services to meet them.
> - Enabling school staff to acquire additional skills to manage and make coordinated, effective use of local, state, and Federal resources (from programs such as Chapter 1, Chapter 188 essential skills and dropout prevention, Chapter 636, transitional bilingual education, special education, gifted and talented, etc.) to reduce fragmentation of regular classroom instruction and unnecessary separation of students. (Massachusetts Board of Education, 1986, p. 2)

Now it is appropriate to become more specific about the steps through which such a new model of urban education could be implemented. Nothing in what follows is without ample precedent in Massachusetts schools and in the work of the Department of Education. Everything that will be proposed is directly supported by research and by experience. The appropriate starting point is this accumulated experience of what works — what can work — in urban schools.

We have learned something about what works and what does not work in desegregation, in creating effective urban schools, and in bringing about broad institutional change.

What Have We Learned From Our Desegregation Efforts?

- It is not enough to assign appropriate numbers of students to a school, and assume that will accomplish either racial integration or improved educational opportunities. A top-down strategy, like Boston's (apart from the magnet district), produces neither solid desegregation nor solid education.
- One of the strengths of a successful desegregation effort is that the staff of a school, and many parents, stretch and grow in response to a clearly articulated challenge. The new energies that become available can be applied directly to educational improvement.
- The central weakness of unsuccessful desegregation efforts is that the energies of staff and parents have not been awakened; instead they become passive and resentful. In short, desegregation only produces the desired results if there is a school-level commitment to making it work.
- Real integration does not occur unless at least two ingredients are present in each desegregated school: (1) a school climate characterized by fairness and mutual respect; and (2) consciously created opportunities for students to work together and learn more from one another. These elements are more important than special curriculum units and activities explicitly concerned with race and ethnicity, but they do not replace them.
- The elements of parent choice were introduced into many desegregation plans as a way of minimizing mandatory reassignments. They have had the largely unanticipated result of strengthening the sense that each school has a clear educational mission, for which it is accountable to parents. Preliminary evidence suggests that it has also had a positive impact on school quality.

- Desegregation can have the effect of raising the expectations for poor and minority students or, unfortunately, of confirming their 'inferior' status through in-school segregation. In other words, it is a high-risk, high-gain strategy for placing them at the top of the educational agenda.
- The factors that make a desegregated school work well also make any school work better!

What Have We Learned From Compensatory Programs?

- Other students make a significant difference; poor students kept isolated with other poor students will not learn as much as poor students who are integrated with middle-class students. As Dean Marshall Smith of the Stanford School of Education writes, 'schools and communities with strong concentrations of poverty have an added negative effect on student achievement above and beyond the student's individual family status' (Smith, 1987, p. 115).
- Schools make a difference. It is not enough to 'plug in' an extra program or resource if the school as a whole remains ineffectual. Some schools serving many poor children are effective, and it is possible to identify many of the characteristics that make them effective, including a clear and shared definition of educational mission, a strong leader who (in what is only an apparent paradox) supports collegial decision-making, continual accountability for results, and a conviction that every child can learn.
- Programs (for example, Chapter 1, special education, bilingual education) are generally only as effective as their setting. It is important that they be aligned for mutual reinforcement with the overall framework within which students are being educated. A recent study suggests that only one classroom teacher in ten knew what the specialist teachers were doing with the children they 'shared'.
- The 'pullout' approach to serving student needs, while it is necessary for some instructional strategies and for some educational needs, has serious drawbacks as the primary mode of providing extra help. Teachers frequently complain about the

disruption of their classrooms, with students coming and going to suit the schedules of specialized programs. Many have the impression that this is somehow mandated by Chapter 1, though it is not.

● Labeling of students for compensatory services can have the effect of enshrining low expectations for those students.

● Our present approaches, while they have been quite successful in their own terms, involve substantial educational costs that were not originally intended when the programs were developed:

(i) Chapter 1 has not only poured billions of Federal dollars into direct instruction of at-risk students, but also has changed the way in which educators think about their responsibilities. It is unlikely that we will ever return to a 'sink or swim' attitude about children from poor families. At the same time, however, the rigid separation of services and centralization of control in the interest of assuring that the most needy students are served — a response to early abuses of the progam — may mean that some schools are actually worse off as a result of the program. 'By increasing the control of the school from the outside', John Chubb (1987) of the Brookings Institution suggests, 'it may discourage' the development of the characteristics of an effective school (p. 244).

(ii) In special education the very success of the individualized approach and intensive additional attention has led to a demand for inclusion of more and more students, and to the development of a poorly understood category of 'learning disability' that can mean almost anything. One critic has remarked that minority students are 'slow' and need compensatory education, while White students are 'learning disabled'. Special education shows signs of being overwhelmed by demand.

(iii) Bilingual education programs are experiencing difficulty connecting with the regular education program. Who should be served? For how long? Is the program's purpose primarily to provide a transition to the use of English, or to develop skills in another language, as well as a cultural heritage? Aren't these desirable goals for every student? Why would any student ever be asked to exit a bilingual program, if — as claimed — it is providing him the best of two educations? The principal may find herself presiding over two schools separated by more than language.

(iv) State compensatory education and urban programs may create additional burdens for harried administrators, to the extent that the funding source insists upon yet another set of goals and objectives to highlight the distinctive contribution of the program.

All of these programs — excellent in themselves — may contribute to the lessening of school-level autonomy. In the interest of quality control for the progam, the conditions for quality in the school as a whole may be undermined. The program may end up serving as a palliative for steadily worsening education.

Schools can only be as dynamic and responsible as their environment will allow them to be. Control and regulation have only a very limited ability to improve education; bad schools don't become good schools by assigning more homework!

Larry Cuban (1987) of Stanford urges that:

Federal or state strategies of school improvement that have goals aimed at changing complex behaviors in children and adults in schools and classrooms should focus less on control and regulation through existing structures and more on incentives and help for those who make on-site judgments. ... In doing so, state and Federal agencies will need to increase schools' capacity to do what they need to do, while holding them responsible for outcomes. (p. 222)

Bringing Together a Coordinated Strategy

How can we put together what we have learned into a strategy that will make a significant difference?

Very little of lasting benefit has been accomplished in education by top-down mandate. Government can, with some success, prevent discrimination and other negative practices, but our ability to mandate real excellence is limited. Excellence in teaching and counseling must happen through individuals in daily contact with students, and it will happen only if they are somehow encouraged and supported to do more than the minimum.

As Edmund Burke observed:

> Our patience will achieve more than our force ... I have never yet seen any plan which has not been mended by the observations of those who were much inferior in understanding to the person who took the lead in the business. By a slow but well-sustained progress, the effect of each step is watched; the good or ill success of the first gives light to us in the second; and so, from light to light, we are conducted through the whole series. ... From hence arises, not an excellence in simplicity, but, one far superior, an excellence in composition. (*Reflections on the Revolution in France*, 1789)

And Cuban (1987) urges that 'state strategies of school improvement that have goals aimed at changing complex behaviors in children and adults in schools and classrooms should focus less on control and regulation through existing structures and more on incentives and help for those who make on-site judgments' (p. 222).

Several operational principles follow:

1   The focus of our efforts should be on the school, not on the school system (which may have a number of fairly prosperous schools as well as schools with many poor and low-achieving students.) This might well mean ranking individual schools state-wide on a measure of the presence of at-risk students (income, home language, identified needs, and other factors included), not on a measure of achievement as the primary selection criterion.

2   The focus of our efforts should be on the school and not on the student who (unless his needs are very specialized) needs an effective overall school environment in order to receive a well-rounded education. It is important to think of the student, not in terms of discrete educational deficiences to be treated, but 'in the round', as an individual to be educated.

3   In order to create an effective school environment for every student, supplemental programs (for example, Chapter 1, special education, bilingual education, state compensatory and

desegregation programs) should be tied closely to the core curriculum.

4   This can happen only if the educational team in each school has the autonomy and flexibility to put together an educational program that makes sense and meets the diverse needs and strengths of the particular students in the school. This has been called 'building commitment to goals among those who actually do the work'.

5   With this autonomy and flexibility must go a strong stress on accountability for results over a reasonable period of time.

6   These 'results' should include the intangibles of citizenship, character, reasoning and creativity, as well as the easily measured skills and knowledge. Note that these intangibles can be taught only in schools where such qualities are manifestly valued!

7   A well-regulated system of parent choice among schools can free each faculty to develop distinctive approaches to excellence, while creating a natural form of accountability for results and for responsiveness to parents.

How Would This Strategy Play Out in a School?

1   The school would have a coordinated system for identifying the educational needs and strengths of each student. For example, a student would not be assessed once for bilingual education and again for special needs. Strengthening the process of entry and exit assessments is a priority for bilingual education officials this year, while special education is planning to identify and disseminate models of student evaluation and placement.

2   The school, not the discrete programs, would function as the basic unit of education, with a cohesive sense of its mission. It would no longer serve as the site for discrete programs with specialized staff 'doing their thing' and controlled from 'downtown'. The principal would be fully responsible for all staff in the school, and for deploying them to assure that every student received the optimal education, taking into account individual needs and strengths.

3   Although the principal would be finally accountable, the staff
    of the school would work together to develop and update
    school-wide educational plans and to share information. As a
    unified faculty, they would set goals and objectives. This
    would require paid planning and coordinating time.

4   In order to put these plans into effect, the staff would be
    encouraged to propose program and schedule modifications
    (such as extended day instruction and year-round or summer
    programs) as well as different ways of grouping staff and
    space.

5   While pullout strategies would still have place, especially for
    students with highly atypical needs, they would be given less
    stress and would in no case be used for administrative
    convenience.

6   The school-level plan would serve as the basis for state and
    Federal grants and plan approvals, as well as for local budget-
    ing. California developed a consolidated form for state and
    Federal grants.

7   Progress in implementing the clear goals and objectives in the
    school-level plan would be assessed every other year. One
    means of assessment would be state-mandated testing, but it
    would be supplemented by other sources of information
    including, possibly, something akin to the accreditation pro-
    cess of peer review.

8   The goals and their assessment would cover more than basic
    skills and knowledge; each school would set goals for the
    development of character and citizenship, as well as for higher
    order thinking and expressive skills.

9   The faculty would be encouraged to develop a distinctive
    approach to educational excellence, not a lowest-common-
    denominator compromise. Parents would have the oppor-
    tunity to transfer their children to another school (without
    loss of services) if it offered an approach to education more
    consistent with their own. In this way parents would be
    specifically empowered and drawn into the educational pro-
    cess of a school with their wholehearted support.

10 Desegregation and integration would continue to be an
    important element of this process:

- for educational progress (avoiding isolation of poor children)
- to assure that students from poor families are taught the whole curriculum, not a 'dumbed-down' inner-city version
- for language development through contact with students whose first language is English
- for self-image (the concern of the *Brown* decision with the 'hearts and minds' of students is not out-of-date!)

What Are the State-Level Actions Necessary?

- identification of target schools;
- discussion of goal setting with each school;
- funding of the planning process;
- training for assessment and planning;
- commitment of program managers to a flexible funding process;
- relating the process to program funding cycles.

References

CHUBB, J. E. (1987) 'Effective schools and the problems of the poor' in DOYLE D. P., MICHIE, J. S. and WILLIAMS B. J. (Eds) *Policy Options For the Future of Compensatory Education: Conference Papers*, Washington, DC, Research and Evaluation Associates.

CUBAN, L. (1987) 'The ways that schools are: Lessons for reformers' in DOYLE D. P., MICHIE, J. J. and WILLIAMS B. J. (Eds) *Policy Options For the Future of Compensatory Education: Conference Papers*, Washington, DC, Research and Evaluation Associates.

MASSACHUSETTS BOARD OF EDUCATION (1986) *Massachusetts Board of Education Commission's Fiscal Year 1987 Operational Plan*, Quincy, MA, Commonwealth of Massachusetts Department of Education.

SMITH, M. S. (1987) 'Selecting students and services for Chapter 1: Reactions in DOYLE D. P., MICHIE, J. S. and WILLIAMS B. J. (Eds) *Policy Options For the Future of Compensatory Education: Conference Papers*, Washington, DC, Research and Evaluation Associates.

11
The Ways that Schools Are: Lessons for Reformers

Larry Cuban

An optimist is a person who sees a green light everywhere, while the pessimist sees only the red light ... But the truly wise are color blind.

Albert Schweitzer (1875–1965)

If colorblindness is wisdom in the above metaphor, amnesia is foolishness. Neither blind optimism nor pessimism is appropriate in making policies to improve the lot of children within organizations called schools. But memory is. Thus, to determine 'the ways that schools are' requires a look at how schools are organized to carry out their assigned roles and a look through the rear-view mirror to see how they were. Policymakers need both historical and organizational perspectives to inform decisions made on behalf of those without power to act, children, for example.

Avoiding Amnesia

Any informed trek through the history of schooling will quickly reveal two facts. First, schooling is a mix of constancy and change in policies, organizational structures, school practices and classroom pedagogy. Second, over the last century and a half, well-intentioned and serious reformers, using the blunt tool of Federal, state, or local policies, tirelessly and repeatedly aimed to improve schooling. These two facts frame any lessons to be drawn for the current crop of well-meaning, hard-working reformers.

216

Trying to improve schools is a great American passion. The expansion of tax-supported public schools in the early decades of the nineteenth century — a social reform movement itself — produced innovations such as compulsory attendance laws, the graded school, and the self-contained classroom which did much to shape the nature of classroom teaching and administrative practice in schools. Since then, wave after wave of serious men and women have tried hard to improve what children receive in schools.

The system-builders of post-Civil War America, such as city superintendents William Torrey Harris and William Maxwell, used the science of the day and the appealing example of corporate growth. They took unorganized districts and imposed a managerial order on schools and classrooms through a hierarchical structure, rules, and specified roles for staff to perform. The modern, graded public school with offerings in many subjects, a teacher for each self-contained classroom, a principal for the school, a district office with special services, and the offices of the superintendent and school board dates back to the closing decades of the nineteenth century. The rule-dominated bureaucracies these reformers built were intended to get masses of children to learn efficiently and inexpensively the skills necessary to best fit into the social order.

What they produced drew criticism from the next generation of reformers who found such systems regimented and inflexible, forcing both teachers and youth into rigid molds of behavior and performance. One group of pedagogical progressives such as Francis W Parker and John Dewey urged a 'New Education' for children. They tried to shift attention from a concentration upon society's needs to the individual child's growth and contribution to the community.

Another set of progressives, drawing from the same wellspring of reform, were more concerned about applying technology and science to the business of schooling children. The search for efficient management and teaching drove professors like Stanford's Ellwood P Cubberley, Teachers College's George Strayer and the University of Chicago's Charles Judd to bring into districts the science of testing, modern ways of measuring progress in everything from teacher evaluation ratings to the proper veneer of wax on corridor floors. These two wings of progressives, interested in child-centered instruction and efficient management, dominated the language of instruction and administration in public schools through the end of World War II.

By the early 1950s, another generation of critics questioned the pedagogy, curricula, and assumptions of their elders. The Cold War and Russian achievements in space accelerated criticism of American science and math curricula. Federally generated policies launched new curricula, advanced placement, programs for the gifted, and the National Defense Education Act in an effort to add vitamins to presumably listless American schools.

Within a decade, spurred by the civil rights movement and federally supported efforts, another wave of reformers discovered the poor, ethnic minorities, and a schooling seemingly hostile to children who were then called the disadvantaged. In seeking remedies, some unknowingly reached back to the progressives in introducing child-centered approaches to schooling (for example, informal or open education); some sought private alternative schools or urged public schools to tailor their offerings to ethnic preferences; others redoubled their efforts to apply rational approaches to management (for example, Programmed Planning and Budgeting Systems). New policies, laws, and rules which spilled forth from Washington, DC and state capitals were targeted on improving what occurred in schools and classrooms. By the mid-1970s, however, this reform impulse was spent.

Since the late 1970s, another generation of reformers has focused upon restoring excellence to public schools by ridding them of what they viewed as excesses promoted by earlier policymakers (for example, social promotion, few requirements for high school graduation, and little homework). In raising academic standards, demonstrating student productivity through test score results, and returning schools to such familiar traditions as homework and patriotic readers, this cohort of reformers leaned less upon Federal initiatives or funding and more upon state law, policies, regulations, and dollars.

This capsule history of periodic surges of reform aimed at school improvement takes little note of exactly what changed and what persisted over the last century. There is little doubt that over the last century substantial changes have occurred in the language used to talk about education, curriculum offerings, the design of school buildings, interactions between adults and children, and the organization and staffing of schools.

The city school of the 1890s had no gymnasium, lunchroom, library, or nurse's office; it had no counselors, reading teacher, or instructional aide; it offered few, if any, vocational courses, physical education, special classes for the handicapped, or the extracurricular array of activities so common in most schools now. In the schools of the 1890s, fear and rules were mainstays of the school. Corporal punishment was common; students stood to recite and would not dare leave their bolted-down desks without the teacher's permission. Today, students frequently move at will within the classroom and informal casualness prevails in many classes although the students know clearly who is the boss.

A century ago, few distinctions among students could be drawn other than that some were older than others; some were immigrants and some were native born; some were of color, and some were not; some were boys and some were girls. Intelligence testing and the battery of psychological tests were unknown a century ago. Today, the categories used by educators to distinguish children go well beyond age, origin, race, class, or gender. The treatment of minorities, expanded access to programs for females and handicapped students — while still imperfect — clearly illustrate alterations in the ways that schools were a century ago and now. Indeed, substantial changes have occurred.[1]

Amidst these changes in policies, facilities, curriculum, and administrative practices much of what existed since the 1890s has proved durable. A dominant classroom pedagogy and persistent school routines, altered somewhat over time, nonetheless have endured in their fundamental forms until the present day. Classroom practices such as lecturing, using textbooks and worksheets, teaching the entire group, grading students' performance, penalizing misbehavior and assigning seatwork dominated teachers' repertoires then and now. School practices commonly done both then and now are grouping by ability, principals' sporadic monitoring and rating of teachers' performance, and the scheduling of time and space in such a manner as to keep students supervised by teachers continually while both were in a building.

These and other practices, I argue, were present in the 1890s, the 1930s, and at the time that Title I of the Elementary and Secondary Education Act (ESEA) became law; they have remained in place through the conversion of Title I into Chapter 1 until now. I further argue that understanding what is constant and what changes in American classrooms and schools (and why both exist as they do over time) is essential foreknowledge for any policymaker interested in improvement. Why?

Because some changes alter the conditions within which teachers, subject matter, and children come together and some don't. Because changes in Federal and state laws, school board policies, and district office regulations get transformed, adapted, or ignored in schools and classrooms where principals, teachers, and students work. And because the final test of an intentional effort to improve what occurs between students and teachers is what happens 180 days a year, six hours a day in classrooms and schools — not when a bill is enacted, an appropriation made, a regulation written, a report submitted, or a multiple-choice item checked.

Distinguishing between visible changes in educators' vocabulary, course titles, and regulations and changes in school routines and classroom structures that shape practices is essential if policymakers ever wish to alter in significant ways children's performance and behavior.[2]

In this chapter, I will initially describe the structural arrangements and expectations that began over a century ago which set the boundaries and shaped much of what occurs in classrooms and schools. I call these structural arrangements and expectations the DNA of schooling; they are imperatives built into the ways that time and space are organized in schools. They are elements that teachers and principals have learned to cope with and adapt to in order to discharge their obligations and gain what pleasures they could from work. Following this description, I will draw from research findings in organizational change and practitioner experience with Federal and state interventions to suggest lessons that policymakers should note when considering changes in Chapter 1 legislation.

DNA: The Classroom Organization

In the early nineteenth century, students who attended public schools were mixed in age and thrown together into one-room schools, where the teacher taught a half dozen or more subjects. In this climate, an innovation imported from Prussia by reformers seeking cheap, efficient ways to expand American education spread swiftly in urban districts. The novel idea of a graded school brought large numbers of students and teachers together into one building with eight or more classrooms. Students were divided by age into grades, teachers were assigned to certain grade levels, and subject matter was split into manageable chunks of content and spread among the grades. Each teacher had a separate class within the grade with specified subject matter and skills to teach. To mid-nineteenth century reformers, the graded school was a remarkable invention for improving education, by standardizing curriculum and instruction for all students while spending public funds in an efficient manner.

A century later, self-contained classrooms were condemned by reformers as counterproductive in achieving the complex goals of the modern school and for keeping teachers insulated and isolated from one another. Nonetheless, the self-contained classroom has survived repeated assaults. Team teaching and open space architecture made temporary dents in its popularity, but by 1980, 95 per cent of all classrooms remained self-contained.

Let us begin with the description of the room to which a teacher is assigned. Between twenty-five to forty students, ages 6 to 16 are required to sit for fifty minutes to five hours daily, depending on their grade, for about 180 days a year. To observers unfamiliar with formal schooling, the first impression of a classroom is its crowdedness. Except in rush hour buses and elevators, no other public place contains as many people who are compelled to be there. Such a setting packed with young people of varying abilities and tastes imposes upon a teacher the fundamental obligation to maintain order.

Except in kindergarten and the primary grades, teachers cope with the crowd by organizing space in a limited number of ways. A teacher's desk, a table for the reading group in elementary schools (or a lectern in secondary classrooms), the chalkboard, and the wall clock usually dominate the front of the room. After the primary years, students generally sit in rows of movable desks and one-arm chairs facing the teacher. Minor variations in seating appear in circular, horseshoe, and hollow square arrangements. A less frequent seating pattern is where students sit at tables or clusters of movable desks facing one another. Except for science labs, art, home economics, and craft shops, these configurations are frequently seen in kindergarten and primary classrooms.

The typical rows-of-desks pattern lessens student contact with one another and fosters one-way communication with the teacher. Moreover, within such an arrangement teachers can scan a room quickly to see who is or is not behaving properly.

If managing a crowd leads to common seating patterns, it also encourages whole-group instruction and reliance on one textbook. Teaching everyone the same thing at one time permits the teacher to manage the flow of information and maintain order simultaneously. Instruction in small groups, an innovation generated by turn-of-the century progressives, appears frequently in the elementary grades for reading and occasionally for math. In secondary schools, small groups appear in performance-based subjects such as laboratory science, shop classes, and art; in academic classes, the dominant practice is whole group instruction.

Teachers organize space, use time, and construct an instructional repertoire to meet the imperative of managing a crowd of students in an orderly, efficient, and civil manner. Each teacher alone, separated from peers and required to teach in isolation, invents ways of coping with the demands of the self-contained classrooms. These responses by teachers to students who are confined to a room in order to learn required subject matter and skills constitute a practical pedagogy, the distilled. experience of generations of teachers who have learned to cope with the structural imperatives over which they have no control. What occurs between teachers and children is shaped not only by the self-contained classroom and the graded school but also by the structures of elementary and secondary schools.

DNA: Elementary and Secondary School Structures

Substantial differences between the two levels of schooling exist in the size of the school, the content that students face in classrooms, the time allocated to instruction, and the external policies and expectations imposed upon each.

Elementary schools are smaller than secondary schools. Most observers label an elementary school large if it has more than 500 students. While some elementary schools have over 1000 pupils, they are uncommon outside large urban districts. Secondary schools commonly have 1000–2000 students, but sometimes as many as 3000 or 4000. Size differences in schools mean that hierarchies, specialization of function, and administrator visibility vary. Most elementary schools will have one principal and no other administrator. An average secondary school of 2000 students will have one principal, three or four assistant principals, almost a dozen department heads who function as quasi-administrators, and a clerical staff that is the envy of an elementary school principal. Finally, differences in size affect student participation in activities and the quality, intensity, and frequency of contacts among members of the school community.

The place of content in the curriculum differs between the two levels of schooling also. Children in elementary grades learn fundamental verbal, writing, reading and math skills. Content, while important, is secondary and often used as a flexible vehicle for teaching those skills. But in the upper grades of elementary school, and certainly in the high school, more sophisticated skills are required of students; these skills are wired directly to complex subject matter that itself must be learned. Literary criticism, historical analysis, advanced math problems, quantitative analysis in chemistry — all require knowledge of complicated facts and their applications. High school teachers of academic subjects adapt to the complexities of content, the number of students they face and the limited time they have each class by concentrating upon whole group instruction, a single textbook, homework, and lecturing.

Also student and teacher contact time differs markedly between the two levels. While the self-contained classroom remains the dominant form of delivering instruction in both settings, elementary teachers spend five or more hours with the same thirty or more students. They see far more of a child's strengths, limitations, capacities, and achievements than high school teachers who see five groups of thirty students less than an hour a day. Over a year, elementary teachers see their students nearly 1000 hours; a high school teacher sees any one class no more than 200 hours during the year or about one-fifth of the time that elementary colleagues spend with pupils. Contact time becomes an important factor in considering issues of grouping, providing individual attention, varying classroom tasks and activities, and rearranging furniture. In elementary schools the *potential* to make instructional changes in these and other areas is present simply because the teacher who is responsible for five or more subjects has more contact time with the children. Such potential is absent for a teacher of one subject with thirty students for a fifty minute daily period in high schools.

Finally, external pressures from accrediting associations, college entrance requirements, state mandates for graduation, and job qualifications have far more direct, unrelenting influence upon high schools than lower grade classrooms. Steady pressures on high schools come from

Carnegie units, college boards, employers, scholastic aptitude tests, and certifying agencies that push teachers to complete the textbook by June, drive students to prepare for high-stakes exams, seek jobs, and take the proper courses for graduation. Of course, not all teachers and students respond in the same manner to these imperatives; variation in response is the norm. The point is that the pressure to respond is both persistent and intense.

While similar urgencies exist in elementary grades, particularly the press to get children ready for the next grade, the tensions seldom pinch as they do in the higher grades. More time is available in elementary schools. Flexible arrangements are possible. The second and third grade classrooms can be combined. Retaining students, for example, keeping a kindergartner for another year rather than promotion to first grade, while uncommon, occurs more frequently in elementary than in high schools.

These three structural differences — emphasis on subject matter, contact time, and external pressures — fundamentally separate the two levels of schooling. One only has to spend time listening to seventh or ninth graders who are in the first weeks of making the leap from a six-grade or eight-grade elementary school to secondary school to understand the ways that the different school structures impact their lives.

While these structural arrangements shape what occurs in classrooms and schools, schools are not islands; they are nested in district organizations (which, in turn, are nested within state systems of schooling). Both districts and states have intentions for what should happen in those schools and classrooms. What is missing from this description of the DNA is the district and state policies that further influence what teachers and principals do.

DNA: Conflicting District and State Goals and Policies

Goals

As a consequence of attending school, the public expects students to:

- master basic skills;
- think rationally and independently;

- accumulate general knowledge in various subjects;
- possess skills to get a job;
- participate in the civic culture of the community; and
- know what values are prized in the community and be able to live them.

Although the above goals are taken from state and local statements, there are other goals that are implicit, that lie in the shadows but nonetheless weigh heavily on public expectations. Schools should:

- house students safely five to eight hours a day;
- shield the adult labor market from competition;
- sort students to fit different socioeconomic niches;
- equip students from low-income families with the means for moving into higher social classes; and
- solve persistent national problems (for example, poverty, drug abuse, racism, defense).

The reach of these goals staggers the unfamiliar observer: creating social mobility, eliminating national ills, and preparing students for college and jobs are expectations that blanket public schools today. Yet the conflict among and between these formal and informal goals is evident. For example, schools should produce graduates imbued with community values who are also critical and independent in their reasoning. Such massive expectations and internal paradoxes echo persistently in state and district policies and permeate structures that set the boundaries for the school and classroom.

State and District Policies

State-mandated courses (for example, four years of English, one year of US History) and district requirements (for example, computer literacy) provide a scaffold for subject matter taught in classrooms. Teachers plan what content to teach, materials to use, and what tests students should take within limits set by state and district directives. Goal conflict arises when teachers are expected to cover in thirty-six weeks content that would take twice as long, given the textbook. Moreover, district policies require teachers to grade students on their performance. In covering content and mastering skills, students receive marks on homework, class participation, quizzes, and tests. Grades are intended to mirror accurately student performance, but practitioners know that an 'A' and an 'F' serve other purposes as well, (for example, rewarding effort, penalizing lack of attention, and keeping order). Furthermore, if a district or state requires a semester- or year-end test, the teacher needs to complete content that would appear on it. The unrelenting impulse to cover subject matter wedded to a requirement to give grades helps to produce the practical pedagogy described earlier.

Furthermore, state and local mandates to use standardized tests also shape classroom instruction and school practices. With the passion for published test scores intensifying since the late 1960s, school officials have sought an alignment of district curriculum, textbook content, and classroom instruction with the content of test items. Some district administrators will realign content taught at certain grades to match what is covered on the standardized test. For example, they will move instruction on decimals from the sixth to the fifth grade because the test including such items is administered at the end of the latter grade. Aware of the increased weight placed upon national percentile ranks, teachers and principals rearrange schools calendars to prepare students for high-stakes tests. Instructional tasks aimed at practicing for upcoming tests absorb large chunks of class time. Thus, standardized tests teach principals, teachers, and students what to expect from classroom instruction and school organizational arrangements.

These goals and policies, cross-cutting as they are, produce expectations among policymakers that what is adopted will be implemented faithfully, yet what occurs seldom yields the highly prized and eagerly sought uniformity in schools and classrooms. The disappointment that policymakers invariably feel over unfulfilled mandates matches the pressures that practitioners feel over being commanded to alter their behavior by those who have little sense of the workplace imperatives that govern their lives between 9 and 3 daily. Practitioners respond to these conflicting goals and policies, although the responses may be both unintended and unsought by policymakers.

The graded school, its classroom organization, the structure of the different levels of schooling, and conflicting local and state policies form the scaffolding of public schools. I use DNA as a metaphor to underscore that these man-made structures define to a large degree the workplace in which the familiar practices of teachers, principals and students have become so evident to observers.

To press the metaphor slightly, just as scientists have begun to reconstruct, recombine the genetic material that constitutes DNA to create new forms of life, the very basic forms of schooling can also be restructured into new forms. To do so, reformers must initially link goals and outcomes to the organizational arrangements that have arisen over time. If there is a mismatch between goals and outcomes and the mismatch can be attributed to familiar organizational arrangements, then framing the problem of improved schooling in terms of altering basic structures appears as a potentially useful strategy with which to begin.

Before moving to recent periodic efforts to improve schooling, I need to make clear that this DNA of schooling, while evident in all settings, has had special impact on the poor and children of color.

The Structure of Schooling and Its Effect on the Poor and Children of Color

Schools for immigrants, minorities, and the poor have been described frequently over the last century. Teacher accounts, journalists' visits, recollections of former students, and an occasional administrator's reflections document the special circumstances of classrooms and schools in which large numbers of children identified as different have attended.

In these classrooms, teacher-centered instruction with fewer variations, fewer hybrids of different practices, dominates both elementary and secondary schools. Maintaining order is the central task from which all else flows. The content and skills taught tend to be minimal, substantively different from what is taught in more affluent, non-minority settings. The emphasis is frequently on steering behavior toward what the teachers and administrators define as acceptable. Using conventional measures of school outcomes (for example, standardized test results, attendance, suspensions, dropouts, college attendance), these schools dominate the bottom quarter of all rankings.

Yet, in most non-poor, non-minority schools, common teaching practices and structural arrangements seem to work. That is, the usual narrow measures of schooling place these sites in the middle or above average categories; most teachers and administrators seek to teach in these schools. This is not the case for places populated by the poor or culturally different.

The anecdotal and research evidence drawn from classrooms and schools of how teaching and administrative practices vary according to race, class, and ethnicity is ample. Teaching practices, such as asking questions, giving praise and blame, and distributing rewards in classrooms, have been correlated with differences in children's socioeconomic status. Secondary school practices, such as grouping students for different curricula and complexity of content taught in classrooms, show strong relationships with the level of family income — a proxy for social status.

Within such schools, cultural differences between teachers and principals representing a version of the dominant culture (English-speaking, white-collar values drawn from Western industrialized societies) intersect with students who may be non-English speaking, of a lower socioeconomic class, with non-Western or rural values or mixes of all these differences.

In a few classrooms and schools, cultural differences become opportunities for increased learning for both adults and children; these become places where both adults and children share a common mission to learn, grow, and share in a community of a classroom or a school. The literature on effective schools has drawn attention to schools populated by low-income, ethnic minorities that removed from despair to determination, instances where socioeconomic and ethnic differences became less important than the overall goals of academic and social improvement.

In most settings in which urban and rural poor children are the majority, cultural differences lead to a cold war. Hostile participants eye one another suspiciously in hallways, across chairs and desks and engage in guerilla tactics prior to becoming school dropouts.

In short the structures of schooling described earlier have special impact upon children who are viewed as different from the mainstream. While some schools and classrooms make mighty efforts to achieve important but narrow ends (for example, raise reading and math test scores, or to have more students take academic subjects) nonetheless they are limited by the classroom organization, elementary and secondary school structures, and conflicting district and state policies. For other schools where token change efforts are made or benign neglect is the rule, those structures become iron cages.

In discussing constancy and change in American schools and classrooms, I have concentrated upon those changes that have altered the face of schooling and those school and classroom practices that have endured. What has persisted for over a century are fundamental organizational arrangements initially introduced to produce cheap, efficient ways of schooling large numbers of children. Although goals have been added and altered, these structures have come to shape to a large degree what occurs in schools and classrooms.

Since 1965 when Federal policymakers launched ambitious efforts to improve schooling for underachieving children of the poor, repeated efforts by different bands of reformers have been undertaken to alleviate the effects of poverty. Given this perspective, it is now time to assess what has been learned from those efforts. Were these Federal and state policymakers optimistic seeing only green lights, pessimistic seeing only red lights or, in Schweitzer's words, were they the truly wise who were color blind?

First- and Second-Order Change

In the mid-1980s, the National Air and Space Administration (NASA) endured a number of grave setbacks with the tragic destruction of the Challenger shuttle and two unmanned rockets within three months. An agency that had soared with the successes of lunar landings and shuttle flights, with space walks and satellite repairs, staggered to a halt with the deaths of seven astronauts and two rocket failures.

With the public awareness of a complete performance collapse in a brief period, its new leadership had to define the problems clearly: was the Challenger accident a design problem, or a lapse in quality control, or some mix of the two? Defining the problem became crucial since the definition charted the direction for changes in NASA's formal structure, relationships with government contractors, and a score of ripple effects. Similarly, for school reforms over the last century there is a need to determine whether school problems were defined as design or quality control issues.

It may help to initially make a distinction among planned organizational changes. *First-order* changes are reforms that assume the existing organizational goals and structures are basically adequate but that deficiencies in policies and practices need correcting. Engineers would label such changes as 'solutions to quality control problems'.

229

For schools, such changes would include recruiting better teachers and administrators, raising salaries, distributing resources more equitably, selecting better texts, adding new (or deleting old) courses to the curriculum, designing more efficient ways of scheduling people and activities, and providing more staff training. When such improvements occur, the results frequently contain the vocabulary of fundamental change or even appear as changes in core activities. Actually, they alter little of the basic school organizational structures for determining how time and space are used or how students are organized and assigned. First-order changes try to make what exists more efficient and effective without disturbing the basic organizational arrangements, without substantially altering how adults and children perform their roles. The compensatory education programs since the 1960s (including Title I of ESEA and Chapter 1) are instances of first-order reforms. The school effectiveness movement with its emphasis on high expectations, strong instructional leadership, academic performance in basic skills, alignment of goals with curriculum, texts, and tests is a recent example of first-order, planned changes.

Second-order changes, on the other hand, aim at altering the fundamental ways of achieving organizational goals because of major dissatisfaction with present arrangements. Second-order changes introduce new goals and interventions that transform the familiar ways of doing things into novel solutions to persistent problems. The point is to reframe the original problems and restructure organizational conditions to conform with the redefined problems. Recombining what I call the DNA of classrooms and schools would be classified as second-order changes. Engineers would call these 'solutions to design problems'.

For schools it was a second order change to go from the one-room schoolhouse with one unsupervised teacher and a gaggle of children ranging in ages from 6 through 16 to an eight-room building divided into grades and a formal curriculum where a teacher is supervised by a principal. It happened throughout the nineteenth century in urban schools and the first half of the twentieth century in rural ones. An example of second-order changes in curriculum and instruction is when teachers and principals choose to embrace a pedagogy rooted in beliefs about children as individuals who need to learn to make their own decisions, as learners who need to connect what occurs outside the school with classroom activities, and as pupils who need to discover knowledge rather than absorb it. Teachers and administrators with such beliefs organize schools, classrooms, lessons, and curriculum consistently with those beliefs. Relationships with students, the utilization of space, and the allocation of time, shift in response to these beliefs.

The history of school reform has been largely first-order improvements of the basic structures (for example, graded school, self-contained classroom with one teacher and thirty students, varied curricula, and fifty minute periods in secondary schools). On occasion, second-order reforms have been attempted (for example, progressive pedagogy, non-graded schools, open-space architecture, and team teaching) without lasting effects other than residual adaptations to the contours of existing arrangements.

Researchers examining past efforts to improve schooling have found common characteristics to those first- and second-order reforms that were institutionalized as contrasted with those that left few or no traces. School improvements that endured were a mix of both kinds of changes with first-order ones dominant. They were structural in nature (for example, graded schools in mid-nineteenth century America) created new constituencies (e.g., vocational educational courses, guidance counselors, and Title I teachers and aides) and were easily monitored (for example, Carnegie units and raising certification requirements for teachers). The researchers concluded that second-order reforms calling for classroom changes such as team teaching, inquiry learning, open classrooms, core curriculum, and individualized instruction were installed and dismantled, barely denting existing practices (Kirst, 1983).

The last two decades have provided more illustrations of more first-order rather than second-order improvements. They have the full force of state and Federal law, ample dollars, and occasional arm-twisting. From the laws (for example, National Defense Education Act in 1958, Elementary and Secondary Education Act in 1965, and the Education for All Handicapped Children Act in 1975), policies, and billions of dollars spent since the late 1950s, the kinds of changes sponsored by Federal intervention that have lasted in states and local districts are as follows:

- organizational changes that created a new layer of specialists in programs that pull children out of their regular classes to receive additional help (for example, remedial reading experts, vocational education staff, bilingual and Chapter 1 teachers);

- procedural changes that guarantee student rights such as due process (for example, P.L. 94–142 mandated new procedures for working with handicapped children and their parents);
- pupil classification systems for categorizing children (for example, limited-English-speaking, gifted and the handi-capped);
- increased teacher specialization that produced new certification categories such as remedial reading, bilingual education, English as a Second Language, and classifications within special education for both teachers and aides; and
- expanded testing to determine student performance.

All of these changes were either rule changes, modifications of existing practices, or further staff specialization. The reforms created new constituencies and were easily monitored but they hardly dented the existing organizational structures. Little or no sustained impact on curriculum or classroom instruction appears to have occurred from these Federal efforts.

Most consequences of Federal efforts to improve schooling suggest first-order changes. Schools were seen as failing to provide necessary resources, much less quality services, for certain populations and had excluded groups of children entirely. To promote quality, that is, provide an equal education, Federal policymakers tried to enhance schools as they were rather than altering substantially the structures, roles, and relationships within states, districts, and schools.

These first-order changes were far from trivial. Expanding equal opportunity in what needy children receive is a massive, if not intimidating, undertaking. The changes that have occurred from these Federal interventions have been superseded in the 1980s by activist state governments. They are filling the vacuum created by the ideology of the Reagan administration in reducing the Federal role in school improvement.

State Efforts at School Improvement

Others have analyzed the origins, spread, and content of state efforts to reform what happens in schools and classrooms. Spurred by national reports on inferior education and its linkage to economic health, governors, legislatures, and superintendents mandated a longer school day, a longer school year, higher graduation standards, more standard-ized tests and tighter linkages between these tests and curricular content. Further, most states legislated higher entry-level teacher salaries and merit pay schemes, competency tests for new and veteran teachers and stiffer evaluation procedures.

Are these first-order or second-order changes? The attempted realignment of local/state relations is an effort to fundamentally alter governance relations. But, the bulk of the state improvement efforts try to make the existing system more efficient and effective, not disturb basic roles and arrangements in districts, schools, and classrooms. The historic design of public schooling instituted in the late nineteenth century, with all of its additions, remains intact. Thus, first-order changes seem to prevail in state interventions heavily loaded with bureaucratic measures targeted at reducing teacher and administrator discretion.

Note that I said 'seem'. Research and experience have yet to determine the cumulative effects of this recent surge of managerially driven state reforms aimed at school improvement. Until that knowl-edge surfaces, I suspect that at least two outcomes are probable. First, the measurement and rule-driven reforms will fail to achieve fully their intentions. Wiring curriculum and instruction to highstakes tests will occur but the business of schooling is for teachers and administrators to make daily decisions about other people. Such human judgments cannot be programmed by others or routinized into a set of rules for all to enact.

In schools, there is a long history of token compliance with external mandates while stable core processes within classrooms persist. Anyone familiar with teacher use of technology knows that machines can be bought, even delivered to schools and placed in teachers' rooms. None of that assures serious use of the advanced technology. Anyone familiar with large bureaucracies knows the ways that principals can comply minimally with district office directives if they find them too intrusive or disruptive for their schools.

A second outcome may well be the partial success of these first-order changes in driving certain teachers and administrators to do pretty much what the policymakers wanted. In some settings where previous reforms have failed to improve students' performance, such as inner-city schools, district administrators will push to put these man-dates into practice.

In some school systems the process is underway. Curriculum is rewritten. Scripts of units and lessons for teachers are produced. Superintendents inspect principals; principals inspect closely whether teachers are teaching what is supposed to be taught. Teachers inspect students through frequent testing. Evaluations of superintendents, principals, and teachers are linked to how well implementation of directives is carried out.

These first-order changes tighten linkages, producing a more efficient schooling that the system-builders of the late nineteenth century would have applauded. Yet such actions raise the strong possibility that what is absorbed by students may be what is tested, i.e., low levels of skills and discrete bits of information, and the broader goals of reasoning, problem solving, and enhanced self-esteem remain unachieved. Such instructional management systems already exist in Washington, DC, Atlanta, Georgia and many other districts. Texas and California are two states that have moved aggressively in that direction.

In states driven to raise standards and student performance on standardized tests, state departments of education try to insure compliance by the hundreds of thousands of teachers, the tens of thousands of principals, and the hundreds of superintendents and school boards. Rivers of paper, occasional inspections, newspaper exposés, complaints, and the publishing of district and school indicators, tell the governor, the legislature, the commissioner of education and state board of education, the degree of compliance.

Not unlike the bold attempt by Federal policymakers to realign their relationship with state and local agencies to effect improvement in classrooms, few can predict with confidence how long such reform energy can be sustained. Let me now consider these largely first-order changes undertaken by the states and Federal government over the last two decades and ask the straightforward question: 'What has been learned from the Federal and state experience about improving schools that might be of use to those interested in improving the schooling that disadvantaged children receive?'

Lessons from State and Federal School Improvement Efforts?

From the enormous body of research findings and practical experience accumulated by teachers and administrators, I have extracted what I believe are primary lessons and converted them into guiding principles for policymakers interested in school and classroom improvement, especially for those schools enrolling large numbers of underachieving poor and minority children. My experience as a teacher and administrator in urban districts, wedded to my research and knowledge of the history of school reform, acted as filters in choosing these guiding principles.

1   *Teaching and administration varies within and among schools. Do not prescribe what should occur in those classrooms and schools.* What teachers in classrooms and administrators in schools do daily is to make decisions about other people. They deal in human judgment. To a great extent their actions are shaped by the general structural arrangements within which they work. These actions are also influenced by the particular conditions, the time that events unfold, and the beliefs and experiences of these teachers and administrators. At some general level clear similarities exist across contexts, time, and beliefs. But classrooms, schools, and districts differ enough in these factors to give pause to anyone who is bent upon generalizing about what should be done.

   Because of these inevitable variations within and between schools, it is impossible to prescribe policies from afar, that is, from state and Federal offices that tell teachers and administrators what they must do about curriculum and instruction or in operating a school. In short, in the face of rich variation in performance, there is no best system of teaching or administering for policymakers or practitioners to adopt.

2   *Improvement is tied to each school site.* Anyone familiar with schooling knows the palpable differences between schools in the same neighborhood. Informed parents shop for schools, not classrooms.

   With all of the criticism of the effective schools movement and its research from both academics and practitioners, one fact has stubbornly emerged as unquestioned: substantial changes that touch the inner core of classroom activities occur at the school site where principal and teachers work together with students to achieve common aims. The literature on effective schools has underscored the importance of building commitment to goals among those who do the work and holding them responsible for outcomes. The intangibles of a school culture that prizes achievement for both adults and children repeatedly turn up in anecdotes by practitioners and research findings. In effect, the organization that can alter teacher and student behavior most directly and in a sustained fashion is the school.

3   *In order to produce enduring improvements at the school site, teachers and principals require a larger degree of independence than is now granted by local and state agencies.* The impulse to control continues to permeate much thinking about change among policymakers. Policies aimed at teachers and principals, especially in inner-city schools, offer little formal autonomy in making decisions about the organizational conditions within which they work. Yet school site decisions spell the differences in how faithfully district, state, and Federal policies are implemented.

Reform by remote control, that is transforming classrooms and schools through regulations, is a familiar strategy practiced by governing bodies. It will yield compliance at some level with easily monitored procedures and the production of paper but will do little to alter the core activities that occur in the workplace.

The more formal discretion for teachers and administrators is in contrast to the negative freedom common in organizations where infrequent supervision occurs and people essentially do what they like, although they worry about bosses showing up unexpectedly. In my argument, I assume that no pool of immense imagination is simply waiting to be tapped at the local level. Nor do I assume that teachers and administrators have a monopoly on goodwill and knowledge of what is best for children; any romantic ideas I may have held eroded in watching my colleagues over the last three decades. I have seen altruism and racism; I have seen fiery engagement with ideas and anti-intellectualism; I have seen colleagues sacrifice money and time for their students and seen others fuse their interests in higher salaries and fringe benefits with the best interests of children.

Yet, these teachers and administrators are all we have.

They do the work. They need to be helped. They need to be seen as potential heroes who perform essential social tasks that cannot be regulated from afar. A better balance than exists now needs to be struck between expanded autonomy for teachers and administrators and ways of demonstrating accountability to the larger community.

4   *Effecting change depends on what the on-site implementers think and do and the quality of help they receive.* The process of adopting, implementing and institutionalizing school improvements aimed at changing what teachers and administrators do is heavily dependent upon their:

- understanding of what it is that needs to be done;
- commitment to doing what is intended;
- having the discretion to make alterations in the changes;
- tailoring the desired improvements to the contextual conditions of the setting; and
- having tangible, sustained help and resources to put into practice the improvements.

The sum of these guiding principles adds up to a reliance upon the infantry of reform, the men and women who staff schools, not the policymakers who legislate and exhort but seldom enter a classroom or school to see the results of their laws or sermons. If proposed changes that are intended to alter what occurs in classrooms are to have a sustained effect, that is, to achieve second-order changes with the educationally disadvantaged of the nation, they must come to grips with the existing organizational structures in elementary and secondary schools. Hence, my final principle for reformers deals with the question of the level of schooling at which intervention should occur.

5   *The site level that offers the potentially highest gain for improvement for those students most in need is the elementary school.* The size of elementary schools and how they generally structure time, space, and student assignments permit more innovation, flexible curriculum, teacher-administrator collegiality, and joint decision making than the current size or organizational arrangements in secondary schools.

The combining of grades in classrooms, team teaching,

school-wide staff and curriculum development, and collaborative decision-making will be observed more often in elementary than secondary schools. Moreover, elementary schools with younger students who have extended contact with only a few adults are able to influence student values, knowledge, and skills in many more ways than secondary schools can with older youth.

All of these guiding principles which I have converted into lessons for reformers say nothing about the goals of reform. Implicit in this analysis is that policymakers and practitioners who wish to improve schooling share similar goals. Because such an assumption is flawed, let me now discuss how these guiding principles fit some goals far better than others.

Reformer Goals and Schooling Structures

Policymakers determined to reform schooling have differed among themselves for decades as to what is desirable. Some have sought increased efficiency in spending public funds; some sought enhanced effectiveness in student performance as measured by standardized achievement tests; some wanted more scientists and engineers. Others wanted schools where intellectual engagement prevailed; others wanted schools where students reasoned critically and solved problems; others wanted schools to take on parental functions such as teaching children proper sexual behavior, the evils of drug abuse, and how to get a job; and others wanted schools where even the slowest and least able student achieved. Among reformers, then, goals expanded, became complex, and were paraded past the public. So what?

Inspired by reformers filled with pocketfuls of intentions and driven by varied conceptions of what schools should do over the last century, a jerry-built architecture of schooling, a jumble of old and new blueprints for the efficient mass production of schooling arose. Different reformer goals produced graded schools and self-contained classrooms, promotion policies, Carnegie units, fifty-minute periods, vocational and sex education, and mandated achievement tests. All were once novel solutions to problems reformers had defined and put into practice.

Over the decades these and other reformers created a Rube Goldberg machine called American schools that were ill-designed to achieve a growing parade of vastly different and contradictory goals. Each generation of policymakers and reformers added goals and organizational mechanisms designed to achieve specific aims. The total effect of these innocent, helter-skelter designs stacked one atop another is a disorderly array of intentions and structures mismatched to certain broad goals for both children and professionals.

The mismatch can be observed in that some aims are consistent with the existing organizational arrangements that have characterized schooling for over a century and some are not. No sandpaper is needed to smooth out the rough edges between what is desired and what can be done within schools when more homework, longer school days, compensatory programs and stiffer graduation requirements are enacted into new rules. These first-order changes fit easily into the scaffolding that frames schooling now.

Goals that are considered important by reformers, researchers, policymakers, and parents are ones that call for students to be treated as individuals and to learn to think for themselves or ones that seek an engaged practice of citizenship or ones that strive for developing a sense of caring for others. Such goals have little chance of achievement within the current structures of schooling except in those instances where extraordinary people overcome the consequences of these structures.

Consider the conflict between the goal of increased reasoning skills and existing structures of schooling. Corporate officials, governors, legislators, superintendents, and district officials share in common the goal of cultivating critical thinking and problem solving in the youth of the nation. National reports repeatedly emphasize the need for graduates of public schools to be flexible, independent thinkers.

But recent state mandates wedded to the existing structural conditions within schools and the practical pedagogy that teachers invented to cope with those conditions are in conflict. Regulations that detail curricular content, specify textbooks, and assess student performance through multiple-choice test items pour molten steel over that practical pedagogy. The core repertoire of instructional practices finds students listening to lectures, doing worksheets at their desks, reciting from textbooks, and seldom asking questions. Such work demands little application of concepts, little imagination, and little intellectual engagement.

Those who would argue that reasoning and problem solving are commonly taught in the schools need to produce evidence that such skills are taught separately or embedded in a discipline; that they are displayed openly, systematically, and persistently within classrooms; and that they are frequently practiced. Of course, such teaching does occur in different places. It is uncommon, however.

Eager reformers, unaware of how practical pedagogy arose in response to difficult working conditions and of the dulling effects of such practices on students' reasoning skills, have repeatedly exhorted teachers to teach students to think. Teachers are caught between using a repertoire that works (given the structures within which they work) and responding to reformers' pleas.

This dilemma has no simple solution. It will not be ended by glitzy materials aimed at producing thinkers, special courses for teachers on how to teach reasoning, new multiple-choice items that supposedly assess students' 'higher order thinking skills'. To teach inner-city students to reflect, to question, and to solve problems, teachers must at least work in settings that allow them ample time and resources to engage in these kinds of activities with students and with each other.

If policymakers desire to have the children of the poor increase their reasoning and problem solving skills, they would need to see clearly the fundamental conflict between school structures and this important goal and then move to realign those commonplace, unquestioned structures to a different pedagogy. To align the classroom setting to teaching that centers on the student's mind, one that concentrates upon cultivating intellectual engagement and student involvement, reformers will have to begin with the organizational imperatives that largely govern teachers' routines, that determine the use of time and space in schools and classrooms, and that shape how and by whom instructional decisions are made. If policymakers become aware of the mismatch between goals and structural arrangements, the DNA of schooling, and if they strive to achieve goals such as improved reasoning skills for inner-city children, they begin the journey of reforming schools for the poor (Cuban, 1984b).

These guiding principles are useful when they fit goals embraced by those who seek to improve what Chapter 1 can do for the underachieving poor and children of color. The overriding implication of all these guiding principles and their linkages to goals is clear. Federal or state strategies of school improvement that have goals aimed at changing complex behaviors in children and adults in schools and classrooms should focus less on control and regulation through existing structures and more on incentives and help for those who make on-site judgments to transform those organizational imperatives to reach those desirable goals. In doing so, state and Federal agencies will need to increase schools' capacity to do what they need to do, while holding them responsible for outcomes.

But in schools there is a structural dilemma over autonomy and accountability. In ending this chapter, I need to discuss briefly this dilemma.

The conventional means of holding teachers and administrators accountable at all levels of government is through rulemaking. Fiscal regulations, for example, call for the production of paper trails that can be monitored in periodic audits. Program regulations and procedures that require the keeping of records and submission of reports are monitored by occasional inspections but more often by systematic examination of the documents. It comes as no surprise that reports in triplicate, files holding records, and massive collections of data that often go uninspected, much less used, fill offices in school districts. This is the common manner of holding educators accountable.

Accountability can also be documented by concentrating on outcomes such as test scores, dropout rates, and similar markers. By examining such numbers, educators and non-educators can supposedly determine whether teachers and administrators have met their responsibilities. Focusing upon outcomes has decided benefits for policymakers with fewer benefits less apparent for those who work in classrooms. Some policymakers have wedded this concentration upon results to the sharing of these outcomes with the public through publishing school-by-school test scores and other performance comparisons using varied measures. The premise is that teachers and administrators will become more responsible if results are available to the community. Undesirable outcomes would trigger community pressure for improvement. This is accountability by bullying. The substantial negatives linked to concentrating upon outcome measures and having them become public signs of success have already begun to emerge.

Another approach to accountability is to simply render an account. Describing what occurs in classrooms and schools, and calling attention to exemplars and misfits, contributes to what teachers and administrators see as their responsibility. Exemplars are recognized; misfits and incompetents are handled. Informally, this occurs in schools and districts where there is sufficient pride in what happens and self-confidence to forthrightly and fairly deal with the exceptions that perform unacceptably. It is uncommon, however.

Also uncommon in public schooling is collegial responsibility. It is rare for teachers to work with teachers to improve performance. Except for occasional schools where solidarity among teachers arises informally and beginning efforts to introduce peer review occur, little of this collegial responsibility exists in public education.

The dominant manner of accountability remains regulatory with occasional mixes of other approaches. In ending this discussion of accountability, I want to make clear that regulations accompanied by familiar forms of accountability are often necessary as a governmental response to certain social problems of injustice, health, and safety. Local agencies may neglect such issues and in a Federal system, another governing body may need to intervene. The point is that a balance is necessary between local, state, and Federal agencies that permits sufficient discretion to those delivering a service while monitoring performance in a flexible manner. It is no easy task to strike that balance, but attention must be paid to it nonetheless.

The primary implication of this discussion of accountability and guiding principles is the need for strategies of school improvement that focus less on control through regulation. Instead, more attention should be placed on vesting individual schools and educators with the independence to reach explicit goals and standards with flexible and fair ways of holding educators responsible.

These lessons and guiding principles suggest that there is an important, even critical, Federal and state role in improving schooling for the disadvantaged. Reformers anxious to help the needy children of the nation must see that role with singular clarity. Somewhere between the green light of the optimistic change-maker and the red light of the pessimist is the flashing yellow signal that colorblind and wise reformers see in the schools and classrooms of the nation before they act.

Notes

1   See, for example, some histories of public schools by David Tyack (1974)

and Michael Katz (1971). Various portions of this analysis are drawn from my writings on this topic over the last few years. The most recent is *How Teachers Taught* (1984a).

2 Milbrey McLaughlin and Richard Elmore (1984) distinguish between policy, administration, and practice and argue that policies as tools for school improvement are blunt-edged, constantly being reshaped by administrators and teachers.

References

CUBAN, L. (1984a) *How Teachers Taught*, New York, Longman.

CUBAN, L. (1984b) 'Policy and research dilemmas in the teaching of reasoning: Unplanned designs', *Review of Educational Research*, **54**, pp. 655–81.

KATZ, M. (1971). *Class, Bureaucracy, and Schools*, New York, Praeger.

KIRST, M. (1983). 'Teaching policy and Federal categorical programs' in SHULMAN, L. and SYKES, G. (Eds) *Handbook of Teaching and Policy*, New York, Longman.

McLAUGHLIN, M. and ELMORE, R. (1984) *Steady Work. The Task of Educational Reform*, Santa Monica, CA, Rand Corporation.

TYACK, D. (1974) *One Best System*. Cambridge, MA, Harvard University Press.

12
Effective Schools and the Problems of the Poor

John E. Chubb

Children who are raised in poverty currently run grave risks of educational failure — of falling far short of even moderate levels of cognitive development, of leaving high school without a diploma and ultimately of ending up in poverty for life (most recently see Kennedy, Jung and Orland, 1986). It is not exactly clear why. It may be the hopelessness of their environments, the disinterest of their parents, or the inferiority of their schools. It may be all of these, and it is probably more. It is clear that the risk of educational failure is tragically large, and that fact has motivated government to try to reduce, if not minimize, that risk.

Not knowing precisely how to break the bond between economic and educational struggle, policymakers have tried many things. They have offered preparatory experiences for pre-schoolers, intensive instruction in the basics for slow learners, and occupational opportunities to potential dropouts. They have spent billions of dollars on educating the economically disadvantaged that would not otherwise have been spent on them. And, to some degree they have succeeded. Modest but favorable claims can now be made, for example, about Head Start, and about the single largest program for the educationally at-risk, namely, Chapter 1 of the 1981 Education Consolidation and Improvement Act (originally, Title I of the 1965 Elementary and Secondary Education Act; for an overview of Title I's improving performance see Kirst and Jung, 1980). Two decades of experimentation with a severe but perplexing problem have resulted in at least some programs that make an identifiable difference.

But this is not to say that the difference is large or even satisfactory. It is probably not as large as the decline in educational achievement that was registered by all students — but especially secondary students — over the first fifteen years of this period (trends in test scores are examined most thoroughly in Congressional Budget Office, 1986). It is not a difference that even half of the at-risk children have experienced.[1] It has not been enough to reduce appreciably the dropout rate among the poor (Hanushek, 1986). And, it has not changed the sad fact that children raised in poverty run a serious risk of educational failure, perhaps every bit as serious as that which confronted them before efforts to help them began in earnest. Notwithstanding the real progress that has been made, there is ample room for improvement.

There is also room for new ideas about how that improvement can be made. Partly, this is because the educational problems of the poor are not well understood. Like the problems of educational achievement generally, they are highly complex involving not only the school (which policymakers can affect) but the family, the economy, and the whole of society (which policymakers cannot affect very skillfully). Educational research, really still in its infancy as a branch of social science, has foreclosed on some ideas for educational improvement — for example, the simple infusion of additional funds — but not on many. And, it is fair to say that for all of the experimentation that has occurred in the field of helping the disadvantaged to learn, there is much that has never been tried. In Chapter 1, for example, more effort has probably been devoted to ensuring that children at risk of educational failure actually receive 'something extra' than to designing something that significantly reduces that risk. But the room for experimentation lies not only within the Chapter 1 program itself; it lies beyond that realm in alternative approaches altogether, in approaches that might not see the provision of specialized and/or supplementary instruction as the key to aiding the disadvantaged.

This chapter will ultimately consider one such alternative, but first it is necessary to lay some groundwork. Most basically, a perspective on educational failure must be developed so that alternative approaches to reform can be evaluated. Somewhat unconventionally, the perspective that will be offered here is not derived from a focus on the problems of the educationally disadvantaged or on the special programs that have been created to solve those problems. Rather, it derives from a concentration on the educational problems of young people generally and on the roles that schools, not programs, play in alleviating or worsening them. This may turn out to be inappropriate given the potentially special nature of the poor's educational difficulties. However, research that treats student achievement, broadly conceived, as a product of school organization and operation has recently proven very promising, and its potential implications for the achievement problems of the poor certainly bear consideration.

After briefly reviewing that research, this chapter will offer a perspective on school performance — and hence on educational failure — that builds not only on the promising results of others, but on the results of a new national survey of public and private high schools. That perspective will then be used to examine the issue of how best to help the disadvantaged, and to suggest that Chapter 1 may not be the most effective way. That line of argument will make clear why a distinctly different approach to the educational problems of the poor should at least be entertained, and will, finally, indicate what such a reform would look like.

The Promise and Problems of Research on School Performance

Two very different bodies of recent research on school performance offer perhaps the most promising insights now available into the problem of student achievement. One is concerned with school effectiveness: what are the characteristics of schools that succeed in promoting academic achievement and other educational goals, and how can we institute reforms that encourage existing schools to develop these characteristics? The other is interested in school sector: are private schools more effective than public schools at educating students?

Research on school effectiveness has contributed to our understanding of schools in two important respects. First, a large and growing literature is building a consensus on some of the basic characteristics that seem to promote school effectiveness (for example, Edmonds, 1979; Brookover, Beady, Flood, Schweitzer and Wisenbaker, 1979; Rutter, Maughan, Mortimore, Ouston and Smith, 1979; Gersten, Carnine and Green, 1982; Farrar, Neufeld and Miles, 1983;

Neufeld, Farrar and Miles, 1983). Generally speaking, these include strong instructional leadership by the principal, clear school goals, rigorous academic requirements, an orderly environment, an integral role for teachers in-school decision-making, cooperative principal-teacher relations, high parental involvement and support, and high teacher and principal expectations about student performance. Perhaps more importantly, this literature is establishing the central significance of one major aspect of the educational enterprise, namely school organization. What goes on inside a school, something that school research traditionally ignored, appears to have an important role in explaining school outcomes (classic 'input–output' studies, weak on organizations, include Coleman *et al*, 1966 and Jencks *et al*, 1972).

Unfortunately, 'appear' is the watchword of effective schools research. Its conclusions, however reasonable and widely shared, can only be regarded as tentative. Partly, this is a problem of method. Most of the work is based on case studies or qualitative analyses of small numbers of schools that gauge school performance impressionistically, i e, without measures of student achievement (Sizer, 1984; Powell, Farrar and Cohen, 1985). Not only does this provide a weak foundation for generalization, it also leaves major doubts about the effects of schools per se.[2]

The largest problem with this research, however, is not one of method. It is a problem of conceptualization. In seeking to identify the causes of school success, this research has accumulated a lengthy list of things closely associated with good performance, but not a single cogent explanation of where, why, and when those things are found. School performance is often conceived very narrowly, for example, as a product of how teachers teach or principals lead. Yet, these things and other proximate sources of student achievement, such as homework and discipline, are bound up with each other, and with qualities of the student body and political, administrative, and economic aspects of the school environment. It is possible, consequently, that many of the familiar 'causes' of school effectiveness may be of only secondary importance, not to mention of limited value as levers of school reform. Unfortunately, there are practical obstacles to broadening the perspective: comprehensive and representative data on school organization and environment are rare, and data that combine these qualities with information on student achievement are virtually nonexistent.[3]

Comparative research on public and private school performance has made equally valuable — but problematic — contributions. The central conclusion of this work, especially the research of James Coleman and his associates, is that school effectiveness depends to some degree on sector; private schools are evidently more effective than public schools at producing academic achievement gains among comparable students (Coleman, Hoffer and Kilgore, 1982; Hoffer, Greeley and Coleman, 1985). Notwithstanding criticism of this conclusion from various methodological, theoretical (and ideological) angles, it has essentially survived (for critiques see Bryk, 1981; Guthrie and Zusman, 1981; Murnane, 1981; Goldberger and Cain, 1982; Heyns and Hilton, 1982). This is important. First, it provides the most reliable evidence yet that schools affect student achievement, that schools really matter. The research by the Coleman team is based on the largest, most extensive, and most appropriate survey ever conducted for analyzing school performance: High School and Beyond (HSB). Second, it suggests that the school environment, in this case public or private, may be closely linked to school organization and, in turn, performance.

The suggestion has not, however, been well investigated. The Coleman group chooses to explain differences in public and private school performance in terms of variables that are logically close to student achievement, namely homework and discipline. But given all that is known about school performance, it is likely that homework and discipline are merely pieces in a large puzzle that only when properly assembled produces an effective school. If reform is to improve school performance, this point must be appreciated. Public schools cannot be made to perform like private schools by mandating that they increase homework and stiffen discipline.

Progress in school improvement demands progress in school theory, and that requires the explanation of private school superiority to be rounded out. The many and related organizational factors that affect student achievement need to be investigated simultaneously. Their arrangement into more and less effective forms of organization, both between and among public and private schools, needs to be assessed in a manner that recognizes their interdependence with each other and with the students and environments they serve. As things now stand we do not know what exactly constitutes an effective organization, or when such an organization is likely to be found. As a result, we do not adequately understand why one school, private or public, outperforms another — and we are ill equipped to do anything about it.

A New Approach to School Performance

In the research I am conducting with Terry M Moe of Stanford University, we are trying to develop a more comprehensive view of school organization and performance (Chubb and Moe, 1986a). We begin that effort by recognizing that a school, like any organization, survives, grows, and adapts through constant exchange with an environment — comprised, in this case, of parents, administrators, politicians, demographic changes, socioeconomic conditions, and a range of other forces that variously generate support, opposition, stress, opportunities for choice, and demands for change. Internally, it has its own distinctive structures and processes, its own culture of norms, beliefs, and values, and its own technology for transforming inputs into outputs. The organization and its environment together constitute an overarching system of behavior in which, as the saying goes, everything is related to everything else, the environment shapes the internal organization, the organization generates outputs and they in turn have a variety of reciprocal effects on both the organization and its environment. The result over time is an iterative process of impact and adaptation.

It is impossible to capture all this richness in theory and research. It is undesirable as well. The key is to put this sort of organizational framework to use in simplified form, retaining only those elements most salient to the explanation. Our focus is on the construction of two interrelated models. The first attempts to explain organizational characteristics, the second attempts to explain outputs. The organizational model allows for the impacts of environment and outputs on school organization, as well as for reciprocal relationships among the organizational elements themselves. The output model explains important school products in terms of environmental and organizational influences.

To estimate these models, and more generally to put our organizational approach to an empirical test, it was necessary to have an unusually comprehensive data set. It had to include reliable quantitative indicators of student achievement and background, school structure, organization, and operation, and school environment, including the influences of parents, administrators, and politicians. No such data set existed when this project was conceived in 1982, but one came close. The High School and Beyond survey, first administered in 1980 and later supplemented by biennial follow-up surveys, provided an excellent data base for analyzing student achievement and measuring school performance in the public and private sectors alike. A data set comprised of the 1980 and 1982 waves could provide measures of actual student achievement for more than 25,000 students in roughly 1000 schools nationwide, and enough information about the 'causes' of that achievement outside of school — for example, parental and peer influence — to gauge reliably the effectiveness of schools. The main problem with any data set derived from the HSB surveys is that it cannot provide adequate information about school organization and environment. Principals in the HSB study were surveyed for data available for the most part in school records — for example, class sizes, course offerings — and teachers were queried only superficially.

The student data in the HSB survey are nonetheless among the best ever collected, so we decided to pursue our organizational approach by supplementing the HSB surveys with a new one aimed at organizational and environmental factors. The result is the 'Administrator and Teacher Survey' (ATS), designed and directed by us and several colleagues. In 1984 it was used to obtain information from nearly 500 of the HSB schools, including most of the more than 100 private schools. Questionnaires were administered in each school to the principal and thirty teachers, among others. The survey permits detailed descriptions of schools — their relationships with parents and outside authorities, their interpersonal relationships, and their educational atmospheres and practices. In other words, the survey provides reliable measures of the gamut of factors identified in qualitative research on school effectiveness, as well as measures of factors that might explain why the qualities of effectiveness arise. When merged, the HSB and ATS surveys provide a promising data base for explaining not only differences in school performance between the public and private sectors, but school performance generally.

Some Suggestive Findings

Evaluating this perspective on school performance is a complicated process, and the work, while well along, is not yet complete. The results we have obtained so far are very encouraging for they suggest that school organization, environment, and performance are bound together in predictable ways. This is well illustrated by a portion of the research that is complete: a comparison of public and private schools (Chubb and Moe, 1986b). The comparison is instructive because public and private schools obviously have very different environments, the former being characterized by political and authoritative control and the latter by market and competitive control. In addition, they seem to have different levels of effectiveness: current evidence suggests that private schools are in fact more effective than public schools at educating comparable students. It is reasonable to expect that private schools already tend to be characterized by precisely those organizational features that reformers have been urging on the public schools — and that it is the environmental differences between the two sectors that largely account for the organizational and performance differences.

For purposes of comparison, we broke down the private sector schools into three types: Catholic, Elite (high performance, college prep), and Other Private (a catch-all category). The results indicate that key aspects of the organizations and environments of public and private schools indeed differ systematically.

External Authorities

If the operation of politics and markets suggests anything, it is that public schools should find themselves operating in larger, more complex governing systems and that these governing systems should tend to leave them with less autonomy and control over their own policies, structure, goals, and operation. Public schools simply do not have available to them the same tools as private schools, namely the forces of the marketplace and the threat of going out of business, to ensure that schools do what clients (and especially voters) want them to do. They must rely on some hierarchical authority structure to set goals and ensure compliance. Of course, it is a foregone conclusion that the public governing system will be more complex when it comes to higher levels of political and administrative authority: public schools are part of state and Federal governmental systems, and private schools generally are not. But what about immediate outside authorities, those best situated to oversee and constrain the school at the local level?

Not surprisingly, virtually all public schools are subordinate to school boards and to outside administrative superiors. Private schools are far more diverse, regardless of type. Most private schools have a

school board of some sort, but many have no accompanying administrative apparatus. Such an apparatus is quite rare among the Elite
schools and nearly half of the other private schools are similarly
unencumbered. It is the Catholic schools that most resemble the public
schools in this regard; some two-thirds of them have both school
boards and administrative superiors.

Still, these patterns tell us only that private schools are subject to
fewer outside authorities; they do not tell us whether the authorities
that private schools actually do face are any less demanding than those
that public schools face. It turns out, however, that they are. On five
basic policy dimensions — curriculum, instructional methods, discipline, hiring, and firing — school boards in the public sector appear to
have more influence over school policy than they do in the private
sector, regardless of the type of private school, and principals, relative
to their school boards, have less. When it comes to the influence of
administrative superiors, the famed Catholic hierarchy (the only private
sector hierarchy worth talking about) plays, by public sector standards,
very little role in setting school policy. On all five dimensions, the
influence of administrative superiors is far less in Catholic than in public
schools, and Catholic principals have more autonomy in setting school
policy than public principals do.

These are, of course, only simple measures of influence. But the
patterns they yield are quite uniform and entirely consistent with the
expectation that public schools, by virtue of their reliance on political
control, will be subject to greater control by external authorities. The
authorities that are so ubiquitous in the democratic context of the public
school are often simply absent from private school settings. Even when
they are an acknowledged part of the governing apparatus, they are less
influential in the actual determination of school policy. Private schools,
it would appear, have more control over their own destinies.

Staffing the Organization

External authorities are by no means the only constraints that limit the
ability of a school to structure and operate its organization as it sees fit.
Two in particular — tenure and unions — restrict a school's freedom to
exercise perhaps its most significant form of control: its ability to recruit
the kinds of teachers it wants and to get rid of those who do not live up

to its standards. Public schools are much more constrained in these regards.

The ATS survey shows that 88 per cent of public schools offer tenure while only a minority of the private schools do. Among the schools that do offer tenure, moreover, the proportion of teachers who have actually been awarded it reflects the same asymmetry: 80 per cent of the eligible teachers in public schools have tenure, while the figure is some 10 to 16 per cent lower in the private sector. The differences in unionization are even more substantial. The vast majority of public schools are unionized — some 80 per cent — while in the private sector, teachers are rarely so organized. Only about 10 per cent of the Catholic schools are unionized; virtually none of the elites and other privates are.

Inherent differences between politics and markets help account for these disparate levels of constraint. Tenure systems in public schools are simply special cases of the civil service systems that exist at all levels of government. Unions are a product, at least in part, of the need among politicians for organization, money, and manpower — real assets in state and local elections where voter turnout is typically low. There is nothing to prevent unions from gaining a foothold in private schools nor to keep private schools from adopting tenure and other civil service-like protections; however, there is nothing comparable to government that drives them in that direction. Whether unions and tenure systems take hold in the private sector is determined to a far greater extent by the market.

But do these constraints perceptibly influence school control over important personnel issues? According to the principals in the ATS survey, they certainly do. Public principals claim to face substantially greater obstacles in dismissing a teacher for poor performance than private school principals indicate. The procedures are far more complex, the tenure rules more restrictive, and the preparation and documentation process roughly three times as long. Their complexity and formality make dismissal procedures the highest barrier to firing cited by public school principals. For private school principals the highest barrier is a personal reluctance to fire.

Even if superintendents and central offices wanted to reduce these obstacles — to delegate greater control over teachers to public school principals — many of these personnel decisions cannot in practice be delegated. In the public sector, tenure protections are usually guaranteed through laws that are written by school boards or state legislatures, and union contracts are typically bargained at the district level. Tenure and unionization tend to settle the question of when and how the basic personnel decisions will be made in the public sector.

Principals

According to much of the new literature on school effectiveness, the principal holds a key to school success. Excellence in education appears to be promoted by a principal who articulates clear goals, holds high expectations of students and teachers, exercises strong instructional leadership, steers clear of administrative burdens, and effectively extracts resources from the environment. According to our perspective, the principal is also critical: he is responsible for negotiating success-fully with the environment — for dealing somehow with demands and pressures from parents, unions, administrators, and school boards.

But this does not mean that schools necessarily will benefit from being headed by an adroit principal. The school environment can have a lot to say about whether the principal is able to practice the precepts of effective leadership. Effective leadership does not simply inhere in the individual filling the role; it is unavoidably contingent upon the demands, constraints, and resources that the principal must deal with. Depending on the nature and strength of these forces, even the 'best' principal may have only a marginal effect on school performance.

The ATS survey disclosed substantial differences between public and private school principals. To begin with, private school principals have considerably more teaching experience — almost four years more for principals in Catholic schools, and over five years more for those in the elites and other privates. Private school principals also come to their jobs with different motivations than their public counterparts. They are more likely to stress control over school policies, while public school principals place greater emphasis on a preference for administrative responsibilities, a desire to further their careers, and an interest in advancing to higher administrative posts.

These differences in experience and motivation appear to shape the principal's performance as a leader. As judged by their own teachers, private school principals are more effective instructional leaders and are more likely to exhibit other basic qualities of leadership — knowledge of school problems, openness with the staff, clarity and strength of purpose, and a willingness to innovate.

From the standpoint of politics and markets, these findings make sense. In the public sector, the administrative hierarchy offers an attractive avenue for career advancement. In the private sector, the governing structure offers fewer opportunities. Private school principals consequently stay in teaching longer, and their view of the principalship focuses more on its relation to the school than on its relation to their movement up an educational hierarchy. Of course, these are not the only determinants of leadership. Public school principals are forced to operate in much more complex, discordant circumstances in which educational success is more difficult to achieve regardless of the principal's (perhaps considerable) abilities. If anything, the public school principal's lack of teaching expertise and his hierarchic career orientation probably contribute to these leadership problems.

Goals and Policies

Given what we know of their environments, there is every reason to expect that public and private schools should adopt very different orientations toward the education of their students. Because public schools must take whoever walks in the door, they do not have the luxury of being able to select the kind of students best suited to organizational goals and structure. In practice this means that the pursuit of educational excellence must compete with much more basic needs — for literacy, for remedial training, for more slowly paced instruction. In addition, the hierarchical structure of democratic control ensures that a range of actors with diverse, often conflicting interests will participate in deciding what the public school ought to pursue and how. Private schools, largely unconstrained by comparison, should find it easier (if they want to do so) to place a high priority on excellence and, whatever their goals, to choose a set that is clear and consistent.

The results of the ATS survey confirmed these expectations. In terms of general goals, public schools place significantly greater emphasis on basic literacy, citizenship, good work habits, and specific occupational skills, while private schools — regardless of type — are more oriented toward academic excellence, personal growth and fulfillment, and human relations skills. These goals are also upheld by specific policies and are clearly discerned by the staff. Private schools have more stringent minimum graduation requirements; their students, regardless of track, must take significantly more English, history, science, math and foreign language than public school students in order to graduate. Private schools also have more stringent homework policies. Finally, private teachers uniformly say that school goals are clearer and more clearly communicated by the principal than public teachers report; and they are more in agreement among themselves on school priorities.

All of these characteristics that private schools possess in greater abundance are stereotypical of effective schools. They are also characteristics that, due to the differential operation of politics and markets, would seem extremely difficult for public schools to develop in the same degree.

Teachers and Teaching

Politics and markets cannot hope to tell us everything we might want to know about organizational structure and process, but they point us in a clear direction. The critical fact about the public school environment is not just that it is complex, but that it imposes decisions about policy, structure, personnel and procedure on the school. Nowhere is this more apparent than in the control over the most crucial agent of organizational performance: the teacher.

As we have seen, the public school principal is far less able than his private counterpart to staff his organization according to his best judgment. This, in turn, should promote differences in staff heterogeneity and conflict. Public school teachers may reject the principal's leadership, dissent from school goals and policies, get along poorly with their colleagues, or fail to perform acceptably in the classroom — but the principal must somehow learn to live with them. When these teachers are represented by unions, as they normally are, leadership difficulties are magnified. Professionalism takes on new meaning: as a demand that decision-making power be transferred from the principal to the teachers. Private schools are not immune from personnel problems and struggles for power. But the fact that the principal has much greater control over hiring and firing means that he can take steps to recruit the kinds of teachers he wants and weed out those he does not. It also means that teachers have a strong inducement to perform.

By comparison to his public school counterpart, the private school principal is better able to create a team of teachers whose values, skills and willingness to work together tend to mirror those qualifications he deems conducive to the pursuit of organizational goals. At the same time, he is in a position to make teacher professionalism work for rather than against him. Without real threat to his own authority or control, he can encourage teachers to participate in decision-making, extend them substantial autonomy within their own spheres of expertise, and promote a context of interaction, exchange of ideas, and mutual respect.

The data from the ATS survey support this general line of reasoning. Private school principals consistently claim that a larger percentage of their schools' teachers are 'excellent', suggesting that these principals are more confident in the abilities of their own staff members than public school principals are in theirs. Private sector teachers, in turn, have better relationships with their principals. They are consistently more likely to regard the latter as encouraging, supportive and reinforcing. Private school teachers also feel more involved and efficacious in important areas of school decision-making that bear on their teaching. They feel more influential over schoolwide policies, and in their classrooms; they believe they have more control over most matters that govern their effectiveness.

Relative harmony between private school principals and teachers is matched by relative harmony among the private teachers themselves. On a personal level, relationships are more collegial in the private sector. On a professional level, private school teachers give greater evidence of mutual involvement and support. It should come as no surprise that private school teachers are much more satisfied with their jobs, have better attendance records, and tend to work for less money. Private schools do look more like teams.

School Control and School Organization

Why private schools tend to develop team-like organizations is a question of potentially great import for school improvement: private schools appear to be more effective than public schools, and the team qualities that distinguish private schools — strong leadership, shared goals, cooperative decision making, collegial relationships, mutual trust, widespread efficacy — are the very qualities that research on

257

school improvement has identified as keys to student achievement. To be sure, private schools may owe some of this organizational esprit de corps to the better students and more supportive parents that, on average, they work with. But not all of it. In analyses that we are currently completing on the merged HSB–ATS data set, we have tentatively found that the school environment is at least as important as the school clientele in determining the organizational climate of the school. Significantly, this appears to be every bit as true of the shaping of school organizations within the public sector as it is between the public and the private sectors: more complex and constraining environments are associated with more troubled school organizations regardless of sector. Still, the differences between the organizations and environments of public and private schools are so striking that they must be understood — not only for what they may say about the influence of school control but, as we shall see, for what they may disclose about the prospects for school improvement both within and outside of public education systems.

It is important to recognize that public schools are captives of democratic politics. They are subordinates in a hierarchical system of control in which myriad interests and actors use the rules, structures, and processes of democracy to impose their preferences on the local school. It is no accident that public schools are lacking in autonomy, that principals have difficulty leading, and that school goals are heterogeneous, unclear, and undemanding. Nor is it an accident that weak principals and tenured, unionized teachers struggle for power and hold one another in relatively low esteem. These sorts of characteristics constitute an organizational syndrome whose roots are deeply anchored in democratic control as we have come to know it.

Private schools are controlled by society too, but there are few, if any, political or administrative mechanisms to ensure that they respond as they 'should'. They make their own decisions about policy, organization, and personnel subject to market forces that signal how they can best pursue their own goals and prosperity. Given their substantial autonomy, it is not surprising to find that principals are stronger leaders, that they have greater control over hiring and firing, that they and the teachers they choose have greater respect for and interaction with one another, and the teachers — without conflict or formal demands — are more integrally involved in school decision making. As in the public sector, these sorts of organizational characteristics are bound up with one another, and they jointly arise from the surrounding environment. Different environments promote different organizational syndromes.

Politics, Bureaucracy, and Chapter 1

In thinking about how best to help disadvantaged children, it may well be instructive to appreciate how much the experience of Chapter 1 (and Title I) has been shaped by the dynamic of public control — and how much that dynamic has itself been shaped by Chapter 1. When Title I was legislated in 1975, it was conceived as a way for the Federal government to provide compensatory educational services to disadvantaged children without becoming involved itself in the delivery of education. As it had in so many other categorical grants-in-aid, the government in Washington would send funds to qualifying lower governments (in this instance, ones with certain concentrations of poor people) on the condition that the funds would be spent for some federally designated purpose. This enabled the Federal government to do what it arguably could do best — raise and redistribute revenue — and left the lower governments to exploit their comparative advantage in supplying services to suit local demands. Cumbersome and costly administrative arrangements would be minimized and efficiency would be maximized.

Unfortunately, things did not quite work out that way. Federal policymakers had underestimated the difficulty of accomplishing national goals through subnational governments and agencies. There was often a conflict of interest between the national and the lower governments and a severe asymmetry of information about what interests were being satisfied. Lower governments did not always agree that Federal funds should be spent directly on serving the educationally disadvantaged; spending on teacher salaries, physical facilities, general school improvements, or even future tax savings were sometimes regarded as more desirable. In addition, since only local governments knew for sure how additional funds (in large fungible budgets) were really being spent, they enjoyed an advantage over Federal authorities who were trying to ensure that their goals were being realized. The problem that Federal authorities faced was a classic one of organizational design, a 'principal-agent' problem.[4] If the 'principals' in

Washington did not take measures to overcome the conflicts of interest and informational asymmetries between them and their state and local 'agents', they were going to find their agents 'shirking' their mandated responsibilities. Because Title I initially included no such measures, shirking indeed occurred.

In theory, this is easy to overcome. 'Principals' can monitor their 'agents' directly to see that appropriate effort is being made to satisfy the 'principals'' goals. Or they can offer their 'agents' incentives for satisfying goals, without prompting a costly amount of monitoring. In the private sector combinations of monitoring and incentives are frequently used. But in the public sector, they usually are not. Incentives tend to be precluded by the difficulty of measuring productivity in the absence of markets for public goods. The public sector therefore relies mostly on monitoring — on rules, regulation, and reporting, i.e., on bureaucracy.

Federal policymakers, alerted by beneficiary groups that Title I funds were not always reaching the disadvantaged, began monitoring state and local educational agencies more carefully in the late 1960s (on the early implementation experience see Murphy (1971) and McLaughlin (1975)). Their intention was not to tell the agencies precisely how to spend their money, but rather, in the spirit of the policy's initial conception, to ensure that the money was spent on the statute's goal, namely improving the educational experiences of the disadvantaged. In time, monitoring proved an awkward and inadequate tool for accomplishing this deceptively simple goal. The Federal government could not afford to supervise directly the behavior of all the state and local agencies participating in the program (though it did increase its auditing sharply in the early 1970s); hence, it opted for specifying in ever greater detail the standards that agencies would have to meet to pass occasional Federal inspections (see Chubb, 1985b). Even these very extensive and explicit regulations — for example, 'supplement, not supplant', 'excess costs', and 'comparability' — did not expressly violate the Federal government's objective of staying out of local educational processes. But in effect they did.

To make these regulations work with a minimum of direct Federal supervision, the Federal government had to find some way to get 'agents' at the state and local level to work with them rather than against them. State and local educational authorities, not to mention general governmental authorities, resisted an alliance because their interest was fundamentally in autonomy. So, lacking any ready converts to Federal objectives, the national government began paying for the employment of state and local 'agents' it could call its own. Title I allocations included funds to establish and maintain state and local offices of compensatory education or any other administrative arrangement that would ensure the financial and educational integrity of the program. Once in place, compensatory education agencies had powerful incentives to see to it that Title I funds were properly allocated and appropriately spent, and that eligible beneficiaries were actually served: their very existence depended on the maintenance of the program, which ultimately depended on its satisfactory implementation. These agencies were also in excellent positions to carry out their mission: they suffered no informational disadvantages and, in time, they developed the political influence — via beneficiary support and their own organizations — to encourage state and local officials to stay in line (see Chubb, 1985c).

The Federal government cultivated these new allies with more than financial support. They interacted with them regularly, encouraged their participation in intergovernmental associations, and ultimately engendered a sense of professional commitment that united administrators from Washington to the lowest level (see Hill, 1979). In the process, the Federal government overcame its 'principal-agent' problem. By 1980 conflict and suspicion had given way to cooperation and trust — or at least healthy measures of these things — and the spiral of regulation and monitoring could be permitted to stop (Kirst and Jung, 1980; Peterson, Rabe and Wong, in press). An intergovernmental bureaucracy, committed to Federal purposes, had been integrated into state and local educational bureaucracies and was operating relatively smoothly. Federal monies were finally supplementing in significant amounts the educations that were being received by the economically and educationally disadvantaged (on the fiscal effectiveness of Title I see Chubb, 1985c).

The process did not, however, leave subnational educational practices essentially intact nor preserve state and local autonomy. To begin with, it contributed to the centralization of school control. While local education agencies — that is, school districts — were designated as the legally responsible officials at the service delivery level, state education agencies were given responsibility for allocating Federal funds and for holding local officials accountable. One effect was to draw local districts increasingly under the influence of state authority. But a more important consequence may have been the shift of authority from the individual school to the district. School districts were given the chore of allocating funds among schools and seeing that these funds, in turn, reached eligible students. In practice this came to mean that schools were less free to choose how best to serve their disadvantaged students, and instead districts were in charge. It also meant that districts had to establish monitoring and reporting procedures and to create jobs and, in large districts, entire offices for performing these routines — not only for compensatory education, but for a host of other categorical programs with similar political and administrative problems.

How much this process of centralization contributed to the general one that was diminishing school autonomy during that time is difficult to say. It is true that Federal assistance facilitated the overall growth of state and local bureaucracy; however, the connection between Federal grants-in-aid and educational centralization has not been well invest-igated.[5] Still, there is no gainsaying the price in autonomy that has been paid by schools on issues and concerns touched by Federal programs. A good case in point is the uniformity of services now provided by schools to students eligible for compensatory education. From state to state, district to district, and school to school educators have converged on a relatively small number of approaches to serving the poor. Among the most common is the concentration of services on the lowest grades of school and the provision of supplementary instruction in reading to children removed from their regular classes for just that purpose (Kennedy, Jung and Orland, 1986; Peterson, Rabe and Wong, in press). While so-called 'pullout' programs may be on the wane with increasing doubts about their effectiveness, uniformity continues to be the rule. It is important to understand why. It is not because educator after educator has concluded that one approach represents the best way to serve eligible students. It is rather because special programs such as 'pullouts' provide the strongest evidence that local authorities can offer to outside authorities that appropriate students are receiving sup-plementary services.

Significantly, there has been little change in this system over recent years — even though Chapter 1 frees lower governments of many of the regulations established under Title I. The administrative apparatus for carrying out Federal purposes is either so well entrenched that forces for change are being successfully resisted, or the fear of re-

regulation is so great that past routines are being continued out of sheer prudence. Whatever the reason, there is little evidence that increases in administrative flexibility have produced innovations in the services that the disadvantaged are receiving. The program and its central objectives are well institutionalized.

Rethinking Reform

The implementation experience of Title I and Chapter 1 illustrates perfectly the potential consequences — often adverse — of trying to improve education through the public system as it is currently constituted. Through an escalating exchange of regulation and resistance between the top of the system and the bottom, a program intended to give resources and discretion to schools with needy children turned into a program delivering highly uniform supplementary services to some of the children in need but offering precious little to the schools themselves. This outcome, it is important to understand, was not the result of considered decisions by educational professionals about how best to educate the poor, nor was it the result of judgments by politicians about the most effective course of action to take. It was not, however, inadvertent. Federal politicians, under pressure from constituency groups to see that eligible children received compensatory education, reacted in the only way they had at their disposal: by demanding that Federal bureaucrats placate those groups. In turn, Federal bureaucrats and their subnational allies used the only tools at their disposal — regulation and auditing — to force local education agencies to help the children of the groups that were complaining. Finally, those agencies responded by providing compensatory education in ways that most readily demonstrated their compliance.

Over time these intergovernmental conflicts have given way to more cooperative implementation routines. But has this adaptive process produced a successful compensatory education policy? Obviously, that is an important question in thinking about improvement. However, it is not the only question — nor perhaps even the most important one. We must also ask whether the process that produced the current policy can be relied upon to generate improvements.

The question of Chapter 1's success has been addressed many

times, and answered in many ways. In recent years, the answers have tended to be positive. It is almost certain that Federal spending has increased the resources devoted to educating the poor. Federal aid for poor students is not only proving to be genuinely supplementary; it also seems to be stimulating state and local spending for the same purposes.[6] In addition, there are favorable signs that students receiving compensatory education are achieving more than they would without it (favorable evaluations are reviewed in Kirst and Jung, 1980; and Peterson, Rabe and Wong, in press).

Still, there is room to question Chapter 1's success and its ultimate desirability. To begin with, many children who are economically and educationally disadvantaged — probably half of the total — do not receive Chapter 1 services, either because they attend schools that have not been designated by their districts to receive compensatory services, or if they attend designated schools, are enrolled in grades that are not receiving services. Second, the schools that Chapter 1 children attend are not demonstrably better off by virtue of offering compensatory services. The children may be, but the schools are not. This has repercussions not only for students who are not receiving compensatory services, but for ones who are. If children are benefiting from supplementary services but otherwise suffering from the poor educational environments of their schools, their educations remain problematic. To be sure, students are better off receiving services than not receiving them. But this is not to say they are being well served.

For one thing, if the centralization process to which compensatory education contributed is in some measure responsible for the deterioration that public education experienced during the time Title I was being implemented, the compensatory services that some disadvantaged students are receiving may simply be making up for ground that the program itself helped to lose. Be that as it may, there is also a firm basis for questioning the very approach to compensatory education that Chapter 1 has come to embody. Both the literature on effective schools and our own research on public and private schools indicate that school performance has more to do with a complex of factors that characterize schools as total organizations than with any particular programs that schools may provide. Successful schools are distinguished by interdependent qualities — strong leadership, a sense of mission, shared decision making, relative teacher autonomy — that bind schools together and foster teamwork. This appears to be as true of schools that teach the rich as it is of schools that teach the poor. Compensatory education as it is currently conceived and implemented does nothing to nurture these qualities. To the contrary, by increasing the control of the school from the outside, it may discourage their development. The implication for reform, then, is quite plain: if research on school organization and performance is on target, compensatory education might be more successful if it were aimed at improving the schools that the disadvantaged attend rather than at increasing the services that some of these students receive.

The remaining question, of course, is how this can be done. How can schools that educate the disadvantaged be encouraged to develop the organizational attributes of effectiveness? If school environments have as much to do with the development of these attributes as the comparative analysis of public and private schools indicates, and as the Title I/Chapter 1 experience suggests, vigorous school organizations may be difficult to cultivate within the current system of public education.

For example, consider the expressed desire of the current school reform movement to create such organizations. The rhetoric of reformers is replete with support for greater school autonomy, stronger leadership from principals, and more respect for the professional judgment of teachers. But what reformers fail to appreciate is that these improvements cannot simply be imposed on schools in the public sector. As the compensatory education experience so well illustrates, politicians and administrators have little incentive to support fundamental reform; their careers are tied to their own control over the schools, and they are unavoidably responsive to interest groups with stakes in the centralized arrangements of the status quo. Reforms that manage to get adopted — for example, tougher graduation requirements and student competency tests — leave the basic structure of the system intact, and, more than that, encourage the further regulation and standardization of educational practices within the school.

In time, it is also likely that whatever reforms are adopted will tend to be neutralized and assimilated. Increases in school autonomy are likely to be restricted once school principals take steps that create political difficulties for superintendents or school boards. Reductions in the number of strings attached to compensatory aid are likely to be turned around once interest groups resume complaining that they cannot identify the additional services that schools are providing.

Public schools did not lose autonomy nor suffer the organizational consequences of that loss by accident or misunderstanding. And, the new-found wisdom that we may be paying a price for a superfluity of accountability is not likely to change things. The various components of the current system are so closely interconnected and so driven toward control from the top that attempts to improve part of the system in isolation from all of the rest — for example, by restructuring Chapter 1 — are likely to set off a series of compensating changes that minimize the impact of the reform.

Where does this leave the prospects for improvement? In rather sad shape — if improvements must be pursued within the existing system. Real improvements may require a different system. It may be necessary to organize the provision of education in some way other than through direct democratic control, as we have come to know it, if the apparent educational problems of centralization, standardization, and routinization are to be avoided. At the very least, the possibility must be entertained.

If schools are to develop the organizational qualities that research now indicates are essential for real educational gains, it may even be necessary to emulate the system of control that governs private schools, where teaching and professional autonomy flourish. Government would still set minimum standards. It would also provide funding, probably in the form of vouchers allocated directly to parents. Students who are difficult to educate, especially the economically disadvantaged, would receive larger vouchers to induce schools to provide for them. But the government, besides providing graduated funding and setting basic standards, would do little else. Virtually all of the important decisions about policy, organization, and personnel would be taken out of the hands of politicians and administrators and given over to schools and their clients: the students and their parents.

In a system requiring competition for students and resources, schools would have incentives to move toward more efficient and effective forms of organization. Schools that clung to costly bureaucratic methods, that did not attract and utilize talented people, that failed to encourage collegial and productive relationships among their members, or that lacked strong leadership toward clearly defined educational goals would tend to go out of business. Effective schools would tend to prosper.

The added virtue of this system for the disadvantaged is that it would provide a way to overcome the considerable professional ignorance about how best to serve those struggling students. Experimentation would be encouraged. Schools and programs that failed to serve the disadvantaged effectively would be weeded out while those that succeeded would grow. The process would almost certainly move schools away from their current reliance on special classes for the disadvantaged and toward a greater variety of services. But even if it did not, there would at least be reason to believe that the programs in place were justified by their educational merits. Today's programs are justified largely by their political and administrative merits. Some will say that parents, especially of the poor, are not wise enough to make the process of natural selection work. But parental wisdom is not a prerequisite for the process to move forward. Even if many parents continued to send their children to the school closest to their home, the neighborhood school would be a better one: the school would have the novel concern that some day parents might find an alternative school more attractive and leave.

Obviously, any change as fundamental as this runs the risk of political infeasibility. Unless the quality or equity of public education declines further, it will be difficult to overcome the opposition of organized groups whose interests are threatened by fundamental reform. Still, there is increasing sympathy among establishment groups — for example, the National Governors Association — for the idea of providing schools with greater autonomy in exchange for schools taking greater responsibility for performance. And, there is even a proposal now before Congress to convert Chapter 1 funds to compensatory vouchers. These are significant developments. To be sure, they do not promise enormous improvements. Even the fairly radical idea of providing Chapter 1 vouchers does little more than increase parental choice by a modicum; it does nothing to increase school autonomy. The significance of the ideas is what they signal: serious interest in basic school reform. If schools are indeed products of their environments, and if the way they are organized really shapes their performance, fundamental reform may be the only type of reform that offers genuine hope for school improvement, and through it, greater educational gains for the poor.

Notes

1   Estimates of the number of eligible children served by Chapter 1 vary, but as Kennedy, Jung and Orland (1986) indicate, 50 per cent is roughly at the center of this range.
2   Even those few studies that analyze actual student achievement (for example, Rutter *et al*, 1979; Brookover *et al*, 1979) rely on limited samples of schools.
3   The best survey on school organization, despite being based on an unrepresentative sample, is probably Goodlad (1984); however, it lacks data on student achievement. The best current survey of students and their abilities is probably High School and Beyond; however, it is weak on organizational measures.
4   This framework is used more formally to evaluate the implementation of Title I in Chubb (1985c).
5   The impact of Federal aid on state and local bureaucracy is discussed and estimated in Chubb (1985a).
6   The growing fiscal effectiveness of the program can be seen by comparing the estimates of Feldstein (1977) for 1970 and of Chubb (1985c) for the period of 1965–1979; the period effect is two-thirds higher.

References

BROOKOVER, W. B., BEADY, C., FLOOD, P., SCHWEITZER, J. and WISEN-BAKER, J. (1979). *School Social Systems and Student Achievement: Schools Can Make a Difference*. New York: Praeger.

BRYK, A. S. (1981) 'Disciplined inquiry or policy argument?', *Harvard Educational Review*, **51**, pp. 497–509.

CHUBB, J. E. (1985a) 'Federalism and the bias for centralization' in CHUBB, J. E. and PETERSON P. E. (Eds) *The New Direction in American Politics*, Washington, DC, The Brookings Institution.

CHUBB, J. E. (1985b) 'Excessive regulation: The case of Federal aid to education', *Political Science Quarterly*, **100**, 2, pp. 287–311.

CHUBB. J. E. (1985c) 'The political economy of federalism', *American Political Science Review*, **79**, pp. 994–1015.

CHUBB, J. E. and MOE, T. M. (1986a) 'Politics, markets and the organization of schools', *Brookings Discussion Paper in Governmental Studies*. Washington, DC, The Brookings Institution, June.

CHUBB, J. E., and MOE, T. M. (1986b), 'No school is an island: Politics, markets and education', *The Brookings Review*, **4**, 4, pp. 21–8.

COLEMAN, J. S., CAMPBELL, E. Q., HOBSON, D. J., MCPARTLAND, J., MOOD, A. M., WEINFELD, F. D., and YORK, R. L. (1966) *Equality of Educational Opportunity*, Washington, DC, US Government Printing Office.

COLEMAN, J. S., HOFFER, T. and KILGORE, S. (1982) *High School Achievement*, New York, Basic Books

CONGRESSIONAL BUDGET OFFICE, (1986) *Trends in Educational Achievement*, Washington, DC, US Government Printing Office.

EDMONDS, R. R. (1979) 'Some schools work and more can', *Social Policy*, **9**, 5, pp. 28–32.

FARRAR, E., NEUFELD, B. and MILES, M. B. (1983) *Effective Schools Programs in High Schools: Implications for Policy, Practice, and Research*, Cambridge, MA, Huron Institute.

FELDSTEIN, M. (1977) 'The effect of a differential add-on grant: Title I and local education spending', *Journal of Human Resources*, **13**, pp. 443–58.

GERSTEN, R., CARNINE, D. and GREEN, S. (1982). 'The principal as instructional leader: A second look', *Educational Leadership*, **40**, pp. 47–50

GOLDBERGER, A. S. and CAIN, G. G. (1982) 'The causal analysis of cognitive outcomes in the Coleman, Hoffer and Kilgore report', *Sociology of Education*, **55**, pp. 103–22.

GOODLAD, J. I. (1984) *A Place Called School: Prospects for the Future*, New York, McGraw Hill.

GUTHRIE, J. W. and ZUSMAN, A. (1981) 'Unasked questions', *Harvard Educational Review*, **51**, pp. 515–8.

HANUSHEK, E. A. (1986) 'The economics of schooling', *The Journal of Economic Literature*, **24**, pp. 1141–77.

HEYNS, B. and HILTON, T. H. (1982) 'The cognitive tests for High School and Beyond: An assessment', *Sociology of Education*, **55**, pp. 89–102.

HILL, P. T. (1979) *Enforcement and Informal Pressure in the Management of Federal Categorical Programs in Education*, Santa Monica, CA, Rand Corporation.

HOFFER, T., GREELEY, A. M. and COLEMAN, J. S. (1985) 'Achievement growth in public and Catholic schools', *Sociology of Education*, **58**, pp. 74–97.

JENCKS, C. S., SMITH, M., ACKLAND, H., BANE, M. J., COHEN, D., GINTIS, H., HEYNS, B., and MICHELSON, S. (1972) *Inequality: A Reassessment of the Effect of Family and Schooling in America*, New York, Basic Books.

KENNEDY, M. M., JUNG, R. K. and ORLAND, M. E. (1986) *Poverty, Achievement and the Distribution of Compensatory Education Services* (first interim report of the National Assessment of Chapter 1), Washington, DC, US Department of Education.

KIRST, M. and JUNG, R. (1980) 'The utility of a longitudinal perspective in assessing implementation: A thirteen-year view of ESEA, Title I', *Education Evaluation and Policy Analysis*, **2**, pp. 17–34.

McLAUGHLIN, M. (1975) *Evaluation and Reform: The Elementary and Secondary Education Act of 1965, Title I*, Cambridge, MA, Ballinger.

MURNANE, R. J., (1981) 'Evidence, analysis, and unanswered questions', *Harvard Educational Review*, **51**, pp. 483–9.

MURPHY, J. T. (1971) 'Title I of ESEA: The politics of implementing Federal education reform', *Harvard Educational Review*, **41**, pp. 35–63.

NEUFELD, B., FARRAR, E. and MILES, M. B. (1983) 'A review of effective

269

schools research: The message for secondary schools', *Harvard Educational Review*, **37**, pp. 61–106.

PETERSON, P. E., RABE, B.G and WONG, K. K. (in press) *When Federalism Works*, Washington, DC, The Brookings Institution.

POWELL, A. G., FARRAR, E. and COHEN, D. K. (1985) *The Shopping Mall High School: Winners and Losers in the Educational Marketplace*, New York, Houghton Mifflin.

RUTTER, M., MAUGHAN, B., MORTIMORE, P., OUSTON, J. and SMITH, A. (1979). *Fifteen Thousand Hours: Secondary Schools and Their Effects on Children*, Cambridge, MA, Harvard University Press.

SIZER, T. R. (1984) *Horace's Compromise: The Dilemma of the American High School*, Boston, MA, Houghton Mifflin.

Contributors

John E. Chubb
The Brookings Institution

Bruce S. Cooper
Fordham University and
The University of London

Larry Cuban
Stanford University

Denis P. Doyle
The Hudson Institute

Richard F. Elmore
Michigan State University
and Rutgers University

Susan Fuhrman
Rutgers University

Charles Glenn
Massachusetts Department of
Education

Paul T. Hill
The Rand Corporation

Michael W. Kirst
Stanford University

Allan Odden
University of Southern
California

Paul E. Peterson
The Brookings Institution

Barry G. Rabe
The Brookings Institution

Marshall S. Smith
Stanford University

Kenneth K. Wong
The Brookings Institution

Index